Fashion's World Cities

Cultures of Consumption Series

Series Editor: Frank Trentmann

ISSN 1744-5876

Previously Published

The Making of the Consumer
Knowledge, Power and Identity in the Modern World
Edited by Frank Trentmann

Consuming Cultures, Global Perspectives
Historical Trajectories, Transnational Exchanges
Edited by John Brewer and Frank Trentmann

Forthcoming Titles

The Khat Controversy
Stimulating the Debate on Drugs
David Anderson, Susan Beckerleg, Degol Hailu, Axel Klein

Governing Consumption
New Spaces of Consumer Politics
Clive Barnett, Nick Clarke, Paul Cloke and Alice Malpass

Alternative Food Networks: Reconnecting Producers, Consumers and Food?
Moya Kneafsey, Lewis Holloway, Laura Venn, Rosie Cox, Elizabeth Dowler and
Helena Tuomainen

Fashion's World Cities

Edited by
Christopher Breward and David Gilbert

Oxford • New York

First published in 2006 by
Berg
Editorial offices:
1st Floor, Angel Court, 81 St Clements Street, Oxford, OX4 1AW, UK
175 Fifth Avenue, New York, NY 10010, USA

Berg is the imprint of Oxford International Publishers Ltd.

This book has been produced with the support of the Economic and Social Research
Council and the Arts and Humanities Research Council

Library of Congress Cataloguing-in-Publication Data

Fashion's world cities / edited by Christopher Breward and David Gilbert.
    p. cm.—(Cultures of consumption series)
    Includes bibliographical references and index.
    ISBN-13: 978-1-84520-413-6 (pbk. : alk. paper)
    ISBN-10: 1-84520-413-1 (pbk. : alk. paper)
    ISBN-13: 978-1-84520-412-9 (cloth : alk. paper)
    ISBN-10: 1-84520-412-3 (cloth : alk. paper) 1. Clothing trade. 2. Fashion.
3. Fashion design. 4. Metropolitan areas. 5. City and town life. I. Breward,
Christopher, 1965- II. Gilbert, David.

    TT497.F37 2006
    391.009—dc22

                                                                2006018530

British Library Cataloguing-in-Publication Data

A catalogue record for this book is available from the British Library.

ISBN-13 978 1 84520 412 9 (Cloth)
ISBN-10 1 84520 412 3 (Cloth)

ISBN-13 978 1 84520 413 6 (Paper)
ISBN-10 1 84520 413 1 (Paper)

Typeset by JS Typesetting, Porthcawl, Mid Glamorgan
Printed in the United Kingdom by Biddles Ltd, King's Lynn

www.bergpublishers.com

Contents

Part III Re-fabricating the Urban Order

Part IV Fashion Cities and Transnational Networks

List of Figures

Preface

The idea of the fashion capital or the world city of fashion is a familiar one. Metropolitan centres of style such as New York, Paris and Milan are routinely incorporated into the advertising of designer brands and retail outlets. Tourism chiefs, trade promoters, planners and public institutions such as museums and galleries have come to see fashion as an important contributor to the broader promotion of the cultural and creative economy of major global cities. Writers, artists, philosophers and designers have also long understood the connections to be made between the sense of place, the experience of modernity and the making and wearing of clothing. Yet, aside from some notable publications that have examined the history of particular fashion cities, there has been a relative lack of work addressing the interplay between the development of fashion centres across the world and their relationship to the production, consumption and mythologizing of fashion in both local and global contexts. *Fashion's World Cities* aims to redress that lack and suggest various disciplinary models for producing further studies in the field.

The book emerges out of a collaborative project titled 'Shopping Routes: Networks of Fashion Consumption in London's West End 1945–1979' hosted at London College of Fashion, Royal Holloway, University of London and the Victoria and Albert Museum between 2003 and 2006. The project was funded by the Arts and Humanities Research Council and the Economic and Social Research Council as part of the 'Cultures of Consumption' programme, which has aimed to 'enhance conceptual and empirical knowledge about consumption and the consumer through the study of the changing natures and dynamic of different cultures of consumption, and the development of new theories and modes of analysis that can be applied to prospective contexts.' One of the programme's key objectives has been to 'identify the commercial, public and social policy implications of the research and to maximize discussion and influence of the findings in relevant fields.' The 'Shopping Routes' project addressed some of these issues through focusing on London's West End as a key location in national and global cultures of fashion, providing a new account of the district's history and a more nuanced understanding of the experience of consumption, particularly in relation to practices of shopping. It organized its approach around four key concepts, considering how the physical landscapes of street and shop produced particular ecologies of fashion; how those landscapes were defined and connected by networks, flows and relationships with other places; how a combination of representations across a range of media created a powerful composite mythology of the fashion city; and how fashionable consumption and personal display in the capital influenced the formation of new class, gender, ethnic and generational identities.

While the work on 'Shopping Routes' was focused largely on London during the 1960s, a period during which the British capital took its place alongside Paris as a world fashion city, we were aware that the changes we were analysing were not necessarily unique. Moreover we wanted to test such developments in a global context and within a longer historical continuum. *Fashion's World Cities* is the result of that desire. It draws on research from a number of leading scholars working across the disciplines of geography, cultural studies, sociology, fashion studies, anthropology and social history. It presents case studies of various centres that at different moments have laid claim to the 'fashion city' mantle. The collection does not pretend to offer a comprehensive overview or historical gazetteer of the world's fashion cities, but instead demonstrates the various contexts in which we can examine the relationship between urban life, practices of consumption and production, and the system of fashion. To do this it extends the focus on landscapes, networks, representations and identities that characterized our work on 'Swinging London' to the diverse centres of Paris, Tokyo, New York, Milan, Moscow, Dakar, Mumbai, Los Angeles and San Francisco, with an introduction that sets these examples in relation to a current reordering of fashion's global networks that has emerged in recent years as a reaction to the rise of Shanghai. Chapters are arranged according to the following rationale. In Part I we address the broad concept of the fashion city and its debt to the complex historical phenomenon of modernity. Part II considers the ways in which key fashion cities have been constituted visually and through processes of design and stylization. Part III looks at examples of economic, cultural and physical change, where some cities have undergone a transformation led by new conceptions of fashion and fashioning. And in Part IV, the connections between cities, forged through trade, colonialism and the movement of labour and ideas are shown to be as important in defining World Fashion City status as any self-conscious policy of 'boosterism'. We very much hope that the resulting collection informs and inspires new accounts of fashion's role in forming a sense of place.

Christopher Breward
London, March 2006

Acknowledgements

This book has benefited from the financial support of the ESRC/AHRC 'Cultures of Consumption' Programme (project RES-143-25-0038) and arises from the related research project 'Shopping Routes: Networks of Fashion Consumption in London's West End 1945–1979' based at London College of Fashion, Royal Holloway, University of London and the Victoria and Albert Museum. The editors would like to thank the 'Cultures of Consumption' programme director, Frank Trentmann, and the project administrator, Rob Lutton, for their invaluable assistance. Several of the chapters in the book were first presented at a 'Shopping Routes' project conference on the theme of 'Fashion's World Cities' held at the London College of Fashion and the Museum of London in 2005. Authors benefited from the astute comments offered at that event by respondents Joanne Entwistle, Peter Jackson, Angela McRobbie, Frank Trentmann, Lesley Whitworth and Verity Wilson. Their insights made a very real contribution to the content of this book. Edwina Ehrman of the Museum of London has also been helpful in opening up a link between the themes of the project, the conference and the book and the holdings and facilities of the Museum. Finally, we would like to thank the contributors to the book, for their forbearance and their stimulating interventions, Lawrence Osborn and Luke Dickens for their work on the manuscript, and the publishers, especially Kathleen May and Ian Critchley, for their continuing faith, even as deadline after deadline passed.

Every effort has been made to trace copyright holders of the images reproduced in this book. If an oversight has been made, please contact the publishers, who will remedy the omission in future editions.

Contributors

Sonia Ashmore is a post-doctoral research fellow based at London College of Fashion. From 2003 to 2005 she was a member of the ESRC/AHRC-funded 'Shopping Routes' project. She has a background in publishing, journalism, museum work and the teaching of design history. She is currently investigating the post-war history of fashion consumption in London's West End, with a focus on the development of retail outlets and has an interest in broader themes of cultural exchange in the decorative arts. Her work on Liberty and Co. and Orientalism is to be published by Yale University Press.

Christopher Breward is Deputy Head of Research at the Victoria and Albert Museum, London and a visiting professor at London College of Fashion. From 2003 to 2006 he was Co-Director of the ESRC/AHRC-funded 'Shopping Routes' project. His publications include *The Culture of Fashion* (1995), *The Hidden Consumer* (1999), *Fashion* (2003) and *Fashioning London* (2004). His most recent co-authored/ edited publications include *The London Look* (2004), *Fashion and Modernity* (2005) and *Swinging Sixties* (2006). *The London Look* and *Swinging Sixties* accompanied exhibitions on the same themes at the Museum of London and the Victoria and Albert Museum.

Claire Dwyer is a lecturer in Geography at University College London. She completed her PhD, 'Constructions and Contestations of Islam: Questions of Identity for Young British Muslim Women', in 1997 at the Department of Geography UCL. She specializes in social and cultural geography and her recent publications include 'Tracing trans-nationalities through commodity culture: a case study of British-South Asian Fashion' in P. Jackson, P. Crang and C. Dwyer (eds) *Transnational Spaces* (2004), and with J. Kneale 'Consumption' in J. Duncan, N. Johnson and R. Schein (eds) *A Companion to Cultural Geography* (2004).

Bronwen Edwards is a lecturer in the Department of Geography at Hull University. From 2003 to 2005 she was a post-doctoral research fellow on the ESRC/AHRC-funded 'Shopping Routes' project based at Royal Holloway, University of London. In 2004 she completed her PhD on West End Shopping Cultures in the 1930s at London College of Fashion.

Pamela Church Gibson is Reader in Historical and Cultural Studies at London College of Fashion. She has published extensively on film, fashion, fandom, history and heritage and co-edited three anthologies, which include *Fashion Cultures: Theories, Analyses, Explorations* (2001). From 2003 to 2006 she was a contributor to the ESRC/AHRC-funded 'Shopping Routes' project and is currently working on the relationship between cinema and consumption in the post-war period.

David Gilbert is Professor of Urban and Historical Geography at Royal Holloway, University of London. From 2003 to 2006 he was Co-Director of the ESRC/AHRC-funded 'Shopping Routes' project. His current research interests include the relationships between fashion and world cities, planning and the West End of London, and the connections between fashion and tourism in post-war London. He has a broader interest in the history of modern London and has published articles on the influence of imperialism on the city, on suburban cultures and tourism. His earlier work focused on local cultures of collective action and political identity in inter-war Britain. He is co-editor of *Imperial Cities* (2003) and *Geographies of British Modernity* (2003).

Susan Kaiser is a professor in the Department of Women and Gender Studies, University of California, Davis. She received her PhD in Textiles and clothing from Texas Women's University in 1977. Her areas of research interest cover the social psychology of clothing and fashion and feminist theory. Publications include *The Social Psychology of Clothing: Symbolic Appearances in Context* (1997).

Yuniya Kawamura is assistant professor of Sociology at the Fashion Institute of Technology/State University of NY. She has published *The Japanese Revolution in Paris Fashion* and *Fashion-ology: An Introduction to Fashion Studies* (2004). She is currently conducting fieldwork research on street fashion in Tokyo and New York.

Hudita Nura Mustafa is a sociocultural anthropologist with interests in West Africa, transnational/urban economies as they relate to cultural productions, gender, and post-colonial cultural politics. She has conducted extensive field research on popular economy, fashion and gender in Dakar, Senegal, over the course of the last decade. Her publications and lectures range through the topics of photography, fashion, South African Indian dance, urbanism and global culture. Future work will examine the relationship between global cities such as Dakar, New York City and Paris as a network for the generation of contemporary African arts and popular culture. She is a research fellow at the W.E.B. Dubois Institute for African and African-American studies at Harvard University.

Leslie W. Rabine is a professor in the Department of Women and Gender Studies at the University of California, Davis. She received her BA and MA in French

Literature from Cornell University and her PhD from Stanford. From 1973 to 2000 she taught at UC Irvine. Her research concerns African literature and culture, nineteenth-century French feminism, feminist interpretations of Western critical theory, contemporary feminism in a transnational context, and fashion. Her recent book, *The Global Circulation of African Fashion* (2002) investigates the alternative, informal economic and cultural networks of African fashion producers in the shadow of dominant corporate globalization.

Norma Rantisi is a lecturer in the Department of Geography, Planning and Environment, Concordia University, Montreal. She received her PhD (2002) from the Department of Geography at the University of Toronto. It examined the geography of design innovation for New York City's women's wear industry. Her current research looks at the innovation system for the Montreal apparel industry and assesses the role government policy can play in promoting design-oriented production strategies for local manufacturers. Her research interests also include the industrial restructuring of mature industries in urban settings, the political economy of innovation, local and regional economic development policy, the cultural economy of cities and the economic value of design. Recent publications include 'The Designer in the City and the City in the Designer' in D. Power and A. J. Scott (eds) *Cultural Industries and the Production of Culture* (2004), 'Cultural Industries and Economic Revitalization Revisited: Lessons from the New York Apparel Industry' *Plan Canada* 44 (2), (Summer 2004), and 'The Ascendance of New York Fashion' *International Journal of Urban and Regional Research* 28 (1), (2004).

Agnès Rocamora is a senior research fellow and lecturer in cultural studies at London College of Fashion. She has published articles on media discourses on fashion and on the work of Pierre Bourdieu. Her current research interests cover fashion journalism and fashion consumption. Recent publications include a Bourdieuian field analysis of London Fashion Week in *Sociology* and an article on Reader's Letters in French *Vogue* in *Fashion Theory*.

Simona Segre Reinach is a social anthropologist teaching fashion studies at IULM University in Milan. She also works as a marketing and communication consultant, specializing in the area of fashion. She has published two books: *Moda: Un'introduzione* (2005) and *Mode in Italy: Una lettura antropologica* (1999), and several articles.

Sonnet Stanfill is a curator of contemporary fashion at the Victoria and Albert Museum, London. She received her MA in dress history from the Courtauld Institute. In 2003 she curated the V&A display on Ossie Clark and in 2004–5 she headed the re-display of the museum's permanent dress gallery. She is currently researching a book and display on New York Fashion scheduled for 2007.

Olga Vainshtein is a senior researcher at the Institute for Advanced Studies in the Humanities, Russian State University for the Humanities in Moscow. She is author of *Dandy* (2005), editor of *Smells and Perfumes in the History of Culture* (2003) and has published widely on fashion history. She is on the editorial board of *Fashion Theory: The Journal of Dress, Body and Culture* and is presently editor of the Russian version of *Fashion Theory*.

Elizabeth Wilson is the author of *Adorned In Dreams: Fashion and Modernity*, *The Sphinx in the City* and *Bohemians: the Glamorous Outcasts*. She was formerly Professor of Cultural Studies at London Metropolitan University and is currently a visiting professor at London College of Fashion, University of the Arts, London.

Part I
Urban Modernity and Urban Orders

–1–

From Paris to Shanghai
The Changing Geographies of Fashion's World Cities
David Gilbert

At the opening of the Shanghai International Fashion Centre on 15 October 2000, the then mayor, Xu Kuangdi, pledged that one of the planning goals for the first decade of the twenty-first century was to build the city into the 'world's sixth fashion centre, alongside London, Paris, New York, Milan and Tokyo' (Xu 2003). Xu Kuangdi lost his job as mayor in 2002, and the annual Shanghai fashion festival that takes place each spring, intended to match the collections of the major fashion centres, has not been an instant success. In 2003 shows by Givenchy, Vivienne Tam, Vivienne Westwood and Ferragamo were all cancelled because of SARS, and the 2004 collections were threatened by scares associated with the avian influenza outbreak. Nonetheless, the idea of Shanghai as a new centre in the global order remains a significant strand of urban policy. Recently, discussing preparations for the World Expo due in the city in 2010, Professor Chu Yunmao, Director of the City Image Institute of Donghua University argued that:

> Fashion is an impulse that leads the trends of the times, a banner of the cultural image of an international metropolis. In the world today, the vanguard of fashion is a city's symbol of dynamism. There are five major cities of fashion in the world. They are New York, Paris, London, Milan and Tokyo.... Given its hard work and opportunities, Shanghai will surely be able to establish its own image as a city of fashion and culture. (Zhang 2005: 87)

The new China is most often interpreted as a potentially dominant player in the global garment industry, undercutting producers elsewhere, particularly in Europe and the United States. This was highlighted by the so-called 'Bra Wars' of 2005 after the mismanaged end of the Multifibre Agreement between the European Union and China. Southern European producers called for emergency quotas on cheap Chinese imports, while major retailers lobbied hard for free trade. The campaigns to promote Shanghai as a fashion capital demonstrate wider aspirations for the Chinese industry, going much further than just consolidating the city's position as a key centre for the trading and sale of Chinese-made goods. Like the recent construction of giant skyscrapers in the city, fashion is being used as a signifier of urban modernity and of world status (Yusuf and Wu 2002: 1227).

The idea of the fashion city is now a feature of the global competition between cities, and has become a part of broader strategies of metropolitan boosterism that give prominence to what have become known as the 'cultural industries'. Shanghai's plans have drawn on specific characteristics of the Chinese garment industry, but the attempts to create the institutions of metropolitan fashion culture (particularly 'collections' on the model of Paris, New York and Milan, and a locally centred fashion press) have parallels in developments from Manchester to Melbourne, and Los Angeles to Lisbon. Such strategies draw upon a long-established popular understanding of a certain urban hierarchy, and particularly of the existence of certain cities with global status in the geographies of fashion. City image-makers often draw upon local traditions and histories, but have also played upon connections or comparisons with established centres. One of the rhetorical goals of Xu Kuangdi's policy was to return Shanghai to its position prior to the Second World War and the Chinese revolution as the 'Paris of the East' (Xu 2003).

Both Mayor Xu and Professor Chu repeat with unquestioning certainty a familiar mantra of fashion's world cities – 'London, Paris, New York, Milan and Tokyo'. Permutations of these cities and a few others have been routinely incorporated into the advertising of high fashion, after the name of a designer or brand, or etched into the glass of a shop window. In some cases the name of the fashion capital is incorporated into a brand name itself (as perhaps most famously in the case of DKNY – Donna Karan New York; see Figure 1.1). The list of cities is an almost transparent sign, only noticed when disrupted. In 2004 as part of an advertising campaign to market itself as 'the Fashion Capital' for the Melbourne metropolitan area, a suburban mall covered the city's billboards, trams and buses with the slogan 'New York, Paris, London, Rome, Chadstone.' This book is intended to have the same disturbing effect on taken-for-granted assumptions about fashion's world cities, though hopefully with rather more analytical force. Despite the widespread use of the term 'fashion capital' in academic work as well as in the fashion press, it has attracted little serious consideration.

The explicit conjunction of major cities and fashion, and claims for the global status of certain cities are of course not new. For example, the concept of 'Paris fashion' must represent one of the most powerful and long-running reifications of place in modern history. But even a cursory examination of the way the term has been used draws attention to the complexity of the notion of the fashion capital, and to the complexity of the fashion process itself. The routine description of the city over the past 200 years as the capital of world fashion disguises the ways in which different aspects of the city's relationship with fashion contribute to this understanding. A dominant representation of Paris has emphasized the clustering of elite designers, the structure of the couture system, and the power of the Paris fashion industry to direct fashion styles far beyond the limits of the city. However Paris's role as fashion

Figure 1.1 The city as fashion brand. Advertising for DKNY at Houston Street, New York City. Photograph taken by Noah Najarian.

capital has also been related to its industrial structure, particularly to the long-term survival of a production sector of specialist workshops and individual craft workers, concentrated in the Sentier district of the city. As Nancy Green has suggested in her comparative study of Paris and New York, both cities had 'flexible specialisation before the term was coined' (1997: 4). Elaborate contracting and subcontracting systems in the apparel industries have been a vital element in sustaining a rapid turnover and adaptation of styles. At other times Paris has been interpreted as a world centre of fashion because of its distinctive metropolitan cultures of consumption, both in the narrow sense of shops and shopping, and in a broader sense of the practices associated with the wearing of fashionable dress in the spaces of the city. Agnès Rocamora shows in her chapter here that Paris has also had a long history of representation, particularly in the fashion press, as the first city in an almost free-floating symbolic order of fashionability. There has been something approaching a naturalization of Paris's relationship with fashion, often around the elevation of a certain construction of fashionable femininity to a symbol of Parisian superiority.

Many of the chapters in this book deal with these dimensions of major fashion cities, as centres of a culture of design, as central points in production networks, as examples of distinctive consumption cultures, or as the subjects of representation in film or the fashion press. The last part of this introductory chapter returns to this question of the multidimensional character of the fashion capital or fashion world city. However this book is not intended as a straightforward exercise in typology or definition. The concern is not to provide a simple list of key characteristics by which a fashion capital can be identified, or a straightforward metric to rate a city's global fashion status. Neither are we seeking to provide a toolkit for city managers or urban boosters looking to make a world fashion city. Instead the concern is to explore the idea of the fashion capital both as a changing historical formation, and relationally as a form of urban ordering or hierarchy. This is significant, as while there have been many excellent studies of the development of individual major fashion cities, much less attention has been given to what might be described as the historical geography of fashion's world cities – the processes by which some cites become identified as central sites of global significance in fashion culture, and the competition and interconnections between those cities.

Fashion and the Geographies of Urban Modernity

For too long fashion has been peripheral in study of the modern city. Yet as Elizabeth Wilson suggests in her chapter in this collection, thinking about fashion takes us to the heart of key questions about the nature of urban modernity, in particular its double-sided character, characterized simultaneously by new forms of constraint and commodification in everyday life, but also by new possibilities for active experimentation and identity formation. Wilson's work (1985; 1991) has been at the forefront in shifting the understanding of fashion from a superficial symptom of modernity to a much more active and creative practice. Fashion's complexity matches that of the modern metropolis itself, and the study of fashion has very many direct points of contact with the study of the city. Christopher Breward has argued that fashion is, like the city, multi-layered, making any attempt at analysis especially fraught:

[Fashion] is a bounded thing, fixed and experienced in space – an amalgamation of seams and textiles, an interface between the body and its environment. It is a practice, a fulcrum for the display of taste and status, a site for the production of objects and beliefs; and it is an event, both spectacular and routine, cyclical in its adherence to the natural and commercial seasons, innovatory in its bursts of avant-gardism, and sequential in its guise as a palimpsest of memories and traditions. (Breward 2004: 11)

A reassessment of fashion's significance has been encouraged by moves within urban studies that have emphasized characteristics of the city that meet these qualities directly. Recent work in urban theory has called for an understanding of the urban that prioritizes embodied experience and treats the city as a haptic, sensory environment, just as work in fashion theory has prioritized the relationship between clothing and the body (Pile 1996; Entwistle 2000; Thrift 2004). Fashion has also been a central focus of a new emphasis on the cultural economies and creative industries of cities – while historians of the fashion industry have been at pains to show that such developments are not late twentieth-century novelties, but have developed from earlier formations particularly in major fashion centres (Green 1997; Jackson, Lowe, Miller and Mort 2000; Scott 2000a; Amin and Thrift 2002; Breward 2004). Studies of urban culture have moved beyond a narrow concern for literary or fine art representations of the city, towards an engagement with other ways in which the city is expressed and performed. This turn has also increased the appreciation of the fashion traditions of great cities as an alternative, more demotic and fragmentary form of urban expression.

These connections between specific city histories and fashion cultures have marked some of the best recent work in both urban history and fashion history (see, for example, Mort 1996; Steele 1998; Breward 1999; Nead 2000; Rappaport 2000). Such work, however, has tended to concentrate on individual cities and on certain defining historical periods. Sometimes this has made for rather inward-looking studies of the fashion city, but there has also been significant work that has sought to think about the wider global position of particular urban fashion cultures. This is the explicit focus of Miles Ogborn's illuminating study of the spatiality of modernity in eighteenth-century London. Ogborn argues that our understanding of modernity is transformed through attention to its geographies. Thus studies of modernity need to acknowledge 'the ways in which there are different modernities in different places', and conceptualize 'modernity as a matter of the hybrid relationships and connections between places' (1998: 17). Ogborn's study of the figure of the 'Macaroni', the ultra-dandy of the period, concentrates both on his territories and routes within London, but also on the way that the Macaroni's fashionable consumption drew upon London's position at the centre of a much wider web of trading and cultural relations. The Macaroni was 'understood within the international chains of commodities that made London itself a dangerous place through the ways in which its endless varieties of consumption brought together the produce of the world' (Ogborn 1998: 139).

Ogborn's comments on the geographies of modernity and his focus on the relations between the urban fashion culture of London and the emergent economic geography of the British Empire are important for the wider study of fashion's world cities. There are a number of responses to this challenge, all of which take us beyond studies of the single fashion city. The first of these takes seriously the idea of different modernities in different places. In Ogborn's study of London this refers primarily to the ways that a range of sites in the city expressed different articulations of the modern. This is an approach that may usefully be taken to other cities at other times, extending our sense of the spaces of fashion culture beyond the salon, designer studio, boutique or department store. But it also invites us to think about the particularities of different urban fashion cultures, even in the same historical period. Nancy Green's comparison of the Parisian and New York fashion industries in the twentieth century is instructive here. She points to similarities in industrial structures and in the general pressures created by the development of new mass markets for fashion, but shows the ways in which the fashion system worked quite differently in the two cities. Such different responses drew upon local fashion cultures and modes of organization, but licensing arrangements and copying also meant that there could be a synergistic relationship between these distinctive urban fashion formations.

Second, our understanding of major fashion cities also needs to think of them as constituted 'through hybrid relationships and connections with other places.' This is a major theme in this volume. Both Sonia Ashmore and Claire Dwyer concentrate specifically on these kinds of connections in their contributions. Ashmore's discussion of the so-called cosmopolitan fashions of 1960s London shows how they were part of a much longer tradition of exoticism and orientalism in the city. For example, the department store of Liberty's in Regent Street opened in 1875, selling Indian silks and Japanese goods, and had an immense influence on late nineteenth- and early twentieth-century taste. The success of Liberty's and its lasting influence on London style drew upon the city's imperial position and culture – Arthur Liberty was said to have taken inspiration for his shop from the displays of Indian fabrics at the 1862 International Exhibition. Mica Nava has suggested that a crucial aspect of modern consumption cultures has been the way that exoticism has been constructed and staged in cities like London and Paris, as part of an imaginative geography that set the imperial cities at the centre and the colonized at the margins (Nava 1996).

Ashmore and Dwyer explore later examples of the consumption of cultural diversity and the marketing of versions of the exotic, addressing London's changing position in what Žižek (1997) has described as 'multicultural capitalism'. There are marked differences between the two periods under consideration, indicating different forms of hybridity and connection, and pointing to wider changes in the city's fashion culture. Ashmore's account of the late 1960s indicates a strong lineage between the fashions for 'ethnic' dress of hippy culture, and earlier forms of imperial orientalism. Although the fashion had strong counter-cultural associations, it was promoted by a young urban elite, many with old family connections to the empire. As fashions like the kaftan moved into the mainstream in the early 1970s, they rapidly lost their specific orientalist meanings, becoming instead rather weakly exotic.

Dwyer's study of contemporary fashion networks between London and India also recognizes the importance of the imperial past. However, she argues that the conventional constructions of 'West' and 'East', of modernity and tradition, and of metropole and periphery have been complicated and disrupted by the emergence of transnational commodity cultures that link London and Mumbai. London's 'Indian Summer' of 2000, marked by mainstream catwalk shows of South Asian influenced designs and by 'Indian' fashions in high street stores, has been seen as just a passing phase in multicultural capitalism's appropriation of cultures, objects and styles with a marketable patina of difference. For Nirmal Puwar, 'those who saunter on Kensington High Street with their pashminas and mojay are playing with the East' in a way that 'refuses to see the power of whiteness as an empty privileged space' (2002: 71). While acknowledging that such neo-orientalism remains a feature of fashion culture, Dwyer also points to the ways in which new transnational connections complicate the imaginative geographies of fashion, challenging established signifiers of 'West' and 'East'.

Dwyer's study of the complexities of diasporic and transnational fashion cultures highlights more general ways that major cities have drawn upon their privileged positions in wider networks. Fashion in such centres has been shaped by flows of people (as cheap skilled labour, designers, entrepreneurs and consumers), materials, capital and ideas. Even Paris, so often represented in the mythologies of fashion as a closed and self-sufficient fashion centre, can only be understood in these terms. (Ironically, as Pamela Church Gibson discusses in her chapter, the representation of Paris as an autarkic citadel of fashion has often been promoted with great vigour from outside of France, particularly in Hollywood's constructions of the city, and in the international fashion press.) From top to bottom, the Parisian industry has been shaped by migration. Charles Worth, Elsa Schiaparelli, Christòbal Balenciaga and Alexander McQueen are all examples of Paris's place in the life-journeys of major designers.

Equally the labour force of the Parisian garment industry has been largely immigrant for over a century. Immigrants to the city have come 'in overlapping succession, from Germany and Belgium, from Eastern Europe, from the ex-Ottoman Empire, from North Africa, and more recently from Yugoslavia, Turkey, South-East Asia and mainland China' (Green 2002: 35). Such immigration has been a feature of the development of most major fashion centres, particularly London, New York and Los Angeles. As Lesley Rabine and Susan Kaiser suggest here, immigrant labour in fashion's world cities has usually been concentrated in small workshops, often at or beyond the margins of legal employment, characterized by poor physical conditions, long hours and low wages. Yet Rabine and Kaiser also suggest that migrants are more than the passive victims of the exploitations of the garment industry. Through the direct participation of migrant entrepreneurs, given opportunities through the complex subcontracting networks, and through a more general influence on the culture of cities, these movements of people have played a vital role in transforming and renewing metropolitan fashion cultures. (See Rath 2002.)

This emphasis on fashion's flows and connections chimes with Amin and Thrift's observation that much recent work on urbanism more generally has had 'a strong emphasis on understanding cities as spatially open and cross-cut by many different kinds of mobilities, from flows of people to commodities and information' (2002: 3). However, Ogborn's observations about the geographies of modernity indicate that this is not enough. London's fashion culture in the eighteenth century and after was also critically shaped by the structured spatialities of imperialism, and particularly by London's position as the imperial capital. In thinking about the nature of fashion's world cities we need to address such networks of power, as expressed in a range of registers from the economic to the cultural. Too often studies in fashion history have taken for granted the wider structures of imperialism or globalizing capitalism, and their consequence for fashion's key urban centres. And, to paraphrase the geographer John Agnew, we also need to think about fashion's active role in actively 'spatializing' the world – dividing, labelling and sorting it into a hierarchy of places of greater or lesser 'importance' (Agnew 1998: 2).

Fashion and the 'World City Hypothesis'

Approaching fashion's world cities from a perspective that emphasizes their position within wider structures of economic and political power draws us towards the literature in urban studies that has focused on 'world cities' or 'global cities'. In 1986, John Friedmann put forward what he described as 'the world city hypothesis' (see Friedmann and Wolff 1982 for an earlier version of these ideas). Friedmann's ideas were less a formal hypothesis than an agenda for research concerning the relationship of cities to the development of the world economy. Friedmann argued that increasing economic globalization had shifted the balance between major cities' roles as centres of territorially bounded political states and as sites for the management of global capital. Increasingly the decisive variable in explaining the nature of key 'world cities' was 'the mode of their integration with the global economy' over and above 'their own historical past, national policies, and cultural influences' (1986: 69). This claim had several consequences for the analysis of cities. First, Friedmann suggested that structural changes in the economies of such world cities (and consequent changes in their physical forms, social composition and urban cultures) were dependent on the form and extent of their integration into the world economy. Second, Friedmann argued that it was necessary to understand cities as part of a world system, thus emphasizing both the significance of connections and interdependencies between major cities, but also their positions within a structured hierarchy.

Friedmann paid particular attention to those cities at the very top of his hierarchy, what he described as 'primary core cities'. In the mid 1980s he suggested that these were London, Paris, New York, Chicago, Los Angeles and Tokyo. Here there is significant overlap with what Saskia Sassen has described as 'global cities' (1991, 2001). In the late twentieth and early twenty-first centuries these cities have developed intense concentrations of 'advanced producer services', typically in sectors such as banking, accountancy, advertising, insurance, commercial law and management consultancy. Sassen argues that financial deregulation and the development of new forms of telecommunications, media and information technology, far from dispersing economic activities as some predicted, has created an aggressive new logic for their concentration of these activities in a few great cities. Sassen further argues that the global cities, particularly London and New York, have been marked by increasing economic and social polarization. Alongside the development of advanced producer services has been a parallel development of a low-paid service sector, often characterized by a casualized labour force with a high proportion of immigrants. In Sassen's account of the distinctive characteristics of the global city, fashion appears only in the guise of the sweatshops of the garment industry.

One response to this emphasis on 'world cities' and 'global cities' has focused on the significance of urban hierarchies, and has attempted to produce different taxonomic strategies for ordering and categorizing cities. At its worst this work has descended into a fixation with league tables and debates about the best way to measure the worldliness of a world city. Beyond consideration of the location of the corporate headquarters of fashion and luxury goods conglomerates like LVMH (Moët Hennessy Louis Vuitton), fashion has rarely been factored into such urban ranking schemes. These have been dominated by analyses of advanced producer services, which have been used to measure the 'global capacity' of various cities. (See, for recent examples of such work, Beaverstock, Smith and Taylor 1999a, 1999b and 2000; Taylor 2004.) Following Friedmann's original arguments such advanced producer services (and financial services in particular) are seen as the primary driving forces of the global urban order. While other activities may demonstrate different kinds of urban networks and hierarchies (see, for example, Taylor 2004 on the global urban geographies of NGOs), these are very much seen as secondary features of the global urban system.

There is clearly a significant overlap between the cities routinely described as world fashion cities, and those identified by Friedmann, Sassen and their followers as primary world cities or global cities. Given, in Friedmann's terminology, the embeddedness of a 'transnational capitalist class' whose 'ideology is consumerist' in such world cities, and given fashion's inherent elitism and consumerism, it would be very surprising if this were not the case (Friedmann 1995: 26). The emergence of New York as a world city of fashion in the early twentieth century, or Tokyo's rise as an international fashion centre from the early 1980s were not unrelated to the position of those cities in rising economic superpowers (see Kawamura and

Rantisi in this collection). However, the major centres of world fashion cannot be simply read off from a list of the main world business centres. For example, within Western Europe, Frankfurt and Milan can be taken as contrasting examples. While the financial centre of Frankfurt has a range of elite designer stores, catering to an affluent, international population, it hardly registers in the wider symbolic or economic geographies of fashion. By contrast, Milan, although certainly one of the most significant business command and control centres in the European Union, has been regarded since the 1970s at least as one of fashion's four or five front-rank world centres (see Simona Segre Reinach's discussions of the development of Milan as a fashion capital in this collection). Viewed historically, there are also significant discontinuities between the development of fashion's ordering of world centres and the urban geographies of global finance, demonstrated most clearly in Paris's long history as the claimed centre of the world fashion industry, despite the vicissitudes of the French economy and catastrophic interruptions by war. The argument here is not that analysis of fashion culture's fixation with urban orderings and world centres can produce a more accurate overall metric of the global significance of certain cities. There are, however, a number of potential insights that can come from bringing the perspectives of the world cities literature together with consideration of the geographies of fashion.

Clearly themes taken from the world cities literature can inform studies of the organization of the contemporary fashion industry. This has underpinned some recent work on fashion that has talked of a historic shift in the balance of power between New York and Paris as fashion capitals. (See for very different examples of this work Agins 1999 and Rantisi 2004a.) This work has argued that the fashion industry has become more locked into the concentration and centralization of advanced capitalism, developing characteristics that make it increasingly like an advanced producer service. In this view, the new fashion world city is less significant as a centre of a design tradition or a cluster of highly skilled manufacturing, than as the organizational headquarters of a global branding industry. Terry Agins has described this as the 'end of fashion' and the 'death of couture' (a demise proclaimed pretty regularly over the past hundred years). This transformation has a number of elements, all of which have altered fashion's relationship with major urban centres, and, Agins argues, has seen New York usurp Paris's position as the dominant fashion centre. The development of American 'designer' sportswear and leisurewear brands in the 1980s and 1990s (such as Calvin Klein, DKNY and Tommy Hilfiger) disrupted the connection between design and skilled, locally based manufacturing. Since the time of Charles Worth modern fashion has always been about the creation of brand identities and the complex relationship between haute couture and the industrial production of copies. But recent developments seem to mark a profound change in the balance between brands and the significance of actual garments, with most production moving to offshore suppliers. In the new organizational order of the fashion industry most elite designers, and certainly most of those shown in the main seasonal collections, are first and foremost global brand identities, part of the portfolio of powerful conglomerates like LMVH, PPR (Pinault Printemps Redoute) or the Prada group. In her chapter here, Norma Rantisi, writes of New York's emergent ascendance in the geography of fashion's world centres, but also of how that shift simultaneously seems to threaten the diversity and vibrancy of the New York fashion scene.

The development of this fashion oligarchy has strengthened the connections between the networks of fashion and corporate finance. At the same time, the primary importance of branding has strengthened the importance of connections with activities like advertising, management consultancy and corporate law. Perhaps the most symbolic site in the development of fashion's recent geography is not a designer shop or department store, but the new American corporate headquarters for LVMH, a spectacular skyscraping office on East 57th Street in Manhattan. This symbol of the increasing corporate control of high fashion is indicative of tensions between the development of global cities (as understood by Sassen) and previously established formations of the fashion industry in its world centres. The overall decline of manufacturing (including with some exceptions, the rag trade) in most major world cities is a well-established feature of their development. Some have described this as a shift towards a post-industrial city characterized not just by the growth of corporate command centres, but also by the emergence of clusters of smaller firms in the 'creative industries', typically in sectors like film, television, music and particularly advertising (Hall 2000). While high-end fashion design working for major corporations is sometimes included in discussions of such clusters, the smaller scale independent sector has suffered significantly from the escalation of property costs in major world cities.

The best work on world cities addresses not just the position of cities in a rank order, but also analyses the nature of connections between cities, and the institutions and processes that work to include, exclude and position cities in the hierarchy (Taylor 2004). Recent work has involved mapping the intercity structures of multinational corporations or the contractual networks of firms in different sectors. Clearly one task for research into the geographies of fashion is to map these kinds of connection. This work has also emphasized the way that even in a world with massive capacity for instantaneous long-distance communication and financial transfer, the relationship between cities is shaped by very basic constraints of time and space. The most common example given is the way that 24-hour trading of shares, currency and commodities has strengthened the position of primary financial markets in different time zones. Fashion's urban world order has worked in different ways, with seasonality as an important factor. As the Australian geographer Sally Weller has noted, all of the conventional world fashion cities, Paris, New York, London, Milan and Tokyo, are situated between 35° and 52° latitude, in the northern hemisphere (Weller 2004: 109). This is not to suggest, like some early twentieth-century proponents of Paris's natural fashion superiority, that the fashion capitals are determined by climate. (Writing in 1908, Edouard Debect argued that France's fashion success came from its perfect climatic position somewhere between the 'cold countries' and the 'blazing'. Quoted in Green 1997: 108.) What it does mean is that the operation of global fashion has become locked into the seasonal rhythms of the temperate northern hemisphere. The major fashion collections are constrained by this seasonality. Given the need to place collections at strategic points in the year, avoiding clashes, there is probably time for no more than three or four collections that can guarantee global media attention, and which can work as part of the travelling circus of the controlling elites of fashion culture.

If the literature on world cities can inform an understanding about fashion's urban ordering, there are also important lessons that travel in the opposite direction, deepening these explorations of urban centrality and ordering. Fashion's slippery character is key to this, stretching standard categories of analysis. Fashion works through a 'never-ceasing play between the processes of production and consumption', it involves both the sale of commodities and the exercise of the creative imagination, and it is at once highly symbolic and yet an intimate part of embodied, everyday experience (Breward 2003: 21). As such it helps us to think about other ways that cities and the spaces within them are ordered and connected. Arjun Appadurai has famously argued that globalization needs to be understood not as a singular process but as multiple and differentiated, working through a series of overlaid '-scapes' or morphologies of flow and movement (Appadurai 1990; 1996). Alongside a 'finanscape' shaped by the shifting global disposition of capital, are other global geographies that he describes variously as ethnoscapes, mediascapes, technoscapes and ideoscapes. Commenting directly on the world city literature, Anthony King uses these ideas to point to different dimensions of the ways that certain cities constitute central places of global significance. For King, 'the problem with the term "world" or "global city" is that it has been appropriated, perhaps hijacked, to represent and also reify not only just one part of a city's activity ... but also has been put at the service of only one representation of "the world" – the world economy' (King 1995: 217). Even within the economic realm, the conventional world city literature gives precedence to one particular dimension, with activities such as consumption and tourism relegated to secondary considerations, although both are economic activities with distinctive geographies of flows and central places.

There are other kinds of urban centrality that are highlighted by King's comments. It has already been noted that one important aspect of fashion's world cities has been their positioning in flows of people, what Appadurai terms movement in the 'ethnoscape'. King also argues that alongside the political economy approach of the world city literature, the nature of urban power and centrality has to be understood within the historical, political and cultural framework of post-imperialism or post-colonialism. The idea of fashion authority, of certain specific urban milieux as the sources of style, has been a powerful form of cultural imperialism. While fashion's world cities have often been examined in terms of distinctive national and metropolitan cultures – in terms of the 'Frenchness' of Parisian fashions, or the edginess of a distinctively London look – they have also worked as a key element of a wider long-running discourse that divided the world into forward and backward regions.

Every bit as much as imperial monuments or the great exhibitions, fashion was used as a means of expressing the superiority of certain places in the world order. (Indeed, the 1900 Exposition Universelle in Paris included twenty displays by couture houses. Lipovetsky 1994: 57.) Versions of 'Parisian' fashions had an extra-ordinary reach in the late nineteenth century, available to elites in urban contexts as different as Meiji Tokyo, gold-rush Melbourne, and the newly prosperous and expanding South American capitals of Montevideo and Buenos Aires. In these contexts, such fashions were understood as expressions of modernity, and their consumption as a marker of belonging and status in a world order centred in the great European capitals. This relationship extended (and indeed still extends) beyond the direct consumption of clothes with some lingering connection with Paris, or the vicarious consumption of the fashion capital in novels, film or the fashion press. Just as more official town planning and architecture attempted to map European modernity into the urban fabric of colonial cities, so the examples of the fashion capitals provided models for the spaces of elite consumption. Shanghai's claims to be the 'Paris of the East' worked through fashions and attitudes towards consumption, but also in the design and culture of the shops and shopping environment of the Bund. In Melbourne, locals have talked of the 'Paris end of Collins Street' for over a century. Both the revived Bund and contemporary Collins Street retain this mimetic relationship with Paris, indicating its continuing force as a symbolic marker of high fashion. (See Figures 1.2 and 1.3.) Clearly this kind of relationship is embedded within the geography of Appadurai's mediascape, dependent on long-running tropes promoted by the fashion press, films and elsewhere that have sustained a powerful imaginative geography of style and sophistication. But it is also possible to stretch Appadurai's concept of globally dispersed ideoscapes to encompass fashion as a particular commercialized expression of the Enlightenment 'image-idea' of progress.

This idea of the continuing cultural significance of certain key cities in a world fashion order is a theme that runs through many of the chapters in this collection. In her chapter, Yuniya Kawamura, argues that the emergence of world-ranked Japanese designers during the 1970s and 1980s placed Tokyo on the fashion map as a significant centre. However their particular career paths via the institutions of Paris, 'the imperial fashion city', locked Tokyo into a subordinate position in the fashion hierarchy, in the opinions of both Japanese designers and consumers. Kawamura notes both the Japanese fixation with Western luxury goods, and the ways that Japanese brands have often adopted French names. Hudita Nura Mustafa charts a more complex response to the cultural hierarchies of cities in Dakar, sometimes given the soubriquet 'Paris of Africa'. Mustafa argues that the mimicry implied in this comparison legitimizes Dakar as a modern cultural centre, but at the same time reinforces constructions of Africa as a culturally regressive space that required the

Figure 1.2 Shanghai's Bund restored and reinvented. Elite shopping in historic architecture at Bund 18 in 2005. Photograph © Wen-I Lin.

'progressive' influence of French high fashion. In her account, Mustafa recognizes the pervasive power of the mythologies of Paris in Africa, and the importance of connections between African cities and migrants in the French capital. Nonetheless she interprets *la Mode Dakaroise*, and particularly the complex sartorial performances of middle-class women in Dakar, not as simple emulation of Paris fashions, but as an actively crafted, cosmopolitan urban style, with a 'remarkable capacity to hybridize, reinvent and resist global hegemonies.'

Fashion's World Cities: The Historical Geography of an Urban Ordering

In its famous 'Swinging London' edition of April 1966, *Time* magazine seemed to suggest that there was a fashion cycle for cities as well as clothes:

> Every decade has its city. During the shell-shocked 1940s thrusting New York led the way, and in the uneasy 50s it was the easy Rome of *La Dolce Vita*. Today it is London, a city steeped in tradition, seized by change, liberated by affluence.... . In a decade

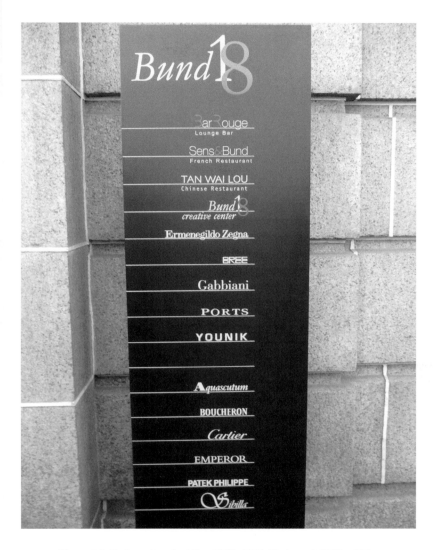

Figure 1.3 Designer brands at Bund 18 in 2005. Photograph © Wen-I Lin.

dominated by youth, London has burst into bloom. It swings, it is the scene. (*Time* 15 April 1966: 32)

Although the *Time* article was picking up on significant changes in London during the 1960s, its tone and style are representative of a common form of fashion journalism, identifying the latest 'hot' place. In its April 2005 edition, British *Vogue* published a new fashion map of the world, subtitled 'Hot in the City', that included

São Paulo, Antwerp, Copenhagen, Kuwait City, Moscow, Delhi and Melbourne alongside the usual suspects. Despite its claims to be the fashion Bible, one piece of editorial filler in *Vogue* does not amount to a definitive list of fashion's current world cities. What it does indicate is the expanding range of places that now might be considered as significant fashion centres. A similar map published twenty years earlier would have been much more focused on the conventional list of fashion cities, concentrated in Western Europe and North America.

Like the *Time* article, *Vogue's* map was predicated on wider changes in the world order. Fashion's ordering does not operate in a vacuum, but instead is shaped by broader economic, cultural and even geopolitical factors. At first sight *Time's* article reads as the most diaphanous hype. It took the format of a storyboard for an imaginary film. Different 'scenes' took the readers out with an aristocratic party at Annabel's nightclub in Mayfair, then, the next day, off shopping in Chelsea, with a coffee bar stop with Mick Jagger, television presenter Cathy McGowan and a teenager in a black and yellow PVC mini-skirt thrown in. This London 'film' was completed with further glamorous lunch parties and art gallery receptions, before a final dinner party with Marlon Brando, Roddy McDowell, Barbra Streisand, Margot Fonteyn, Warren Beatty and other stars in the Kensington home of the actress Leslie Caron (Breward 2006). Yet behind this confection of a city peopled by the famous and beautiful, all dressed in the latest cutting-edge fashions, was a sense that the new London was a key site in much broader changes taking place across the Western world: increasing consumer affluence, particularly among teenagers and young adults, changing intergenerational relationships, and new attitudes towards popular culture, leisure and the body.

Vogue's 2005 map is a similarly superficial indicator of major changes in the contexts of urban fashion, drawing attention particularly to the emergent economies in South America, East Asia and the Gulf, or the resurgence of high-end fashion in post-communist cities. Olga Vainshtein in her chapter here points to the re-emergence of Moscow as a fashion city. This 'wild' stage of capitalism in Moscow focuses on the conspicuous consumption of luxury goods in a city marked by staggering inequalities of wealth. While the majority of the population struggle to make ends meet, Moscow now boats the biggest Armani store in Europe, and the boutiques in Tretyakovsky Proezd shift Gucci, Dolce e Gabbana and Prada by the lorry-load. This new Moscow looks not to Paris as its exemplar, but to an imagined Milan characterized by the kind of ostentatious vulgarity most often associated with the excesses of Gianni and Donatella Versace.

Such connections between 1960s London, contemporary Moscow and wider changes in the economic and political contexts of major cities are indicative of a much longer interplay between fashion and urban ordering. Although much of the world and global city literature has focused on recent developments in capitalism, others such as Peter Taylor (2004) and Anthony King (1990) have pointed to the significance of the long-term development of a network of key cities. Elsewhere I have argued that the continuing status of London, New York and particularly Paris has to be understood through just such a long-term history, which places fashion at the intersection of key cultural and economic processes that shaped the urban order (Gilbert 2000: 15). Put in very broad historical terms, the development of the major fashion centres before the mid twentieth century was shaped in turn by the urban consumer revolution of the late seventeenth and eighteenth centuries, by the economic and symbolic systems of European imperialism, by the development of rivalries between European fashion cities, by the growing influence of an American engagement with European fashion, and finally by the emergence of a distinctively modern fashion media system, that was focused on a few key urban centres.

Gilles Lipovetsky (1994: 20) argues that modern fashion, in the sense of the 'systematic reign of the ephemeral', was a European invention 'scarcely existing before the mid fourteenth century'. Early innovations in European fashion anticipated the development of later fashion systems in the great metropolises. The fashion cultures of early modern Italy were closely associated with the rise of cities – Milan, Florence and Venice – and with the complicated politics of status and display that came with a growing merchant class. These Italian cities, like later centres of mercantile capitalism in the Low Countries, were characterized by concentrations of commercial activity, and by public areas that promoted the spectacle of fashionable consumption, encouraging the demand for novelty. 'Streets, squares, arcades, and promenades offered places where crowds might congregate, classes intermingle, and individuals compete for attention' (Breward 2003: 169).

However, the geography of fashion in Europe worked not just through this emergence of a bourgeois 'city' system, but also through a 'courtly' system of royal and aristocratic display that was concentrated in the great national capitals. These 'dual paths' of fashion converged in late seventeenth-century Paris. A standard interpretation of the long-term development of French fashion emphasizes the power and prestige of the court at Versailles under Louis XIV, operating as the centre of a system of instruction and emulation (Roche 1994: 48). However in part through the demands created by the court, and in part through Colbert's deliberate strategy of import substitution (aimed particularly at excluding Italian luxury goods in favour of French products), the Parisian economy was transformed. By the beginning of the eighteenth century, thousands of tailors, dressmakers and milliners were producing not just for courtiers, but also for a new Parisian bourgeoisie, and for an increasing number of French and foreign visitors to the city (Steele 1988: 25). In terms of fashion culture at least, Paris was becoming a more open society, characterized by trends that emerged from different strata of its urban culture, rather than trickling down from the court (Steele 1988: 27).

Put in the broadest of terms, there was a long-term shift in the locus of fashion between court and city. In Norbert Elias's terms, the 'civilising and cultural physiognomy' of aristocratic court society 'was taken over by professional-bourgeois society, partly as a heritage' (1987: 40). Buckley and Gundle (2000: 335) indicate that a key element of this 'heritage' was the continuing importance of conspicuous consumption, its association with status, and its increasingly widespread use as a marker of consumer sophistication. Discussions of the emergence of modern consumption patterns now conventionally stress the importance of an urban renaissance and 'consumer revolution' of the late seventeenth and early eighteenth centuries, rather than the later industrial revolution. Glennie and Thrift (1992) suggest that European and new North American urban contexts were central both to the learning of new consumption practices and to their pursuit.

Yet not all cities were equally suited to the development of the fashion process. If, as Glennie and Thrift argue, knowledge of consumption was essentially practical, acquired less through instruction or advertising, as through 'quasi-personal contact and observation in the urban throng', then some cities (particularly London and Paris) were more thronging than others (1992: 430). And if the rise of fashion was dependent on the prioritization of novelty, then some cities (and again particularly London and Paris) were in positions in the networks of world trade that enhanced the supply of novel experiences, and encouraged the acceleration of the fashion cycle. Albeit in rather different ways, eighteenth and early nineteenth-century London and Paris were both sites that combined long traditions of elite fashion (and associated specialist urban producers of fashionable goods), strongly growing 'professional-bourgeois' markets, and increasingly significant central roles in imperial structures of political control and trade.

As has already been argued here, the growth and systemization of European imperialism was an important phase in the development of fashion's world cities. Most obviously this worked in terms of the relationship between the great metropolises and the colonized world, especially the world of the settler colonies. London and Paris came to be understood as sites of both innovation and of fashion authority. This worked through the actual export of clothes and designs, but also through the symbolic projection of these cities as avatars of fashionable modernity. Other kinds of flow and connection between the colonies and the imperial metropolises also reinforced their status. The new department stores of London, Paris and other European capitals promoted themselves through a rhetoric and performance of world significance and centrality. Guidebooks and other promotional literature for those arriving from the colonies stressed the significance of London as a capital of style and luxury (Gilbert 1999). The spheres of influence of imperial fashion trade were of lasting significance for the major fashion cities. While the international sale and licensing of haute couture designs underpinned Paris's reputation as the predominant fashion capital, the French colonies formed an important market for its ready-made clothes from the late nineteenth century until decolonization in the 1950s and 1960s (Green 2002: 32).

The age of Empire was marked not only by highly unequal relations between Europe and the rest of the world, but also by intense economic, political and cultural competition between the European powers. High fashion became another of the ways that European national cultures could measure themselves against each other. Berlin, Brussels, Vienna and Milan all combined significant local fashion production, distinctive design traditions and spectacular shops with the public display of fashion among the crowds in their streets, squares and arcades. However, even within Europe, such competition took place within a developing hierarchy of fashion cities, in which Paris was increasingly best able to position itself as the world capital of fashion. Anticipating the twentieth-century relationship between the French and American industries, from its origins the European fashion system was marked by an uneasy mixture of competition and synergy between its major centres. Neil McKendrick has argued that the veneration of Paris was a significant dimension of the consumer revolution centred on eighteenth-century London. Fashion that was 'expensive, exclusive and Paris-based' was translated into something that was 'cheap, popular and London-based' (McKendrick 1983: 43). It was vital that the process of translation from exclusive Parisian fashion to popular London fashion was incomplete, and that a residue of Parisian origins remained on clothes that were intended for consumption outside the traditional elites.

Despite London's incontrovertible economic and political supremacy, it is Paris that is remembered, in Walter Benjamin's phrase, as the 'capital of the nineteenth century', not least because its cityscape was remade as a global object of desire and consumption (Hancock 1999: 75). The 'Haussmannization' of Paris changed more than its street pattern and its architecture; it also altered the imagined geography of the city, locking together a strong visual trope of the material city with ideas about its cultural life, in which the consumption and public display of high fashion were key elements. London and Paris represented different sides of the modern city, with the feminized 'capital of pleasure' routinely contrasted with a more masculine city of work and business. This gendering of urban identities corresponded with a division in the dominant characterizations of the cities as fashion centres, with London associated with elite male tailoring, and Paris the dominant centre for women's fashion.

By the late nineteenth century, tourism was an increasingly significant element in fashion's urban order. European and North American cities promoted themselves as centres for luxury shopping, and magazines and tourist guides were increasingly significant in the production of international understandings of the fashion cultures of major cities. International tourism was one of the growth industries of Second Empire Paris, and by the end of the nineteenth century developments in transatlantic travel helped to turn the city into the hub of the European tour for thousands of upper- and middle-class Americans. More than the clothes of particular designers, the fashion object that was being consumed was the city itself, and the spectacle of high fashion *in situ*. Those Americans who travelled to experience Paris were just part of the wider popular consumption of the idea of the city as an elite space.

The development of the international fashion system in the early twentieth century was marked both by an unprecedented democratization as more and more people had access to fashion clothing and fashion imagery, and also by a concentration of the control of style and design (Craik 1994: 74). Lipovetsky (1994: 50) may be guilty of polemical exaggeration in suggesting that 'with the hegemony of haute couture, a hypercentralized fashion appeared, entirely indigenous to Paris and yet at the same time international: Parisian fashion was followed by all the "up-to-date" women in the world.' Other fashion centres did retain independent significance, and the geographies of male fashions were always more complex. Nonetheless, the institutionalization of the couture system strongly reinforced Paris's claims to be the world's capital of fashion. In the second half of the nineteenth century, Charles Frederick Worth particularly had reinvented the role of the couturier, placing it at the core of the Parisian fashion system. Worth inaugurated the cult of the designer, producing a figure that was seen as the author of new styles. This owed something to Worth's design talents, but much more to his innovations in marketing and business organization, effectively creating the first designer brand (see De Marly 1980). The same period saw the development of strongly enforced systems of licensing and legal restrictions on copying in France that further concentrated the industry in Paris and enhanced the sense that fashion was something that was diffused from the city's designers.

In the early twentieth century there was a formal institutionalization of the distinction between couturiers and other fashion professionals with the establishment of La Chambre Syndicale de la Couture Parisienne in 1910. Organized fashion shows and seasonal collections also began in this period. These developments had a number of implications for fashion's geographies. The first shows with live models and music were criticized in *L'Illustration* as part of a 'hideous crisis of bad taste' (quoted in Steele 1988: 228). However, what seemed likely to be a short lived gimmick became an integral element of modern fashion promotion, turning the launch of new fashions into a focused performance. The fashion show worked both to focus attention on key spaces within the city, but was also a perfect fit for the requirements of the new fashion and news media. The Paris fashion system became more structured in its annual timetable in this period. After the First World War, seasonal shows presenting the new collections of the major couture houses were organized at more or less fixed dates in the calendar. This new systematized haute couture system regularized the rhythms of fashion, with a normalization of change brought about at fixed dates by specialized groups (Lipovetsky 1994: 58). The biannual collections gave precedence to foreign agents and buyers, who were able to purchase reproduction rights.

In this new formation of the international fashion system there was a strong interdependence between Parisian and American fashion. The American film industry recast the mythologies of Paris for a global audience (see Church Gibson's chapter in this collection). However, Paris, or more accurately the aura of Parisian fashion authority, was also a critical feature in the systematization of the American fashion cycle, used to organize seasons into particular looks and colours. The sale of patterns to foreign ready-to-wear companies (illegal in France itself) underpinned the mythology of Paris as the authoritative source of fashion edicts. This system reached a high point in the post-war accommodation between the French and American fashion industries that was aggressively promoted in American *Vogue*. The period after Christian Dior's 'New Look' of 1947 was marked by an unprecedented penetration of Parisian designs and influences into the American market. At the top end these were officially licensed copies, but the rapidly expanding American middle market was dominated by copies of the season's Parisian looks, taking advantage of the USA's more liberal laws on style copyright (Green 1997: 120). As the Broadway musical *Sweet Charity* put it, what many American women wanted was a 'copy of a copy of a copy of Dior.' As the designs were copied and recopied, making their way down the social hierarchy, the patina of Parisian design became thinner and thinner, but what was important was that there was still some lingering connection to the authentic original in the Paris collections.

In the early twentieth century, New York City became established as another place that existed both as an actual site of elite fashion consumption and as an imagined space of fashion fantasy (see Rantisi's chapter in this collection). Since the late eighteenth century New York had been the dominant economic city of the United States, and a public culture of socially choreographed displays of fashion, taste and difference on Broadway and Fifth Avenue was well developed by the 1860s (Domosh 1998). By the late nineteenth century, the city was the match of London and Paris in both its scale and its 'intensely urban qualities', which stimulated the development of a vibrant commercial culture (Hammack 1991: 37). Like the great European capitals, it also possessed a highly flexible local manufacturing sector able to respond rapidly to changes of style, at least in part due to the heterogeneity of a population in which immigrants were a majority.

A number of factors pushed New York into the front rank of fashion cities in the early twentieth century. To some extent, this was a direct reflection of the rise of American political and economic power. The development of New York's international fashion prestige depended on the development of a class of the super-rich resident in the apartments and hotels of the city. As the novels of Edith Wharton and Henry James indicate, this new elite often sought to validate and consolidate their status through connections with established European aristocratic families. High fashion formed part of the performance of this new status; but what was significant was that this performance was increasingly one with a global audience. The image of elite New York consumption was one element in an unprecedented promotion of a city as a spectacle of commercial culture. Alongside the emerging vertical city of skyscrapers, and Broadway's 'great white way', the high fashion shops of Fifth Avenue became a familiar part of a cityscape that was celebrated in film, song, literature and indeed in tourist literature for those now making the journey across the Atlantic from East to West (Gilbert and Hancock 2006).

In the twentieth century, the hierarchy of fashion cities was mediated particularly through the fashion press. Although fashion's metropolitan centres had long been consumed vicariously through magazines and other forms of publicity, the development of the modern fashion press reinforced the idea that a very few cities had a distinctive global importance. The *Vogue* titles were particularly important in this respect. American *Vogue* USA was founded in 1892, but was only dedicated to fashion from 1909. It was followed by London and Paris editions in 1916 and 1920 respectively. It was not until after the Second World War that other international editions appeared, for example in Italy in 1950, and in Australia the same year. Such magazines became desirable consumer objects in their own right, disseminating knowledge about elite design far beyond the elite customers of Paris, London and New York. However the world represented in *Vogue* was tightly constrained. Not only were readers shown designs and collections that came almost exclusively from the main fashion centres, they were taught about the detailed shopping geographies of those cities, through columns like British *Vogue's* 'Shophound' (Edwards 2006). Newer fashion and lifestyle magazines, like *Elle* published in France from 1945 or *Cosmopolitan* (UK 1963), may have had a more democratic view of affordable fashion, but still retained a fixation with certain key sites in fashion's world order. Agnès Rocamora's study in this collection shows the remarkable consistency in the ways that cities and their fashion cultures have been represented in magazines and other parts of the media. In the case of Paris, the city has long been naturalized as a place where style and creativity are in the atmosphere, or even anthropomorphized as a sentient force, the ultimate creator of fashion.

The post-war period saw significant shifts in fashion's ordering of cities, both in the institutional organization of the industry, and in the symbolic promotion and understanding of fashion capitals. For some, the international success of the 'New Look' seemed to presage a lasting return to Parisian domination of the international fashion system. However, a number of changes were undermining the long-defended division between couture and ready-made copies. During the 1950s, Parisian originated fashions came under sustained competition from Italian fashions, also targeted at the lucrative American market. Italian style, as Pamela Church Gibson argues in this volume, was well suited to the mythologizings of Hollywood and the fashion press, and an imagined Rome played an important part in its promotion. The structure of the Italian industry was distinctively different, with its cutting edge consisting not of handmade couture, but designed ready-to-wear fashions. In the 1960s, London was the locus of a different kind of challenge to the established order that drew on a newly affluent youth market. The significance of designers like Mary Quant was that they showed that cutting-edge fashion could be very different from the Parisian model. In place of the wealthy, elite and mature couture customer, Quant promoted the Chelsea Girl, a figure defined by her youth (and her skinny body shape), her casual confidence in the city, and her willingness to experiment with a rapid succession of new looks. London fashion in the 1960s, while still in part about the work of a group of designers identified with the city, was as much about the development of a distinctive urban fashion culture, seemingly more spontaneous, and associated with the boutique, street and club.

The post-war period, and particularly the period from the 1960s onwards, was therefore characterized by a less concentrated and more differentiated ordering of fashion's major centres. The Parisian collections were joined by others, and the biannual journeys of international buyers turned into a moving road show of events. The first shows in Florence were organized in 1951, and 1958 saw the first London fashion weeks. Other cities formed organizations to protect and promote local design traditions, such as the Council of Fashion Designers of America founded in New York in 1963. However what was taking place was not that other cities were threatening to usurp Paris's established position, but that the whole geometry of fashion's urban ordering was changing. For a time in the 1960s, particularly when viewed through developments in London or the West Coast of the USA, it looked as if this might see a transition to a new fashion order that was less controlled and hierarchical (see Kaiser and Rabine in this collection). However, what did take place between the late 1950s and the 1980s was a reconfiguration of the relationship between elite fashion and mass-market clothes that redefined the role of key cities.

Sally Weller (2004) has suggested that the crisis in the couture system brought about responses that reconfigured the global geographies of the fashion system in the second half of the twentieth century. These she argues marked a fundamental break in the relationship between fashion design as a form of commodified knowledge and the actual production of clothes. The first major development was the expansion of licensing and branding. There is a long association between couture houses and licensed perfumes and accessories; Ernest Beaux developed the 'No. 5' fragrance for Chanel in 1921. However, the 1950s and 1960s saw a significant extension of perfume ranges, and of the direct licensing of ready-to-wear fashions marked with designer names. Weller argues that licensing is a commodification of elite designers' reputations, and that its viability 'depends on continued public recognition of designers' names and the maintenance of designers' elite status in the public arena, through the media and through events that create media interest' (2004: 97). This development placed even greater emphasis (and clear economic value) on the constructed traditions and mythologies of the great fashion cities: 'It is hardly a criticism to say that Paris is but a myth, because this in fact is one of its strongest selling points.... . fashion houses make their money on perfumes, cosmetics and accessory items that sell precisely because the mythical place of their origin, 'Paris' is part of their logo' (Skov 1996: 133).

Fashion's world order was also transformed by the international restructuring of elite garment production. As Simona Segre Reinach argues in her chapter here, the rapid rise of Milan as a fashion capital in the 1970s was due to its position in this process. Between 1971 and 1978, established Italian fashion designers abandoned the Florence shows to display their work in Milan. At the same time a new generation of entrepreneur designers who had trained in the industrial and commercial enterprises of Northern Italy became established in Milan. Milan's position as a fashion city drew upon its established traditions in design, and the developing 'flexible specialization' and 'vertical integration' of the industrial regions of Northern Italy. Segre Reinach suggests that Milan's position in fashion's world order was as the central city for prêt-à-porter. However, the 1970s and early 1980s also saw a broader shift in the geographies of production of elite fashions. Italian manufacturers, particularly the giant Gruppo GFT, contracted major French designers to produce ready-to-wear fashions, alongside the emerging Italian names. While the fashion press emphasized the rivalries between Paris and Milan, this new prêt-à-porter system of internationalized production networks drew upon the design reputations and symbolic power of both cities.

The creation of this new axis between Paris and Milan was part of a wider late twentieth-century reordering of fashion's world cities. As Norma Rantisi and Sonnet Stanfill argue in this volume, a more general shift towards ready-to-wear fashions converged with an increasing demand for a more 'American sensibility' in high-end fashion, and increased New York's significance as a centre of design (Rantisi 2004a: 103). Tokyo's rise to prominence, and London's continuing status as a significant centre of fashion innovation, underpinned the contemporary cliché of the five great fashion capitals. Yet hidden behind the routine recitation of this list of five cities are significant changes in fashion's urban order.

Fashion's World Cities in the Twenty-First Century

Throughout this history of their development, the nature of fashion's world centres has been complex, cutting across boundaries of the categories cultural, social and economic, combining both consumption and production, and fusing the material and the symbolic. The most systematic work on their contemporary characteristics that attempts to encompass these dimensions comes from those focusing on the 'cultural economy' of cities (see, for example, Lash and Urry 1994; Scott 1997; 2000a; G. Evans 2003). This approach concentrates on the growing significance of sectors concerned with 'goods and services that are infused in one way or another with broadly aesthetic or semiotic attributes' (Scott 1997: 323). The cultural economy approach to cities emphasizes precisely the kinds of cultural connections between place and goods that has been a feature of the long-term history of fashion's central places. Molotch indicates the way that the 'positive connection of product image to place yields a kind of monopoly rent that adheres to places, their insignia, and the brand names that may attach to them... Favourable images create entry barriers for products from competing places' (1996: 229).

While this connection between the symbolic qualities of places and product is given primary significance in the cultural economy approach, it also recognizes the different ways that particular industries are embedded in particular urban contexts. Fashion's role as a creative industry has been addressed most explicitly by Allen Scott (2002), at the end of a discussion of the 'competitive dynamics' of the Southern Californian clothing industry, where he turns his attention to Los Angeles's position in fashion's world order. Scott asks whether Los Angeles can emerge as 'a credible and distinctive competitor, not only of New York, but also of other notable international centres of the fashion industry such as Paris, London and Milan' (2002: 1304). The main substantive interest of the paper is the potential development of a creative cluster of high status garment design in the Los Angeles area, but in his policy recommendations for the emergence of a new world fashion centre ('a policy imperative of the first order', no less), Scott shifts attention towards broader issues concerning the institutional organization and symbolic promotion of the city's fashion culture. He sets out a checklist of the characteristics required for southern California to move to the front rank of world fashion centres, competing directly with 'New York, Paris, Milan and London' (2002: 1304):

- a 'flexible' manufacturing basis (in the case of early twenty-first-century Los Angeles this is increasingly 'offshore', but with strong subcontracting networks centred in the region);
- a core cluster of specialist and skill-intensive subcontractors capable of high quality work on short turnaround times;
- a dense 'groundwork' of fashion training and research institutes in the city region;
- a new infrastructure of regionally based but internationally recognized publicity and promotional vehicles (these include the development of the fashion media, major fashion shows and other fashion events);
- an evolving fashion and design tradition with strong place-specific elements;
- formal and informal connections between the fashion industry and other cultural products industries of the region (in the case of Los Angeles, the relationship with Hollywood is particularly important).

What is remarkable about this list, for all the emphasis given to the newness of the cultural economy of cities, is the way it also seems to accord with the long-term characteristics of fashion's world cities. Indeed the combination of flexibility, spectacle and elite validation would certainly be understood by Charles Worth, and might even be recognized by Jean-Baptiste Colbert. Scott's analysis depends on a characterization of urban economic development – from an earlier era of mass consumerism to a post-1970s age of cultural or symbolic capitalism – that corresponds rather poorly to precisely those places that have long histories as major world centres of the fashion industry (notably Paris, London and New York). Instead we might think about the 'creative economy' as having a long-term history in such cities rather than something that emerged in the late twentieth century. As such, we need to think about Scott's list as a particular urban complex combining production, culture and consumption that has moved through a series of distinctive inflections in the modern histories of major metropolises. Some chapters in this volume develop and give historical context to these themes of production flexibility, place-specific design traditions and the significance of the media and institutions in the promotion of particular urban cultures. However, other chapters also raise important alternative dimensions to our understandings of fashion's world cities.

One theme strongly present in the studies in this volume indicates the significance of world centres of consumption. In the cultural economy literature this is often treated as a rather passive consequence of the geographies of production, both in the conventional sense of the design and actual fabrication of clothing, and in the broader sense of the production of symbolic meanings of a city and its fashion culture. Many of the studies in this volume are concerned with what might be described as world cities of shopping. In a world of ever more similar shopping spaces, the traditions and symbolic significance of certain districts and streets become increasingly valuable. While the clothes sold in the shops may be available elsewhere in regional malls, or online, the practices of consumption are altered (and the prices of commodities raised) in a few key locations. One way of thinking about the long-term trajectory of the fashion capital explores the changing importance of the location of production, the location of design and the location of purchase. Fashion consumption – or perhaps more precisely the experience and consumption of places traditionally associated with elite fashion – has also made a significant contribution to the massive growth in urban tourism. Such sites of fashion work as tourist 'honey-pots' alongside galleries or historic landmarks.

As Bronwen Edwards suggests in her chapter in this volume, another significant dimension of the major fashion city is its distinctive built environment. This again is often seen as secondary to the design and production of clothes, but the physical nature of the buildings and streets of fashion culture have also contributed to the identification and understanding of the centrality of certain cities. There is a complex and long-standing relationship between architecture and fashion design. While Wigley has written of mid twentieth-century modern architecture's guilt-ridden relationship with fashion, recent times have seen a much more willing synergy between architecture and high status fashion (Wigley 1995). A special edition of *Architectural Design* on architecture and fashion in 2000 was dominated by commissions in a few global cities, with one article even introduced with a blunt reference to New York as 'a global fashion capital … alongside London, Paris, Milan and Tokyo' (Merkel 2000: 63). New York has seen perhaps the most developed examples of the ways that fashion and architecture work in a symbiotic relationship of endorsement by association, notably in Richard Gluckman's work for YSL and Helmut Lang, John Pawson's design of the Calvin Klein flagship store on Madison Avenue, and indeed through the 1999 Armani retrospective held in the architectural 'holy of holies,' the Frank Lloyd Wright spiral gallery at the Guggenheim (Pawley

2000: 6; Merkel 2000). However Edwards's study of post-war London moves beyond this connection between architecture and fashion at certain flagship stores. Edwards's detailed analysis of the established micro-geographies and routes of fashion consumption in the city and of planning strategies, is suggestive of broader questions about the relations between fashion culture and urban space as experienced and imagined, planned and used.

Many of the studies in this volume also point to the complexity entailed in what Scott briefly describes as 'a design tradition with strong place-specific elements' (2002: 1304). There have been plenty of studies of the histories of individual cities that point to the difficulties of establishing new design traditions without such lineages (or as in the case of both Moscow and Shanghai, places with strong discontinuities in political and economic structures.) Sonnet Stanfill's chapter in this collection draws attention to another facet of the design tradition. From her perspective as a curator of fashion history, Stanfill discusses the way that London's Victoria and Albert Museum has represented the design tradition of another major fashion city, using a limited selection of garments to construct a narrative about a 'New York look'. As Fiona Anderson (2000) and Valerie Steele (1998) have argued, museums play an increasingly influential role in the construction of popular understandings of design traditions. We might think about the ways that museums of clothing, and indeed certain iconic garments, work as what Pierre Nora (1989) calls 'lieux de memoire', or as sites or realms of collective memory. Such collective memory works not just within national cultures, but also internationally. Unsurprisingly, it is the established fashion capitals that have the strongest cultural resources to elaborate and rework the invented traditions of their own design heritage. The recent major exhibition on 'the London Look' at the Museum of London worked in this way, reinforcing 'London's reputation as a guardian of the bespoke and the edgy' (Breward, Ehrman and Evans 2004: 5).

Scott's analysis of Los Angeles is written in part as a policy recommendation for the promotion of the city and its region – approaching the kind of city booster toolkit recognizable to Professor Chu at the Shanghai City Image Institute. As such it works within a resolutely top-down model of the fashion industry. As Kaiser and Rabine remind us in this collection there has been another dimension, more popular and less controlled, to the fashion cultures of California's cities with a global significance since the late twentieth century. As has been discussed above, a significant strand in the discussion of fashion and metropolitan modernity has stressed the importance of the vitality of urban life, the creativity arising from the intermixing and chaos of the city, the performance of fashion on the streets, and the position of great cities in wider flows of people, ideas and images. While it is easy to over-romanticize street style and more democratic influences on fashion innovation, these have clearly been significant in the story of major fashion centres. Angela McRobbie (1998) has pointed out in her study of the 'mixed economy' of fashion design in late twentieth-century London, that this has often involved crossovers between the subcultural consumption of fashion in the city and informally organized design and production sectors.

From the chapters in this volume therefore, we can supplement Scott's 'cultural economy' model of a fashion capital with a more active sense of the significance of sites of consumption, with an awareness of the distinctiveness of architecture and urban space in such cities, with a more sophisticated understanding of the construction of city-based fashion heritages, and with more attention to the creative potential of great cities. However, there is a sense in the early twenty-first century that this long-running conjunction of fashion and great city may be at a moment of crisis. Some of this comes from rather precise geopolitical circumstances of our times. The attacks on New York City in 2001 and the subsequent 'war on terror' have had their effects on the geography of fashion's world order, with US buyers in particular reducing their presence at the international collections in Paris, London and Milan. At the same time, a move to stricter immigration controls in Europe and the United States has effects on production sectors that have long been dependent on cheap migrant labour and the know-how of immigrant entrepreneurs.

However the fashion world city is also threatened by more fundamental changes in the world economic order. While Paris, London or New York retain their symbolic potency, there is a danger that the modern world fashion city formation – a combination of creative clustering, flexible production and vibrant consumption culture – is being replaced by new 'Potemkin cities' of fashion, characterized by little more than the corporatized surface sheen of fashion culture. Cities like London and New York are characterized by very high rents, right across their central districts. The intensification of property markets, brought about by the kinds of development discussed by Friedmann and Sassen has affected more and more spaces in the city. Not only have rents for prestige sites increased dramatically, but these cities have lost many of the more marginal sites that were important for innovation in design and retailing strategies. It is, for example, impossible to imagine the kind of fashion revolution that took place in London in the late 1950s and early 1960s in a city that has now lost the more affordable backspaces that operated as laboratories of style.

In 1990s' London, Angela McRobbie's young independent designers found a precarious space for themselves in the interstices of the city, working part-time, selling in markets, and moving in and out of the formal fashion system. In the 2000s such opportunities seem much more limited, with many of the key markets replaced by more conventional commercial developments, with the continuing rise of global big-brand designer clothes, and with the strengthening grip on the mass market of major high street stores like Top Shop and H&M. In New York, Sharon Zukin (2003) makes parallel points about the growing corporatization of consumer culture, highlighting the loss of distinctive, independent shops alongside greater control and ordering of the spaces of the city. And in this volume, Simona Segre Reinach presents contemporary Milan as a city increasingly unsure of its place in fashion's world order. The specialist industrial clusters of Northern Italy that underpinned the city's rise as a centre of elite ready-to-wear are now threatened by cheaper imports, particularly from China.

In the twenty-first century the established fashion city formation seems endangered by both the globalization of the luxury goods sector, and by the emergence of new forms of fashion production, marketing and retailing, that have short-circuited the established structures and rhythms of the fashion system (Segre Reinach 2005a). While there were long-term shifts and synergies in the relationship between couture and prêt-à-porter systems that had ramifications for the ordering and internal structure of fashion's world cities, this 'fast fashion' system threatens more radical change. Companies like Zara, Mango and H&M work with flexible suppliers in China to produce rapidly changing ranges. These operate outside of the conventional patterns of the collections and seasons of the fashion establishment, but are also relatively independent of local urban cultures.

At the same time new technology also threatens to disrupt many of the significant institutions of fashion's world cities. Just as the production schedules of fast fashion seem to be breaking the rigid seasonal rhythms that were built into fashion's twentieth-century world order, with its controlling citadels in the capitals of the northern hemisphere, so the institutional apparatus of the fashion system is threatened with revolution. Perhaps the internet poses less threat to the major centres as spaces of consumption, than as spaces for the institutions of fashion. Recent times have shown that attendance at the Paris, Milan and London collections is not the sine qua non that it was in the twentieth-century fashion formation. Internet fashion portals, notably Worth Global Style Network (WGSN), currently operate as remote information sources. WGSN is still rooted in major fashion centres, with 'real' bureaux in London, New York, Milan, Paris, São Paulo, Hong Kong and Tokyo. Yet the network has the potential effectively to circumvent traditional fashion collections and shows, and to orchestrate simultaneous international launches of collections online.

Under such pressures, the tendency towards Potemkin fashion cities seems likely to strengthen, but there are potential sources of disruption. As Kawamura stresses here in her study of street fashion in Tokyo, even in the most seemingly contained and corporatized fashion environments there are possibilities for upwellings of independent, influential design. It would be dangerous to suggest that the current passivity of street fashion in London and New York will be permanent features of their fashion cultures. Another model for the fashion city has been pioneered in Antwerp, where increased state support for local designers has promoted fashion design not so much as a creative industry, as a part of the creative infrastructure of the city, with anticipated positive consequences for gentrification and urban regeneration. Maybe, as Mustafa and Dwyer suggest, this is an era where dynamism in fashion shifts to the margins of the corporate fashion system, to transnational populations in the established world cities, and to the hybridizations of local and global influences in emergent fashion centres.

But we must return to Shanghai to think about the possibilities for fashion's world cities in the twenty-first century. China possesses not only huge manufacturing capacity, but also the largest ever emerging market, with possibly 250 million luxury brand consumers by 2010 (Dodd 2005). Shanghai's position in one of the main manufacturing regions of the country suggests parallels with the transformation of Milan in the 1970s and 1980s. However the relations between the fashion culture of this rapidly growing city and the heartland of fast fashion manufacturing are likely to be very different. For all the efforts that its planners and politicians are taking to make Shanghai fit the mould of the fashion world city, this is the place where that mould is most likely to be broken.

–2–

Urbane Fashion
Elizabeth Wilson

There was for a long time an assumption that modernity, urbanization and the growth of fashion went hand in hand. This was one aspect of the idea, so influentially developed by the German sociologists of the late nineteenth century, Georg Simmel and Max Weber, that modernity represents a decisive break with the past. They developed the contrast – which must indeed have been startling to the agricultural workers flocking to the new industrial cities in the nineteenth century – between rural life, tradition and stasis; and urban change, fragmentation and mobility. These highly generalized accounts were summarized and perhaps over simplified by Anthony Giddens (1991). He argued that the discontinuities of modernity lay in the pace of change, the scope of change and in the nature of modern institutions, in the way that time and space become abstract entities, replacing the old sense of place and the rural time cycle. All aspects of life, including leisure, are institutionalized, bureaucratized and commodified, yet modernity is dynamic. Its dynamism is produced in part by two processes. Giddens terms these disembedding and reflexivity. Traditional ways of doing things are disembedded and replaced by new ways in a process of continual change; while reflexivity is also the opposite of tradition, meaning that social and other practices are subjected to a continual process of examination and modification. Experiment replaces tradition.

It isn't hard to see how fashion systems came to represent these processes and how the life of cities provided a culture ideally suited to the expansion of fashion. Georg Simmel, who, like other later writers, understood the curious feature of fashion: that it embodies a contradiction – that is, that in dressing fashionably we aim simultaneously to stand out and blend in with the crowd – understood also that the urban *audience* is necessary for fashion to flourish. True, there had always been audiences of some kind for fashion or elaborate dress generally, aristocratic courts in particular, but it was the rapidly growing cities of the nineteenth and twentieth centuries that provided the ideal ecology for fashion.

Over time, increased mobility, both physical and social, the development of mass production and mass markets and the growth of a fully monetarized and commodified social formation enabled fashion to become less expensive and extravagant and for fashions to change much more rapidly. There is, writes Michael Carter in his discussion of Simmel 'a preference for the new over the traditional; an emphasis upon the present as a moment disconnected from any other point in time and a sense that time consists of fleeting moments rather than a continual flow' (2003: 75).

Urban life became a huge experimental laboratory. It may seem odd to introduce the subject of pornography or erotic literature in this context, but Lynn Hunt has made a powerful argument for the development of such a literature as part of the development of early modernity with the urban culture of the Renaissance. She argues firstly that 'pornography was closely linked with political and religious subversion' (Hunt 1993: 3). Long before de Sade, it offered a critique of conventional morality and religious orthodoxy, the Church and aristocracy and it therefore had a democratic dimension. It was part of a more mobile society in which not only men but also some women were travelling more freely and independently and even if most of the female characters in pornographic narratives were prostitutes they are 'most often portrayed as independent, determined, financially successful and scornful of the new ideals of female virtue and domesticity' (Hunt, 1993: 38). It was only with the reordering and reinforcement of gender difference at the close of the eighteenth century, Hunt argues, that sadomasochism and the victimization of women came to be dominant features of pornographic literature.

Seen thus, pornography becomes a dimension of the experimental freedom of urban life, in which the streets are thronged with strangers and where erotic encounters become more possible. The city becomes a locus of desire, of transgression and of the exploration of the body. It is to be expected that fashion and adornment will achieve great importance in such a situation. Dress will signify the erotic dimension of life as well as social status and economic calling. Women, and men too, will wish to call attention to their charms and individualize themselves.

It does also seem likely that, then and later, urban life offered some possibilities, however restricted, to women in terms of emancipation from the family and possibilities for independence. This was, in fact, the basis for much of the criticism of city life and of the ambivalence of many writers towards it. And indeed, the literature of modernity and the city has in general been ambivalent towards the nature of urban life, although the contrast between rural virtue and urban worldliness theorized by Simmel and Weber, even if they reconfigured it, did not originate with them. Bunyan's *Pilgrim's Progress* presented a powerful picture – an antidote to the pornographic literature, if you like – of 'Vanity Fair', the wicked city full of temptations to vice of all kinds. The eighteenth century saw the development of the idea of the peaceful rural life as closer to godliness than the city, so that by the nineteenth century the city was increasingly depicted as a dangerous labyrinth, a jungle, a cesspit, source of vice, crime and disease, although there were always some Victorians who celebrated the city (see Wilson 1991).

Today, economic globalization has transformed relationships both between country and town and between nation states. The contrast between town and country may have lost some of its force in Western societies, as the suburbs encroach ever further, but the contrast as an *idea* has retained its salience, and nineteenth-century *images* of the urban seem to resist change. These images persist in the media. The British edition of the listings magazine, *Time Out* continually peddles the idea of the cutting-edge, bohemian inner city, and similar ideas continue to be reproduced in popular music, in fashion and in film. In the 1980s there was a whole sub-genre of 'yuppie nightmare' films, in which, typically, a hapless young yuppie underwent the hell of a night in lower Manhattan, menaced by drug dealers, gangsters and the mentally ill; a more light-hearted version was Madonna's *Desperately Seeking Susan*, in which, perhaps significantly, a garment, the Madonna character's funky leather jacket, stood in for, or represented, urban cool in general. Today, *Sin City* continues the love affair with *Film Noir*. In the world of fashion, the youth directed cosmetics range, Urban Decay for some years neatly summed up the idea that pleasure and danger in the city are intimately linked and that precisely the charm and magic of urban life lies in its proximity to disintegration, and even if that brand has disappeared, there is still the fashion chain, Urban Outfitters. Given the choice, Europeans may migrate to Cotswold villages or Provence, but they evidently still also wish to consume this romantic image of the city of dreadful, but alluring night.

This vision of the city, or rather of an exciting urban lifestyle is rather at odds with what has actually happened to the Western metropolis. There has come to be a perception (although it may be debatable to what extent it represents actual change) that as city centres have been gentrified they have lost their authenticity and edge. Both journalists and academics have written of New York, or at least Manhattan, of Paris, Dublin and Glasgow specifically and of the gentrification of city centres more generally, that these city centres have become what François Maspero (1994), writing of Paris, called Disneyfied cities, city centres whose famous landmarks have been repackaged for tourists, while the real life of the city has moved elsewhere, in his case, or so he argues, to the tower blocks and dismal estates beyond the *péripherique*.

Christopher Breward (2004) has mapped a historical trajectory of the production *and* consumption of dress on to specific changing districts of London – Covent Garden and the Strand at the end of the nineteenth century, Chelsea in the 1960s. He described how Camden Market was the locus of all that was streetwise and edgy during the last quarter of the twentieth century and eloquently charts its prehistory as well as the glamour it exuded in its best years. But that street style, too, had declined by the millennium and – again – today Camden Lock is largely the hunting ground of tourists. Only the covens of Goths cling doggedly on. A similarly cynical view of the decay of bohemianism has been developed more theoretically by Jean Baudrillard (1993), while Sharon Zukin (1982) demonstrated empirically the economic imperatives underlying these shifts as they played out in lower Manhattan in the 1950s to 1970s.

It was, in fact, paradoxically, an *unchanging* feature of cities that their bohemian and chic districts were continually mobile (see Wilson 2000). Siegfried Kracauer remarked how familiar streets in 1920s Berlin disappeared from one day to the next under the imperative of the developer (see Frisby 1985: 139). And even those districts of which the actual fabric remains intact completely change their usage and ambience, as the cool and fashionable migrate like flocks of birds in the direction of the latest hot spot. Urban space itself comes under the dominion of fashion. Such perceptions might be in part due to sentimental nostalgia, a grim or at least banal present contrasted with some lost golden era of authenticity. Yet it is pertinent to ask the question: what is happening to cities? Where are the new places? More specifically, what is the contemporary relationship of the urban and fashion? Is urbanity still urbane? Is fashion still fashionable?

The dynamic of modernity has changed cities, paradoxically, in attempting to freeze them at a certain point in time, which becomes picturesque as it is embalmed. But the people who populate these cities are not the citizens who once gave them life and variety. Can fashionable dress play the same role in these contemporary city centres that it is alleged once to have played in the nineteenth-century city?

What then was the role of fashion in the great metropolis? In the Regency period in Britain the assembly rooms, theatres and pleasure gardens at Bath, Covent Garden and Vauxhall were all spaces of personal display. American writers described the passeggiata up and down Broadway in the 1860s. Even right down to the 1980s there were clubs and venues where, in London, the New Romantics theatricalized their lives, and where, on the Lower East Side, the circles memorialized in the photography of Nan Goldin dressed up and flaunted their deviance. And these were all examples of Simmel's fluctuating dynamic, whereby fashion oscillates between, or rather combines the opposites of uniformity and, in Quentin Bell's (1947) term, 'outrage' or differentiation.

It may be that as urban centres have become reprogrammed for tourists, their role as a theatre of display has diminished. Tourist dress, which so far as I know, has not been extensively researched, is hardly distinguished by its elegance and fashionability and also tends to be more distanced from formality than other kinds of urban day wear, the general casualization of dress notwithstanding.

If we accept that modernity is ongoing and continues to be dynamic – if, that is, we can agree that postmodernity is, as Giddens suggests, a new moment in modernity – this must have effects for the nature of urban life and the city fabric (in all senses of the word). Are we too reliant on outworn conceptions of the urban, such as those elaborated by Weber and Simmel? Do the Situationists and their heirs, the psycho-geographers (I'm thinking of writers such as Iain Sinclair) tell a more contemporary and relevant story of urban life (see Kerr and Gibson 2003), or are they, too, locked into an essentially romantic vision derived from Charles Baudelaire and Walter Benjamin? Theorists of dress, and of the city, have certainly continued to draw on Benjamin's vision as a key to the understanding of modernity and its relationship to the city, drawing extensively on the often gnomic fragments in *The Arcades Project* (Benjamin, 1999).

To ask a rather different question: what is the way to dress for city life today? And does it matter? Andrew Hill suggests that everyone now dresses badly, that the sartorial efforts of the urban crowds are utilitarian and uniform. Street wear can be divided into casual wear and office dress, both equally dreary. 'There is little or nothing that stands out as distinct ... you could swap people's clothes around and it would not make much difference – they would look virtually the same' (Hill 2005: 68). Anecdotally, this observation tends to be confirmed when the observer walks through central London or New York. It may be that now that so many women are in paid employment women's day wear is approximating more closely to the relative stability and uniformity of men's business and casual wear. It may also be that actually – and perhaps counter-intuitively – we are living in an increasingly conformist society. Ethnically different dress may be increasingly visible on city streets (which is a whole other topic in itself) but Western dress and customs seem in some ways to be increasingly circumscribed (and Muslim women's covered dress aims to conceal rather than reveal both individuality and the body). This is paradoxical, because the dominant political discourse is about choice and individualization, but – and this is even more noticeable in the United States – the more our society talks about the individual and individualism, the more alike we all seem to become. The strange paradox of consumer society seems to turn out to be that the more our desires are commercialized and differentiated, somehow the more the parameters of acceptable behaviour are narrowed rather than widened, even as our choices seem to contract rather than expand.

It is certainly the case that the high street itself, at least as a retail venue, has become increasingly uniform. It is sometimes difficult to remember whether one is in Oxford or Oxford Street, Stafford or Stanford, California Shopping Mall, for the same chain stores are everywhere to be seen, and for that matter Nanjing Road more closely resembles Bond Street or Fifth Avenue than it resembles Shanghai in the 1930s. The development of China and the Chinese fashion industry is relevant in this regard. In a recent article, Simona Segre Reinach (2005a) has fascinatingly explored two important and interrelated aspects of metropolitan fashion today, which also link production and consumption. Her perspective still positions the production – and consumption – of fashion as an urban phenomenon, although production may also take place in the countryside in particular cases. She describes the collaboration between Chinese clothing producers and Italian firms. One point she makes is the suggestion that a new fashion culture is emerging. On the one hand, she writes, 'to refer to the Shanghai lifestyle implies evoking the spirit of the new and distinctive type of capitalism that characterizes communist China, one aspect of which is an attitude towards copying that differs from the western attitude' (2005a: 46). This, says Segre Reinach, is part of the new emerging fashion culture. It might be seen as postmodern (whatever our difficulties with this term), but whether or not we give it that label it is 'the culture of instant or fast fashion, born of the globalization of trends, of a global concept of production and domestic marketing. Quick and easy brands capable of answering the needs of a new consumer who is fickle and changeable, and quite different from those desires prompted by life-styles and the democratization of luxury' (2005a: 47). This she contrasts with the two previous systems: of haute couture, which represented high bourgeois taste; and the post-1945 system she terms prêt-à-porter – the good style of the diffusion line, when lifestyles were replacing the more rigid divisions of class. Both these systems nevertheless paid obeisance to quality and the desire for clothes that would 'last'.

Today, no one wants clothes that 'last' any more. As recently as a generation ago there were still young men who boasted that they were wearing the bespoke suits their fathers had had made for them in the 1940s. Now, it is difficult for the great Savile Row firms even to recruit the bespoke tailors of tomorrow. Instead, Segre Reinach suggests, we inhabit very temporary identities and 'fast fashion' caters to these. She also says a very great deal more about the many complex relationships of Sino-Italian fashion production than I could possibly summarize and in any case, I should then finally lose the focus on urbanism. But 'fast fashion' does have implications for urban life. Segre Reinach describes a new fashion world in which fake brands and the real thing are hardly distinguishable (and what does that mean anyway?), in which Italian firms export 'market stall' fashions to China and Chinese brands are produced and made 'as if in Italy'; where unknown, new, small brands arise as an antidote to the blandness of the Gap model and where the new retailers, such as H&M and Urban Outfitters offer a huge variety of fast fashion styles. She concludes by questioning the assumption with which this chapter began: the Weberian belief in privileged links between modernity and the West, particularly the Western city. We should be looking at the new huge cities of the Pacific Rim for a view of the future and the future of fashion.

Now these cities are in some respects very different from the classic Western metropolis. The traditional Chinese city never developed a bourgeois public space along Western lines. Instead, the urban fabric itself was subjected to cataclysmic change in the twentieth century, the result of which has now been seen in the razing in Beijing and elsewhere of the old narrow, labyrinthine residential quarters, which have been replaced by the kind of monumental tower blocks that we in the West consider to have spectacularly failed to provide housing on a human scale. Of course the history of the tower block is more complex than the stereotype allows, but still, that stereotype is a central plank of our discourse on housing, which makes the enthusiasm of the Chinese for this form rather baffling. But then again after the Second World War, many Western architects and planners were equally enthusiastic about the streets in the sky.

The violent Chinese rush for change from medieval *quartier* to twenty-first-century utopia is echoed, or finds a parallel in the gulf between classical Chinese culture and the new China. This seems far deeper than the gap that has developed in the West between high art and mass culture. At the end of the day both these share much common ground, whereas the disjuncture between old and new in China does really seem immense and the appeal of the new less nuanced with the ambivalence of aesthetic nostalgia (though political nostalgia there may be). There is, for example, a whole new district in Shanghai that has been created as a slightly fake-seeming little Italy, where Shanghai 'yuppies' drink cappuccinos or cocktails, eat ice cream and cheesecake and dance in a Western-style clubbing scene. Here too the separation of old and new seems sharper and more definitive. But although it might seem like a simulacrum of a Western city, there is somehow nothing Disneyfied about it.

Breward's *Fashioning London* and the conference upon which this current book has been based have placed the relationship of urban fabric and (literally as well as metaphorically) fashion fabric at the centre of fashion systems. I have tried here to reprise some of the ways in which this relationship was configured in the classic sociology of modernity. Vivienne Westwood's biographer, Jane Mulvagh (1999), argues that it was punk and Malcolm Maclaren that fully integrated pop music and fashion for the first time, marketing the two simultaneously and inseparably. The relationship between urban life and fashion does not provide an exact parallel or analogy, but just as at an earlier period of cultural studies the exploration of youth cultures inaugurated a fruitful period and an exponential growth in the field – with the work done on teddy boys, mods and rockers – so now, albeit in a different way, it is to be hoped that our heightened awareness of the fashion/city symbiosis will be the spur for another leap forward in our understanding, so that we can transcend the generalities of classical sociology, while building on Simmel's refined and subtle aesthetic insights with the combination of empirical and theoretical work that fashion studies is today achieving.

Part II
Styles and Representations

–3–

Paris, Capitale de la Mode
Representing the Fashion City in the Media
Agnès Rocamora

Drawing on the work of Pierre Bourdieu I have insisted elsewhere (see Rocamora 2001, 2002, 2006 forthcoming) on the significance of the process of symbolic production of fashion. Fashion is both a material and a symbolic reality. Its institutions, players, objects and practices are invested with a variety of meanings and values whose 'truth' is a constant object of struggle. Central to this process is the discourse of the media. As Foucault argues, discourses are not mere 'groups of signs [... but ...] practices that systematically form the objects of which they speak' (1997: 49). In France, the discourse of fashion journalism has long participated in the production of Paris as fashion capital, as I discuss in this chapter, looking first at the way, in contemporary texts since the late 1980s, *la mode* has been anchored to the Parisian territory, to then turn more specifically to the figure of *la Parisienne*, the Parisian woman.

Producing fashion, producing Paris: *Paris c'est la mode*

The first French paper to devote space to fashion, *Le Mercure Galant*, created in 1672, offered articles telling an imaginary woman from the provinces about Versailles and Paris fashions (Jones 2004: 26–7). However, soon the French capital overtook Versailles as fashion centre, with the style of Parisian women reported in the press for both provincial and foreign readers (Jones 2004: 181–2). Similarly, the French journal *La Mode*, created in 1829, and where Balzac published his *Traité de la vie Elégante* (2002 [1830]), defined itself, Fortassier (1988: 43, 45) observes, as 'Parisian, fashionable [*mondaine*], aristocratic'. The collocation of the three adjectives illustrates here the homology that Bourdieu argues exists between social and geographical spaces. (1993: 160–1) More generally throughout the nineteenth century and up until the 1950s, Wargnier suggests that fashion can be considered 'an orderly pyramid which, based on the undisputed authority of Paris and its couturiers, progressively diffuses changes down the social scale' (2004: 15). During this period the press taught readers how to reproduce Parisian dress patterns ['*modèles parisiens*'].

Today the Parisian model is no longer conveyed through the principle of patterns to reproduce, but it is no less overt. In the French media, fashion still means Paris. Regularly anchoring fashion to the Parisian territory, the media have long naturalized the signifying relation between the French capital and *la mode*. The centrality of Paris in all things cultural is consecrated, as it has been since the seventeenth century with the Parisian academies' leading role in the definition of culture, the split between court society and the provinces being replaced by the opposition between Paris and provinces in the eighteenth century (George 1998: 11–16; see also Jones 2004: 73–4). The one TV fashion programme, for instance, that established itself throughout the 1990s as a dominant player was called *'Paris Modes'*, the title clearly encapsulating the link that regularly binds the two signifiers 'Paris' and 'Mode' together, as in the title of another TV programme 'Paris c'est la Mode', broadcast on the Paris Ile-de-France TV network

Fashion magazines have often borne in their title a reference to Paris as indicated with *Parisiennes*, or *Paris-Mode* in the nineteenth century, for instance, and *Les Elégances Parisiennes* in the early twentieth century (see Gay-Fragneaud et Vallet 2004: 53; Lecercle 1989: 27–28). Today the two key institutions *Vogue* and *L'Officiel de la Couture et de la mode de Paris* (hereafter *L'Officiel*) still carry in their title the word 'Paris', encased, for the former, in the letter 'O'. Of all 15 national issues of *Vogue*, the French one – *Vogue Paris* – is the only one bearing the name of a capital city (Rocamora 2006; all subsequent references to *Vogue* in this chapter are to *Vogue Paris*). Through its very title, but also through the many articles that privilege Paris over the rest of France, *Vogue*, like the other key French media institution *Le Monde* (see Rocamora 2001: 138–9), contributes to the superior positioning of Paris in the 'geography of fashion' (Steele 1998: 136).

However, Paris in the French media, is not simply the French capital of fashion but the fashion capital *tout court*, the *'capitale de la mode'*, as daily *Le Monde* (13 October 2004) and fashion magazine *Jalouse* (June 2004), for instance, tell their readers. This is an expression the media mobilizes regularly. Thus an advertisement for L'Oréal in *L'Officiel* reads: 'For this spring-summer 2001, through their collections, designers translate Parisian chic with audacity, allure and impertinence. The French touch will gratify lovers of femininity ... Paris, *capitale de la mode*, becomes centre of the world again' (April 2001). Here, designers are depicted as mere translators of Parisian chic, as if the style unveiled during the collections was not so much the creation of the designers themselves as of the French capital itself.

A certain naturalization of fashion culture is a common feature of coverage in the press. Cities like Milan are often portrayed as somehow naturally stylish (see Gilbert 2000: 20). However, in the French media, such organicism is pushed further in statements where the city itself is invoked as an active agent in the making of fashion. As in the French literary discourse that has constructed the Paris myth, the French capital is anthropomorphized (see Stierle 2001:18). Not only is the creativity of designers said to be rooted in Paris, their true source of inspiration, but the city itself is depicted as an author of fashion. Thus *L'Officiel* notes that Paris 'sets the tone for fashion, and gives all *couturiers* talent' (May 1990) and *Vogue* observes that 'it is Paris, the best perfumers say, that inspires them and breathes this spirit into them, this inimitable lightness' (November 1996). One perfumer, Jacques Cavalier, is quoted saying: 'the city, itself, predisposes one to create'; in another issue of *Vogue Paris* photographer Henry Clarke states that 'Paris has taught me everything, Paris has inspired my whole life' (August 1996).

Foucault, who defines 'the term discourse ... as the group of statements that belong to a single system of formation', draws attention to the 'statements formulated elsewhere and taken up in a discourse' (1997: 107), and which constitute 'a field of presence' (1997: 57) in which statements coexist. In the same way that he speaks of economic and psychiatric discourses one can speak of the fashion discourse, with the media one site where its statements 'breed and multiply'. (Foucault 1997: 100) The fashion discourse, of which Cavalier's and Clarke's assertions are an element, enunciates statements in existence in a field of presence that stretches across a variety of sites, including literary discourse. The idea of Paris as source of inspiration has informed the work of many French authors (see Stierle 2001). For Zola, for instance, Paris was 'the fermentation tank, the alembic, where ideas and the future world are elaborated' (cited in Noiray 2002: 8). Similarly, for the poet Breton, in works such as *Nadja* and *L'Amour Fou*, 'the great purveyor of materials for the processes of the psyche to derive energies and modes of representation is the city of Paris' (Sheringham 1996: 95). Sheringham discusses 'Paris-as-subjectivity'; more than an author's subjectivity being connected to the city, in such works Paris itself gains subjectivity (1996: 96).

Bound to the city, designers' creativity is an outcome of Paris, of its *esprit* – a recurrent notion in discourses on the French capital: *l'esprit parisien* – the Parisian spirit – is perceived as the original creative source, 'the spirit of time that determines all things', as Stierle observes of the Paris of Mercier's seminal *Tableaux de Paris*. (2001: 92) Similarly, in *Vogue*, for instance, Lacroix's Director observes that 'the work of designers needs a kind of environment, a climate, something that may be in the atmosphere of Paris and must come from a heritage, a patrimony, a disposition of *esprits* [minds]' (April 1997). (In French the words 'spirit', 'mind', 'wit' and their related connotations are all captured within the one term 'esprit'.) 'Paris has a gift for perpetual invention', French writer Louise de Vilmorin argued in her fashion writings, 'Paris changes women without ever changing its *esprit*' (2000: 27).

Instrumental in the creativity of fashion designers, *l'esprit de Paris* expresses itself in their creations. An *Officiel* cover (November 2001), for instance, reads 'Fashion: the Left Bank spirit'. At Chanel's show, French glossy *Stiletto* observes, 'rarely has what defines Paris's atmosphere been better captured: a group *esprit* offset by a rebellious spirit *esprit*' (Autumn 2004). 'The famous phrase "that's Paris"', *Elle* writes, 'no one can pronounce as well as a designer on a catwalk' (24 January 2005).

Objectified in clothes, the city's spirit is made visible. Hedi Slimane, *Le Figaro* notes, has 'the Parisian spirit', and the designer is quoted saying 'I've read two or three things to absorb the idea of Paris' (26 January 2001). The spirit of Paris melds with that of designers to materialize as clothes. As fashion magazine *Jalouse* writes, in a statement that captures this melding of identities – geographical, authorial and visual – into one another: 'Robert Normand and Mélodie Wolf: 2 styles, 2 Parises' (March 2004).

Paris becomes the central character of the fashion stories narrated by journalists, a thinking being and the ultimate creator of fashion. For instance, while the French *Elle* notes that 'Paris, known for its experimental reflections on fashion, didn't want to rush' (March 2004), the *Journal du Textile* states that 'Paris is reflecting on its economic development that seems to be stuck' (23 February 2004). The French city, like an artist, even has its 'muses', as *Vogue* writes of women pictured modelling haute couture clothes (September 1995), the fabric of their outfits that of the city. 'It's Paris which dominates, simplifies, measures, decorates, balances Haute couture' the French author Madeleine Chapsal writes in *Vogue*, adding: 'when Christian Lacroix unites brocade to embroidery ... it's a 'number' where Paris's spirit reintroduces balance' (September 1989).

This anthropomorphizing of Paris also draws attention to the news value attributed to fashion events such as the collections. Fashion involves a whole capital, and, implicitly, through the capital, a whole nation, as is made clear by *Le Figaro*: 'Threatened by Milan and Hanover', the daily writes, 'Paris fights to remain the capital of fashion [in textiles]: the French unite against Italy' (24 January 2001). *L'Officiel*, however, reassures its readers: 'the other fashion capitals seem to look pale' compared to Paris (May 2001).

In the early twentieth century, as Wargnier observes, the French press produced fashion as 'a collective phenomenon', a Zeitgeist incarnated in the Parisian dress patterns (2004: 15). In the contemporary press, as the examples above suggest, fashion is still given a collective spirit, one situated in time but also anchored in place. Thus if fashion journalists draw on high cultural references to legitimize fashion in the hierarchy of cultural productions, reference to the collectivity, invoking the traits of Paris, also contributes to this process of legitimization (see Rocamora 2001, 2002, 2006). No longer derided as what is often seen as an individualistic and narcissistic practice, fashion's status is raised to that of representative of a collective being, a matter of collective pride.

The media discourse on *la mode*, then, is also a discourse on Paris, and in the same way that the process of symbolic production of fashion entails the production of the value of designers and their creations, it also entails the production of the symbolic value of Paris. Absorbed, like its derivative 'Parisian', into the fashion rhetoric, the word 'Paris' no longer simply refers to a geographical origin. Rather, it is turned into a fashion signifier whose value resides in its power to evoke the world of fashion, with the word 'Paris' now a synonym for 'chic' and 'elegance', the latter being a 'recurring spiel of French fashion', as Remaury observes (*Paris Vogue*, October 2004).

Finally, in the French media, not only is Paris promoted as the centre of elegance, but it is also turned into one 'vast department store' (see Wilson 2001: 65). This is captured in the many pages devoted, in magazines such as *L'Officiel* and *Vogue*, to Parisian retail sites. In *L'Officiel*, for instance, a feature on luxury fashion shops reads: '*L'Officiel*'s Paris: the mood of the time and of fashion, trends, Parisian symbols, and capital institutions from the right bank to the left bank are to be discovered throughout these pages in the form of an address book, like a very official guide' (September 1990). *L'Officiel* guides the readers through the Paris streets, but the symbols mentioned are not major historical sites as in traditional tourist guides but shops. '*L'Officiel*'s Paris' is here reduced to a series of sites of luxury consumption, and the city's diversity reduced to an abundance of designer brands.

Enjoying Paris has become synonymous with enjoying consuming in Paris. In the French fashion media, this is best illustrated with the newcomer *Bag* – 'Beautiful Address Guide' – whose presence in the field also signals a blurring of the distinction between fashion magazines and tourist guides, evidence for 'the close relationship between shopping and urban tourism' (Gilbert 2000: 21). As *Bag* puts it, Paris is both the 'capital of fashion and tourism'. Launched in 2004, it focuses on guiding readers through Paris's fashionable shops and goods. The French capital, like a fashionable commodity, is permanently updated, forever made new. Some articles are translated into English, the 'lingua franca' of the transnational field of fashion, promoting the goods mentioned throughout the magazine, and, in the process, Paris itself, to foreign tourists/consumers. A whole section – 'shopping route' – is devoted to maps allowing readers to locate the stores while also highlighting possible shopping breaks, such as what the magazine calls 'arty breaks' during which 'the ultra contemporary artistic heritage Paris abounds in' can be uncovered (*Bag* 3 2004). An editorial reads: 'because shopping is not simply 'buying'. Because it is not necessarily futile' (*Bag* 2 2004). Small maps are also provided next to some of the products photographed: to find them, 'follow the map', as the magazine puts it (*Bag* 3 2004). Paris's geography provides the connections between fashionable objects and retail sites. Thus, in *Bag*'s 'shopping route' section, the Paris maps are superimposed on details of fashion fabrics (*Bag* 3 2004). A visual metaphor is here created that turns the fabrics shown into that of Paris, as if the French capital was made of fashion, its streets and buildings sewn together like the diverse fragments of an outfit. For *Bag*, Paris is fashion, and vice versa.

Fashion journalists are 'cultural intermediaries' who participate, alongside advertising, in the creation of the aesthetic value of fashion and the symbolic production of cities (Bourdieu 1996: 359; Gilbert 2000: 13–14). Paris is turned into 'an image designed to foster consumption of the city itself' (Miles and Miles 2004: 52). Through a reading/writing of the city that reduces its many layers into two-dimensional street maps, journalists also facilitate readers' access to different kinds of commodities, including both those laid out in the various stores that the magazines recommend, but also the reified Paris commodified into a landscape of shopping sites and fashionable objects.

La Parisienne in *Vogue*

'When I put on a trenchcoat' a fashion journalist writes in *The Guardian*, 'I think I'm being very chic, very Parisienne, very Deneuve' (13 November 2004). The French daily paper *Le Parisien* praises the Parisian woman's '*état d'esprit* [way of thinking], this famous 'French touch' ... which sets trends, immediately inspires the provinces and amazes foreign women' (8 August 2003). This fashionable figure *la Parisienne* is not an invention of the fashion media. It is the object of a discourse which has stretched across a wider 'formation' of texts, most famously perhaps in the work of Balzac, where she is contrasted with the provincial woman (Fortassier 1988: 139). The ultimate incarnation of fashionability, *la Parisienne* is the woman who, as in Feydeau's *La Dame de Maxim*, sets trends and incarnates Parisian distinction (Heinich 2003: 30). Today, this figure features most notably in the discourse of the key institution *Vogue Paris*.

Vogue frequently refers to *la Parisienne*. This archetypal Parisian woman is at once the essence of French femininity but also a superior being whose identity resides in her belonging to the Parisian territory. For perfumer Guerlain she 'is the height of femininity' (*Vogue* November 1996). *Vogue* writes that 'La Parisienne is the most beautiful mistress of haute couture' (September 1996), evoking 'the preciousness of Parisian elegance, the classic eternal feminine.' (May 2003) The magazine's editorial for February 2000 declared that the new season 'will be chic. But a sublimated and never immediate chic. A symbol of that elegance captured through the prism of idealization: la Parisienne'. *La Parisienne* is perceived as the ultimate fashionable woman precisely because Paris is seen as the ultimate fashion capital, but also as a feminine capital (Wilson 1991: 47; Hughes 1994: 126; Gilbert 2000: 18; Peers 2004: 41). Flaubert described the city as 'women's paradise' while Louis Octave Uzanne argued in 1894 that 'in every class of society, a woman is *plus femme* in Paris than in any other city in the universe' (Flaubert 2000 [1881]: 73; Uzanne cited in Steele 1998: 75).

Vogue often attempts to define French women. However, in such articles one figure is recurrently singled out, *la Parisienne*. As Bernstein observes, '[Paris] alone stands for Frenchness as we know it today' (1991: 72), a comment certainly true for *Vogue*. In a 'special French woman' issue (September 1996), for instance, the author Laure Adler invites her readers to 'sit at the terrasse of one of St Germain's cafés and watch girls passing by. In this territory, which remains the symbolic heart of an intellectual and creative France'. The freedom, 'rebellious *esprit*' and 'irony' she praises are embodied in *les Parisiennes*. Similarly, Catherine Deneuve is celebrated not so much for her acting but for her Parisian qualities highlighted in

Vogue's 'Itinerary of a Chic Parisian' (December 2003). The French *Elle* gives equal status to celebrities and *les Parisiennes* in an article promoting Ayurvedic therapy, which observes that both groups have adopted it (8 November 2004). *La Parisienne*, like the celebrity is a model to emulate. In *Vogue* this is most clearly epitomized in the section *'Fille en Vogue'* and the more recent *'une Fille, un Style'*, where the sophisticated style of women from the capital is unveiled to the readers. These are the holders of high 'cultural capital' demonstrated through knowledge, as they share fashion tips and addresses, but also through their possessions, as they display their favourite items. Appearing alongside pages featuring professional models these women are turned into models in their own right, posing in their fashionable clothes. Their presence in *Vogue*, the high point of the French fashion media, is legitimized by place on the French fashion map.

However, Steele observes, a contradiction informs 'the mythology of Paris' (1998: 74). On the one hand, *la Parisienne* is, Steele notes, '"every Frenchwoman"'. But on the other hand ... there was a rigid dichotomy between Paris and everywhere else. There were Parisians, and then there were "barbarians and provincials"' (1998: 74). *Vogue's* discourse on *la Parisienne* reflects the exceptional status of Paris, at once the epitome of France, but also, and in its claimed superiority to the provinces, above France, somehow detached from it. As Bernstein suggests, 'to be Parisian is to have an identity that transcends social class, economic distinction; it is to belong to a world apart, to an intellectual and moral category, not of class, race and gender, but of a qualitative difference from the rest, an essential worldliness' (1991: 73). This translates into the figure of the Parisian foreigner, a figure that has long informed discourses on Parisian women. In the Goncourt brothers' work, as Fortassier notes, *la Parisienne* 'can equally well be a foreigner: freed from the provincial ties all French women have, she will the more easily be a fully-fledged Parisian' (1988: 140). In Balzac's *La Peau de Chagrin*, Foedora is 'the most beautiful woman of Paris' but also 'a half-Russian Parisian, a half-Parisian Russian!' (1974 [1831]: 153). According to Théodore de Banville's 1881 *Le Génie des Parisiennes*, *les Parisiennes* are 'women born or living in Paris' (2002: 7) while for the periodical *La Vie Parisienne* (1889) the fashionable woman was 'not always French, but almost always Parisian or she becomes so very quickly. She is sometimes even born a *Parisienne* on the other side of the ocean' (Steele 2004: 319).

This discourse continues in our times. In *Vogue*, while *la Parisienne* is the ultimate French woman she is not necessarily French, for one can be 'Parisian by birth or at heart' as the magazine puts it (November 1996). Thus *Vogue* asks: 'how does the American Nan Legeai dress to be, from morning to evening, the quintessence of a *Parisienne* in the Céline style' (August 1990) also invoking 'a borderless chic seriously redolent of *la Parisienne*' (November 1999). In *Vogue* Hiroko Matsumoto can be 'the most Parisian of Japanese women' (December 1995), and Minami Goto is 'the most Parisian woman from Osaka' (September 1994). As *Libération* argued Parisian women have 'no need to be born in the capital to personify the spirit of the city' (27 January 2001). Borderless, the Parisian woman is above '*les provinciales*', who, as Balzac (1984 [1843]: 303–4) once put it, are 'in a permanent state of blatant inferiority'. The French dictionary *Le Petit Larousse* (1994) reflected this long-running hierarchy defining 'provincial', as: 'Pejorative: lacking in the ease usually attributed to the inhabitants of the capital'.

In contrast with *les provinciales*, Parisian women have been endowed with a creativity which has for long been established as one of their main attributes. The eighteenth-century fashion journal *Le Cabinet des Modes*, for instance, 'perpetuated the notion that the creativity of the fashionable women of Paris remained fecund and abundant and constantly praised the 'riens' [little nothings] that the women of Paris created' (Jones 2004: 192). For Banville, writing in 1881, Paris 'is the artist and poet city *par excellence*; but the greatest artists and the greatest poets of Paris are les Parisiennes' (2002: 7). Balzac celebrates their 'inventive *esprit* [mind]' (1984 [1843]: 307). In modern *Vogue*, the *Parisiennes* of '*Une fille, un style*' are presented as individual and original: '[Masako] mixes styles, juggles with the basics' (March 2003) while Clarisse likes 'scrambling the signals' (March 2003) and Laurence enjoys customising her T-shirts (April 2003). Like Certeau's (1988) hero of consumer culture, *la Parisienne* is the everyday artist who, at once consumer and author, has mastered the art of consumption.

However, although *la Parisienne* is a creator, she is the fashion artist that Paris makes her, for it is the city, as discussed earlier, that is the source of her inspiration. The journalist Claire Chazal, for instance, is depicted as being 'a pure product' of the 16th *arrondissement* (May 1991). The Favier sisters have 'a 16th *arrondissement* side' (August 1996) while actress Anouk Aimée, photographed at a café terrasse 'is Left Bank, at the Deux Magots' (August 1994). This *Parisienne* is an incarnation of place: she *is* left bank, her identity indissociable from that of the city.

The idea that it is Paris that gives Parisian women their identity is best illustrated in a *Vogue* feature from October 1998, where models walking down the catwalk are shown with their faces covered by a blank oval matching the *arrondissements* on a Paris map reproduced next to them. The women's individuality is 'a pure product' of the *arrondissements* they live in. Commenting on the work of the French poet Reda on Paris, Sheringham (1996: 105) notes that 'the city manifests itself in endless traits which confer on it, by analogy, certain kinds of personality but do not alter its profound anonymity', an idea conveyed, in the feature discussed, through the representation of faceless, anonymous, models. The women's identity – their name – is only that which Paris gives them. They are, the headline tells us, *la Parisienne*. The singular form of the noun itself, a form frequently used in discourses on Parisian women, brushes aside essential differences in favour of formal sartorial variations. 'This elegant woman is plural', *Vogue* writes in the feature. But, *la Parisienne* is first and foremost a 'she', not a 'they', the ultimate woman who stands in for the others, as in Breton's *Nadja* where 'woman' is 'incarnated by the generic "Parisian woman"' (Sheringham 1996: 94).

The women's look, their 'plastic self', is expressive of a wider collective self, that of Paris, whose spirit manifests itself through its female inhabitants (Jenkins 2004: 29). 'In Tokyo, in New York', for instance, *Vogue* writes, Isabelle d'Ornano 'is the spirit, the chic of Paris' (December 1989), while 'the spirit of these two Parisians by adoption [Alaia and the model Farida], as Parisian as you can get, suggests there's no need to despair of the future: Paris will always be Paris. It must be the climate' (May 1990). Thus although after the industrial revolution, as Sennett argues fashions in cities assumed the role of 'direct expressions of the "inner" self ... guides to the authentic self of the wearer' (Sennett, cited in Wilson 2001: 64), they also seen as an expression of cities themselves. The self of the wearer is a situated self, Paris's spirit melding with that of its inhabitants. Parisian women, do not simply *habitent à* Paris – 'live in Paris' – but *habitent* Paris – 'inhabit Paris'.

La Parisienne embodies Paris's *esprit*, a virtue already conferred on her in her nineteenth-century toy version, known as a *Parisienne* or *Poupée Parisienne* (Fortassier 1988: 140; Peers 2004: 43). As Peers observes of the Rochard doll: it 'performs most clearly a duty that Octave Uzanne devolved to all living *Parisiennes*: to be specifically fashionable and thus to represent "the spirit of Paris"' (2004: 42). This idea is also captured in the theme of the Parisian passer-by – *la passante* – to whom Baudelaire dedicated a poem in his *Tableaux Parisiens* of 1860. In *Vogue* Adler refers to such a *passante* when she praises the style of the women walking by Saint-Germain's cafés. Similarly *L'Officiel* notes that '*la Parisienne* has chic... . Heads turn when she passes by ... she *is* fashion' (May 1990). A central element in the Paris myth, the *passant* contrasts with the *flâneur* in that the former 'has no gaze for the city', and is 'no longer a type or a personality, but only an abstract, fugitive element of the city itself' (Stierle 2001: 153, 15). However, Bowlby draws attention to the gendering of the figure of the *passant*: 'the *passante*, the female-passer-by', she writes, 'may have a certain something that is lacking in her neutral or male counterpart, the ordinary *passant*. In Baudelaire and Proust, the *passante* appears romantically as the momentary object of a longing look' (Bowlby 2000: 52). In Philippe Soupault's *Les Dernières Nuits de Paris* of 1928, the *passante* is Georgette, who the narrator follows through the Paris streets. When she stands in front of the protagonists, 'Paris was before our eyes' (Soupault 1997: 141). In *Vogue* the *passante Parisienne* is also invoked in fashion shoots featuring models walking in Paris streets, as on the September 1989 cover '*Haute Couture: l'esprit parisien*', for instance, where two women are photographed walking briskly by Paris café Les Deux Magots (Figure 3.1).

La Parisienne, material embodiment of the French capital, also has *esprit*. And, in the same way that the spirit of Paris has often been celebrated, so has that of its fleshly manifestation. Banville (1881) for instance, praises the Parisian mademoiselle Rachel: in her eyes can be seen 'the subtle flame of the *esprit* [mind]' (2002: 11). More recently, Hélène and Irène Lurçat note in their guide *Comment devenir une vraie Parisienne* [How to become a true *Parisienne*] that *la Parisienne*

Figure 3.1 Passantes Parisiennes, cover of *Paris Vogue* September 1989, Photograph Peter Lindbergh © Vogue Paris.

'*a de l'esprit*' ['has wit'] (2002: 5). One of the defining traits of French women, according to *Vogue*, is their spirit: 'Women's spirit [*esprit*]: it's known, French women are racy, talented and amazingly classy' (September 1995). However since *la Parisienne* is perceived as the ultimate incarnation of *la Francaise*, she is also the best representative of this spirited womanhood, the 'speciality' of Parisians being, according to *Vogue*, '*de faire de l'esprit*' [to display wit] (April 1990), a statement that recalls Vilmorin's comment that '[in Paris] nothing is done without *esprit* [wit]'

(2000: 35). The 'Parisian nose', the magazine tells the readers, is known to be a 'little nose full of *esprit*' – while '*La Parisienne*' Inès de la Fressange is 'an ideal of the active, elegant, *spirituelle* [witty], ardent French woman' (September 1995). This ideal, according to *Vogue*, is not unattainable to the reader. It can be appropriated through the purchase of commodities, allowing consumers to fashion themselves as *Parisiennes*. In *Vogue*, I suggest borrowing from Hughes's comments on Leduc's *La Batarde*, readers are 'seduced into embracing Parisian feminine selfhood – a selfhood that is very much for sale' (1994: 127).

Promoting an exhibition in the Paris department store Le Bon Marché, *Vogue* ran a feature bearing the title of the exhibition: 'Portraits of Left Bank Women' (October 1995). On the pages a selection of clothes and accessories are laid out in a manner recalling cut out paper dolls. However, the doll is not shown, only referred to, as a *femme Rive Gauche*; a *Parisienne*. It no longer exists in the form of a doll, as in the nineteenth century, but in the no less powerful form of a category of the mind whose simple evocation brings about the idea of ultimate fashionability. A background image shows Paris. Projecting their own body onto the pages, readers can visualize themselves wearing the clothes while projecting themselves into the French capital, becoming *Parisiennes* by inhabiting a Parisian look. *La Parisienne Rive Gauche* is assimilated to a doll's outfit, the doll the reader herself.

Vogue draws on the analogy with dolls and costumes through the repeated use of the word '*panoplie*', the French for a doll's outfit or a child's costume, as in the section '*Une Fille, un Style*'. Of Masako Kumakura, who lives in Paris and Tokyo, *Vogue* writes that she 'keeps a little girl's spirit, and functions through *panoplies*' (March 2003). Kumakura is quoted saying 'I compose my look as though with a Barbie doll'. Similarly, a fashion story is entitled 'Paris, France: … jewellery, accessories, the *panoplie* of *la Parisienne*' (September 2005). In *Vogue*, what Lury refers to as 'the work of femininity' is turned into the playful experience of the feminine 'masquerade', through the appropriation of the *Parisienne*'s *panoplie* (Lury 1999: 144). The *Parisienne* identity is attainable through 'performative' enactments, in Judith Butler's sense of 'fabrications manufactured and sustained through corporeal signs and other discursive means' (1999: 173). Here the signs are conveyed through the goods promoted in *Vogue*. In the section '*Une Fille, un Style*' such goods are also juxtaposed with the pictures of the selected *Parisiennes*, again like paper clothes next to a paper doll. Laid out beside the woman, they become associated with the identity of their wearer, while at the same time the woman herself become objectified into goods, a take on femininity characteristic of fashion discourses. In the fashion industry, 'women are constructed as consumers of themselves *as possessions or commodities*' (Lury 1999: 127). Thus in *Vogue*, actress Lou Doillon is described as 'a prototype of the underground *Parisienne*. Cigarettes, whisky and reggae: the *coup de coeur* [the selection] of the magazine' (November 1998). Doillon's object-like quality – she is a prototype – is also established in the expression '*le coup de coeur*', only usually applied to objects and frequently used by

French fashion magazines to draw consumers' attention to the products they favour. Doillon's identity is reduced to one journalists have selected – have had a *coup de coeur* on – as they would with any other fashionable object.

Alongside the *femme fatale*, the *garçonne* or the *femme active*, La Parisienne is one of the feminine identities on offer in the fashion press. And like the word 'Paris', it has been appropriated by the fashion rhetoric to signify fashion, or, as Barthes puts it of 'written clothing', 'to convey a message whose content is: *Fashion*' (1990: 8). Turned into a fashion category, *la Parisienne* is the outcome of a process. Categorization, as Jenkins suggests, 'may be more significant for categoriser(s) than for categorised', that is, for the fashion industry selling images of fashion and their related products (2004: 85). 'In our contemporary consumer society', Finkelstein notes, 'women's identities have been fractured, divided, redivided and newly created in order to multiply the opportunities and niche markets for fashion driven products' (1996: 64). The commodification in *Vogue* of *la Parisienne* is only one instance of a phenomenon that reaches across various sectors from Yves Saint Laurent's *'Parisienne'* handbag to Vosges's chocolate drink *'Couture Cocoa la Parisienne'*.

However, as Finkelstein also argues drawing on the work of Rabine, 'to enjoy the moment when fashionable clothing and a well-groomed style give one a sense of being attractive is also to be aware of having failed to replicate the perfection displayed in the fashion photograph. The perfect image can never be achieved' (1996: 47). The *Parisiennes* featured in the pages of *Vogue* ultimately *are* unattainable models – 'inimitable to the point of irreality' as Rabine suggests of most fashion images (1994: 63). The proximity to the *Parisienne* identity that the appropriation of goods is said to enable is ultimately denied by the very nature of the media that promote them. Paris, through *La Parisienne*, remains firmly placed in the sphere of all things superior. The aura of Paris is further strengthened, and, thereby, its dominance over the rest of France further legitimized.

–4–

Placing Tokyo on the Fashion Map
From Catwalk to Streetstyle
Yuniya Kawamura

This chapter focuses on the evolution of Tokyo as a fashion city. The history of Western clothing in Japan is still new. Ever since it first appeared in Japan in the mid nineteenth century, the Japanese have been fascinated by Western dress. One hundred and fifty years later that fascination persists but Japan's position in the global order of fashion is in transition. Tokyo is emerging from a history where it featured as a city of consumption, where people competed with one another to purchase expensive Western brands for status, to becoming a city of production where some of the most innovative designers in the world are establishing themselves. It is also attracting attention as a city that creates a unique form of street fashion.

The chapter suggests that there is a significant contrast between the idea of Tokyo as a new fashion centre in the 1970s and 1980s that worked through the exoticization of Japanese designers in established Western centres, and the new street fashion in the 1990s. Two different ways of placing Tokyo in fashion's world order are thus discussed, in addition to the practice of purchasing brands that originated from major fashion centres in the West, Paris in particular, among women in Tokyo. French fashion is universally believed to be the epitome of high fashion because of haute couture. Paris has always represented modernity in fashion, and it holds an exclusive symbolic status in the minds of Japanese consumers. Yet Tokyo today holds a unique position in the urban hierarchy of fashion where consumption and production take place simultaneously with much intensity, making Parisian models less relevant. Tokyo is no longer just a city in which Western fashion is widely appreciated and consumed but is becoming a centre that produces innovative fashion ideas in its own right.

Western Clothing in Japan as a Symbol of Modernization since 1868

After a long period of isolation from foreign and neighbouring countries, Japan opened its doors and moved towards Westernization in the Meiji era (1868–1912). This was a period of radical economic, social and political reforms. The emperor supported and encouraged the modernization and military build-up of Japan. The government's new slogan was 'Civilization and Enlightenment' following Western patterns. The most visible transformation was seen in clothes. This new cultural phenomenon, a shift from kimonos to Western styles, was a sign of sophistication and membership of the upper class. They were first adopted for men's military uniforms, and French- and British-style uniforms were designed for the Japanese army and navy since this was the style that Westerners wore when they first arrived in Japan. After 1870, government workers, such as policemen, railroad workers and postal carriers, were required to wear Western male suits. The emperor and the empress took the initiative and wore Western clothing and hairstyles at official events. By the end of the nineteenth century, the court adopted Western clothes and formal imperial kimonos were worn only in traditional ceremonies.

During the Taisho period (1912–26) wearing Western clothing continued to be a sign of sophistication and an expression of modernity. Working women, such as bus conductors, nurses and typists, started wearing Western clothes as occupational uniforms. After the Second World War, fashion information from the USA and Europe began to spread throughout Japan. People in metropolitan centres in Japan, especially in Tokyo, began to consume Western fashion at a very rapid pace in the 1950s and 1960s, and whatever trend was popular in the West was imported to Japan or exact copies were reproduced locally.

However, no matter how fashionable Japanese consumers became, Tokyo was never included in the global hierarchy of fashion centres nor did it receive any recognition as a fashion city in the same way that Paris, Milan or New York did, until the 1970s. For decades, Tokyo was considered a market for Western corporations to invest in. Helped by the booming economy in Japan in the 1980s, companies from the USA and Europe were aggressively entering into Tokyo, either setting up subsidiaries or opening up freestanding stores. For Western designers, the Japanese market, especially in Tokyo, provided a great commercial opportunity, but for Japanese designers, it was never a country or a city where fashion was produced. According to Akira Baba (in Lockwood 1995: 8–9), the president of Kashiyama, a major Japanese apparel manufacturer, there are two types of merchandise in Japan: (1) products used for daily consumption and (2) fashion goods. For Japanese consumers, 'fashion' is still a Western concept. As Koenig (1974) indicates, in democratic societies, people feel the need to make subtle differences with others, and in a society like Japan where people believe in homogeneity and conformity, they use fashion and clothing as the means to indicate those slight differences. Similarly, Wilson (1992b) also suggests that the need to distinguish oneself is perhaps strongest with regard to the group to which one has the strongest affiliation.

French luxury goods function as a status symbol because, first and foremost, they are expensive in Japan. The image of French companies in Japan is very strong in consumer goods (Thuresson 2002) and this explains the fact that in 2001 the largest importer of French luxury products of the Colbert Committee,[1] an organization that represents French luxury brands, was Japan, which accounted for 51 per cent of the member companies' total sales in the Asia-Pacific region (*Le Comité Colbert* 2002/2003).

The Exoticization of Japanese Designers in Paris since 1970

Tokyo as a fashion city and Japanese designers gradually began to attract attention vicariously through the emergence of Kenzo Takada (known as Kenzo) in Paris in 1970. He was the very first Japanese designer to take part in the biannual ready-to-wear Paris fashion collections. Kenzo was famous for mixing plaids, flowers, checks and stripes, a combination that no Western designers ever imagined (Figure 4.1). The quilting technique he used was rooted in Japanese traditions, and square shapes

Figure 4.1 Kenzo Spring/Summer 1996 Collection. Photograph: Courtesy of www.FirstView.com

and straight lines that derived from the kimono were also used. There was something particularly Japanese in the way he reconstructed Western clothing. Immediately after his first show in Paris in June 1970, it was one of his designs in *Sashiko*, the traditional Japanese stitching technique, which appeared on the cover of *Elle*, one of the most influential magazines in France.

His biographer Ginnette Sainderichinn writes: 'Kenzo is a magician of color. Since the mid 1960s, when he moved from his native Japan to the city of Paris, he has devoted himself to the creation of wearable, vivacious clothing: a fashion without hierarchies' (1998: 17). He has made a major contribution to the democratization of fashion. However, his identity as a Japanese designer was the focal point of his position and career in Paris, and he was constantly reminded of his ethnic background in the Western press. Kenzo's sudden appearance and his almost overnight success in Paris as a designer provoked an interest in Tokyo among the fashion professionals in the West, as an exotic, mysterious city, where there could be more creative designers, like Kenzo, hidden or waiting to be discovered.

As Georg Simmel pointed out in the traditions of modern Western fashion there 'exists a wide-spread predilection for importing fashions from without, and such foreign fashions assume a greater value within the circle, simply because they did not originate there.... . the exotic origin of fashions seems strongly to favor the exclusiveness of the groups which adopt them' (1957 [1904]: 545). Fashion needs to be exotic and foreign, and Japanese designers, such as Kenzo and those who followed after him, fulfilled that definition. So-called Japanese fashion was different and completely new to the eyes of French fashion professionals.

At the beginning of the 1980s, the placement of Tokyo on the fashion map became even more pronounced when the three controversial avant-garde Japanese designers, Issey Miyake, Yohji Yamamoto and Rei Kawakubo of Comme des Garçons, rocked the Paris fashion world by introducing clothes that were creative and unconventional to say the least, and their designs were definitely not Western. Miyake had been in Paris since 1973, but when the other two arrived, the three together created the Japanese avant-garde[2] fashion phenomenon, although it was never their intention to do so.

They destroyed and reinterpreted Western conventions of the clothing system, by suggesting different ways of wearing a garment. They also redefined the nature of Western clothing itself. Western female clothing has historically been fitted to expose the contours of the body, but these Japanese designers introduced large, loose-fitting garments. Like Kenzo, the integration of kimono elements into their designs is clearly evident, especially in their earlier works. It was a combination of Japanese and Western elements that forced the destruction of both in order to reconstruct something completely new. In this way they also redefined the nature of fashion, not only clothing. The conception of fashion is synonymous with the conception of beauty. Therefore, by introducing a new fashion, they simultaneously suggested a new definition of aesthetics.

Hanae Mori was the first Japanese couturier to be officially named by the Chambre Syndicale de la Couture Parisienne[3] in 1977 and introduced something that the other ready-to-wear Japanese designers did not. Her style, methods of dressmaking and the clients she catered to in and outside Japan distanced her from any other Japanese designers. She recognized that haute couture is the product of high culture and a phenomenon of an elitist society. Thus Mori did not challenge the Western clothing system as the others had done. Nor did she use fabrics bought at a flea market or worn by Japanese fishermen or farmers. Until her retirement from the couture organization in July 2004, she stayed within the realm of Japanese high culture and introduced the ultimate luxury and beauty of Japan to the West using Japanese cultural objects, viewed through the rules of Western aesthetics.

Jennifer Craik (1994: 41) points out that during this period the Japanese influence partially redrew the boundaries of fashion away from 'Western' ideals of the body, body–space relations and conventions of clothing. The principles of Western fashion increasingly incorporated non-European influences, traditions and forms into mainstream practice, and Western appreciation for Japanese fashion, which many believed to have originated in Tokyo, quickly intensified. At the same time, the 1980s were the decade when Tokyo appeared to have been included in the order of major fashion cities along with Paris, Milan, New York and London. Coincidentally, it was the time when Japan became economically powerful. Because of the strong exchange rate, Japanese tourists were flocking to expensive designer label stores on the street of Champs-Elysées in Paris and were buying the merchandise literally by the dozens.

The Marginal Status of Tokyo as a Fashion Centre until the mid 1990s

The 1970s and 1980s were not the first time that clothes with oriental inspirations appeared in the West. In the late thirteenth century, Marco Polo had brought the first marvels of China to the West (Martin and Koda 1994) and in the early twentieth century famous French designers, such as Jeanne Lanvin, Paul Poiret and Coco Chanel incorporated Asian- as well as Japanese-inspired textiles, prints, calligraphy and pattern constructions, such as kimono sleeves, into their original designs. What was different in the late twentieth century was that the Japanese designers of the 1970s and 1980s came from the East. What made them unique was not only their clothes but their position and status as non-Western fashion outsiders. The marginality of these Japanese has become an asset. Before Kenzo, there were virtually no Asian designers on the Western fashion scene. Tokyo was considered an exotic city that produced very different but talented and creative fashion designers. After the first generation of Japanese designers, such as Kenzo, Miyake and Mori, other Japanese were arriving in Paris one after another.

Tokyo became known indirectly through the marginal status of these designers. At the same time, they were brought to the centre with French legitimization. But the Japanese fashion phenomenon was not enough to include Tokyo among the major fashion centres. For instance, Tokyo was not strong enough to attract Western journalists to attend and cover the Tokyo collections. As Lise Skov accurately points out (1996: 148): 'It is ironical ... that Rei Kawakubo, as one of the designers who brought 'Japanese fashion' to fame, simultaneously reinforced the interest in the Paris collections.' Designers flocked to Paris because Paris provided and still provides the kind of status that no other city could provide, and there was no way that Tokyo could provide the same added value.

Furthermore, it was believed that the widespread popularity of 'Japanese fashion' in the 1980s was a decisive factor in placing Tokyo on the list of international fashion capitals (Skov 1996: 134). Yet Tokyo was still falling far behind Paris in the production of fashion and setting of trends until the 1990s. This was due to the fact that there was a lack of an institutionalized and centralized fashion system in Japan (Kawamura 2004a). Tokyo as a fashion city did not have the kind of structural strength and effectiveness that the French system took for granted. Through the exoticization of Japanese design in Paris, Tokyo did find a place on the fashion map, and many buyers and fashion insiders went to Japan but were disappointed to see Japanese consumers wearing Western brands.

As Wilson states (1985) fashion is an outstanding mark of modern civilization, and Craik (1994) questions whether fashion can be confined to the development of European fashion and argues that the term 'fashion' needs revision because fashion is too often equated with modern European high fashion. It was not possible, until recently, to produce, market and distribute fashion that was not baptized or consecrated by the West. However, this has been changing over the years with the emergence of street fashion creating a separate system of fashion with a new business model. Modern fashion, which is consumer driven, comes not only from the West but also from the streets of Tokyo.

Tokyo's Efforts to Create a Stronger Fashion Identity

Japan's neighbouring countries in the Asian region have fallen behind in building credible fashion centres because their cities have a reputation for garment manufacturing that has nothing to do with the local fashion culture. Unlike other Asian countries that are known for their cheap labour rather than for their design creativity, Tokyo's fashion identity had been strong among the Asian countries while its position was weaker in the broader context of the world's fashion cities. Among Asian countries, Tokyo is the fashion capital. Japanese fashion magazines are widely read in Korea, China and Taiwan, and tourists from neighbouring countries regularly visit Tokyo to purchase Japanese brands.

What fashion cities need is the symbolic production of fashion. The material production of clothing is less important. Tokyo still needs to reinforce place-based resources or images to establish fashion as a symbolic cultural product. Tokyo is becoming a true fashion city not only by consuming fashion but also by producing fashion, both of which are the necessary characteristics of a fashion capital.

One way to promote a fashion centre is to organize fashion shows on a regular basis. Tokyo has done this but has not been successful. When the Council for Fashion Designers (CFD) was formed in 1985 to systematize all fashion-related events and activities in Tokyo and also to facilitate the relationships among designers, buyers and the media, a French journalist wrote sarcastically:

> Is Paris going to have its Oriental rival soon? Those Japanese creators who do not look for the consecration on the Parisian podium are hoping some day to have the same power to replace Paris with Tokyo ... Japanese are trying to include Tokyo among the traditional route of fashion, such as Milan, New York and Paris. But isn't it ironical that many of the Japanese brands have French names, such as Coup de Pied, C'est Vrai, Etique, Madame Hanai, Madame Nicole and so on. How can Tokyo replace Paris? (Piganeu 1986: 3)

The CFD organization is now rebuilding its internal structure and is collaborating with the Japanese government (Fujita 2005). Yet, they have managed to invite only fifty-two designers and apparel companies for the Tokyo collections in November 2005, which is fewer than half of the participants in the Paris or New York Collections. Thus, the structural weaknesses of fashion production in Japan forces Japanese designers to go overseas, especially to Paris which remains supreme, at least in the minds of the Japanese consumers as well as the designers.

Street Fashion and Subcultures: Bringing Tokyo to the Centre

Street fashion has been in existence on the streets of Tokyo for decades. Especially in Harajuku, where between 1979 and 1981, there was a group called *Takenoko-zoku* (literally translated as the Bamboo Tribe). A number of different teenage subcultures and fashions followed, such as the *New Wave* that was influenced by the British rock scene, *Karasu-zoku* (the Crow Tribe) who were the followers of Rei Kawakubo and Yohji Yamamoto, and *Shibu-Kaji,* which was a casual look worn in Shibuya, a fashion district in Tokyo. However, these subcultures were short-lived fads that did not spread far, remained within their own group and gradually disappeared.

What is new and different about the current street fashion that emerged at the beginning of the 1990s is that different institutions of fashion got together to make use of and take advantage of the marketing potential of the teenagers. There is a strong interdependent relationship between the industries and the individuals involved. Trends that were spread by teenagers were completely independent of the

Western fashion system or the mainstream fashion establishment in Japan. They have led the way in a creative mixing and matching of contrasting eclectic styles that have been extensively copied in the West (Polhemus 1996: 12). High-school girls in Tokyo are the key to any trend. The popularity of a pair of white loose socks amongst this group was one of the first such trends to emerge.[4] Dick Hebdige, in studying subculture in 1970s and 1980s London, explained that girls have been relegated to a position of secondary interest within both sociological accounts of subculture and photographic studies of urban youth, and that the masculinist bias was present in the subcultures themselves (1988: 27). But in the case of subcultures in Tokyo, they are dominated by women, and by teenage girls in particular.

Fashion has always been a reflection of the current situation of the society. Ironically, Japan's economic slowdown over the past decade may have played a role in today's longer-lasting street fashion. There is a widespread feeling of disillusionment, alienation, uncertainty or anger, which has spread through Japanese society from adults to children. This has led to the breakdown of traditional Japanese values, such as perseverance, discipline and the belief in education, especially among children. Their norm-breaking attitude is exhibited through their appearance, which is a way to make themselves seen and heard.

Diana Crane explains that the fact that, in the past decade, the major Japanese companies have been investing in young and exceptionally innovative Western designers suggests that the Japanese have not been able to satisfy their enormous demand for fashion talent (1993: 70). This was true until ten years ago, but the new type of fashion, that is street fashion, has a different structure. Furthermore, as Crane (2000) points out today's fashion is consumer driven, and market trends originate in many types of social groups, especially adolescent urban subcultures, and this is exactly what is happening today in Tokyo. The most recent fashion phenomenon in Tokyo originates from various subcultures. Since the mid 1990s, teenagers in Tokyo have been producing and guiding fashion trends that are unique and original, and many fashion professionals in the West are now paying attention to the latest styles in Tokyo.

This again placed Tokyo on the fashion map but in a different way. Attention is no longer on fashion designers who were professionally trained or have formal experiences in the industries but on the amateur, untrained teenagers on the streets, who simply love directional, expressive clothing. They are the producers, marketers and distributors of fashion. Pop culture trends, including fashion, are extremely fickle, and tastes can change overnight, but to find out what is hot and popular, the industries rely on Japanese schoolgirls.

Tokyo in the 1970s and 1980s was not the place where the trends were created, but that presumption has changed. Tokyo is becoming a city that engages in producing creative and new ideas. It is becoming a true fashion force.

Segmentation and Diffusion: The Case of Harajuku in Tokyo[5]

Street life is made of multiple subcultures and each has its own taste, lifestyle, attitudes and fashion. Shibuya used to be the place where street fashion was found because of the emergence of the Kogal phenomenon.[6] At weekends, these girls occupy the Shibuya 109 Department Store,[7] which is the landmark of Shibuya. Today, each district within the city of Tokyo is very much segmented according to different groups of teenagers. Besides Shibuya, street fashion in Tokyo is found in Harajuku, Daikanyama, Ikebukuro and Jiyugaoka, among many others, and each district has its distinctive look. One girl in my fieldwork study said: 'If you are in Jiyugaoka and dressed in a Shibuya style, you would be totally out of place. That's something really embarrassing, and no one would do that.'[8] The teenagers know how they should dress depending on where they are going. The physical environment of an area helps street fashion to grow and spread, and it provides a space or a stage for the teenagers to be fashionable. It gives them the opportunity to socialize, communicate and interact with each other, all of which are necessary for any subculture to form. Furthermore, those behaviours must be repeated for the group to continue and be maintained, and the same style and fashion need to be exposed repeatedly for the public to recognize them as a subculture.

One of the primary reasons that the youth culture came out of Harajuku, which has become known as Tokyo's teenage town, was *Hokosha-Tengoku,* or *Hokoten* (literally translated as 'pedestrian paradise'). Between 1977 and 1998 a section of the main road in Harajuku was closed to traffic on Sundays, and this place became a public sphere, which was a new idea in Japan. Many young people who were dressed in their often handmade creative fashion gathered there. *Hokoten* was terminated in 1998 and Harajuku gradually returned to its original state, but Harajuku remained a place where teenagers congregate to meet and chat with their friends who want to dress in certain styles.

Harajuku now produces distinctive subcultures. In the back streets of Harajuku known as *Ura-Hara*, there are many so-called select shops, small boutiques where the owners' tastes in selecting, mixing and remixing merchandise are highly valued by customers. The stores are run and managed by semi-professional designers, those who just graduated from fashion schools or artists, such as graphic and textile designers. There are a number of collaborative projects between the store owners and the artists. Those who shop in *Ura-Hara* are the most fashion-conscious teens, and the street style in Harajuku is a hybrid of original handmade items and styles that are reminiscent of Western subcultures, such as London punk fashion with plaid, bondage pants or skirts and spiked belts, or American Harlem hip-hop styles with baggy T-shirts and jeans that fall down to the hips. Many of them sew their own outfits because creating a one-of-a-kind style by combining them with ready-made items is important.

Another subculture emerged from the teenagers that hang around with their friends on the bridge near the station. They wear clothing based on cartoon characters in anime, and this trend is called Costume Play, abbreviated as Cos-Play. This movement refers not only to dressing as a specific character but also as a waitress or a nurse. The Gothic Lolita is one of the most popular costumes found in Harajuku since 1999 (Figure 4.2). The girls are photographed by magazines and scouted by model agencies.

No fashion is diffused locally or globally without the mass media. The production process of fashion is always strongly connected to fashion magazines (Moeran 2005). In any type of fashion, magazines are the most important medium to build the status and the reputation of a designer, to spread specific fashion trends and promote new merchandise. The dissemination process is a crucial stage between production and consumption. An object is first manufactured, and then it is transformed into fashion through the process of dissemination. In this respect, street fashion in Harajuku has been well documented by the monthly magazine called *Fruits* published in 1997 by photographer, Shoichi Aoki. His goal was to report on cutting-edge street and youth fashion. His photographs depict a revolutionary Japanese fashion movement since the mid 1990s. The attention was not on the designers but on the consumers who have become the producers of street fashion. The diverse styles in *Fruits* are continuously evolving and often unique. Aoki writes:

Figure 4.2 Gothic Lolitas on a bridge near Harajuku Station. Photograph: Yuniya Kawamura.

Because Western clothing has a short history in Japan, there is a strong tendency for people to dress in the same style as each other. Essentially this tendency has not changed. In Japan, having a different style is a kind of risk. Even the designer brand boom of the 1980s did not change that. People only took suggestions from the designers in the same manner as everyone else.... . Therefore the fashion movement that came about in Harajuku was a revolution. This kind of fashion was not suggested by designers, but rather, the fashion of the young inspired the designers. On the streets of Harajuku, there was no risk in having a different style. In fact it was considered worthwhile. (Aoki 2001: 2)

Almost all street fashion magazines published in Japan are distributed only domestically, but with the wide influence of the Internet, and through word of mouth, Japanese fashion is steadily going global. For instance, the street magazines are found in Japanese bookstores in New York and are read not only by Japanese but also by local teenagers and fashion students. Similarly, some of the Japanese magazines published in English, such as *International Katei Gaho*, are featuring Japanese fashion. What is now required is to create the diffusion mechanism which has internationally recognized publicity and promotional vehicles, such as fashion press, major fashion shows and events that are noticed by fashion professionals worldwide.

The Harajuku teenagers' radical fashion has become the inspiration for young designers known as the street designers. Some of them, for example, Jun Takahashi of Undercover or Keita Maruyama, now take part in the Paris collections, because for the Japanese, French legitimization and recognition are the fastest way to success. Those who are not going to Paris, such as the brand Bathing Ape, are now arriving in New York, seeking the legitimization of other fashion cities.

The Significance of Paris among Women in Tokyo

While Tokyo is now being placed on the fashion map and being acknowledged and included in an urban hierarchy of fashion, Japanese consumers still have a voracious appetite for Western brands, and Japan has undoubtedly been playing a major role in the global surge in fashion consumption. Western designers are generally favoured by Japanese consumers more than their Japanese counterparts. As the concepts of fashion and modernity are closely linked (Wilson 1985; Breward and Evans 2005) the increasing number of Western brands in Tokyo can be interpreted as a sign of modernization as well as Westernization, and it also meant that Tokyo was transforming into a major metropolitan city. Despite more than a decade of economic downturn, consumers are still purchasing European luxury goods. No matter how bad the economy gets in Japan, there are those who are willing to pay hundreds or thousands of dollars for big names like 'Gucci' and 'Prada'.

Paris is the imperial fashion city. It has become the symbol of fashion that adds values to designers' names because of the efforts taken by the system to maintain and reproduce that ideology and maintain the belief. Paris as a fashion city has held an exclusive place in the minds of modern Japanese consumers ever since Pierre Cardin visited Tokyo and introduced his brand in the 1950s. It carries far more weight than London, New York or Milan, where biannual collections are held. Even for Kenzo himself, the Japanese market was only secondary to his business, and his core customer base was in France because their acceptance and legitimization guaranteed his worldwide fame and reputation, which were followed by financial rewards. One of the Japanese magazine editors in my study said: 'Every time we do a feature story on Paris or French fashion, the circulation figures go way up for that particular month. It may seem redundant sometimes, but we do that a few times a year for that reason. Milan and New York come next. London is so, so.'[9]

In contrast to street fashion, which is a teenage phenomenon, statistics show that 94 per cent of women in Tokyo who are in their twenties own something made by Louis Vuitton, according to Saison Research Institute, and goods made by Gucci sit in the closets of 92 per cent of women in Tokyo in their twenties; almost 58 per cent own Prada and almost 52 per cent Chanel (Prasso and Brady 2003). The country has developed a leisure class, known as parasite singles, who still live at home with their parents, giving them plenty of disposable income. The most popular brand among this group is undoubtedly Louis Vuitton, and the company has been actively investing in the Japanese market, by increasing the number of stores throughout Japan, especially in Tokyo. When the world's largest Louis Vuitton store in the Omotensando district, which is near Harajuku, opened in September, 2003, it set a single-day sales record for the company, selling 125 million yen, or about 1.05 million dollars worth of merchandise, and more than a thousand people waited in a long line for the grand opening (Prasso and Brady 2003). Other luxury retailers, such as Salvatore Ferragamo, Cartier, Christian Dior and Gucci, have also opened new stores or are planning to do so soon. French companies have been very successful in entering into the Japanese market. Despite Japan's weak economy, consumers remain passionate about imported brand-name goods.

Conclusion

Japanese street fashion used to be explained by the existence of one or two conspicuous subcultures, such as *Ganguro* in Shibuya in the mid 1990s, but today they have multiplied in different directions and fragmented into smaller groups, and thus, the phenomenon appears to have slowed down. However, much of Japan's cultural output that travelled mostly to other parts of Asia is now transcending cultural boundaries and is spreading worldwide. Japan's street fashion influence on popular and youth cultures is spreading globally. Paris as a fashion capital has been successful because its institutions accepted the fusion of the local and the distant, and there was international exchange of clothes, design and designers between Paris and other cities. The Japanese designers who became successful in Paris took advantage of the system in Paris while Japanese teenagers are creating their own fashion with their own force making a major contribution to the construction of Tokyo as a fashion centre. Fashion's world cities are determined by the flows of goods, ideas and people. This is what Tokyo needed for a long time, and it is finally happening.

Notes

1. The Colbert Committee (Le Comité Colbert) is a trade association for French luxury products that organizes promotional activities for its member companies. It was founded in 1954 by Jean-Jacques Guerlain, a perfume manufacturer, and Lucien Lelong, a couturier and the former president of *La Chambre Syndicale de la Couture Parisienne*. There are sixty-one member companies among ten industry sectors as of December 2004.
2. The general meaning of the term avant-garde implies a cohesive group of artists who have a strong commitment to iconoclastic aesthetic values and who reject both popular culture and middle-class lifestyle, They are often in opposition to dominant social values and norms (Crane 1997: 1).
3. The Chambre Syndicale de la Couture Parisienne, which was officially set up in 1911, is part of the larger organization called the Federation Française de la couture, du Prêt-à-Porter des Couturiers et des Créateurs de Mode, which was established in 1973. For details, see Kawamura (2004b).
4. The loose socks were probably the first trend that the teens in Shibuya created. Unlike the other street fashion, which was very much influenced by Western designers, this was typically Japanese. They are pairs of white, baggy knee socks, which are deliberately pushed down to the shin like leg warmers. This trend was started not by the fashion industry but by high-school teenagers, and the marketing potential of these girls became strongly apparent. Fashion trends can no longer be dictated only by the designers or the industries.
5. This is based on my ethnographical study conducted in Harajuku during January, July and August 2005.
6. Tokyo's distinctive street fashion is said to have begun in the mid 1990s by young teenage girls known as *Kogal*. They are known for wearing short plaid skirts that look like their own school uniforms and knee-high white socks, and occasionally with heavy makeup and artificial suntans.

7. The stores inside the department store cater to Japanese teenagers. It is the fashion mecca where fashionable teenagers shop and where well-known sales girls who have appeared in street fashion magazines work. Street fashion in Shibuya functions in conjunction with the building. These girls are the trendsetters, merchandisers, stylists and designers.
8. Kumiko Okuma interviewed in Tokyo, on 22 July 2005.
9. Yoko Sato interviewed in Tokyo, on 1 August 2005.

–5–

Curating the Fashion City
New York Fashion at the V&A
Sonnet Stanfill

The coveted status of 'fashion capital' is closely associated with the perceived benefits of cultural tourism, whose transformative power can produce an increase in visitors, investment and prestige. Encouraged through such initiatives as the European-funded City of Culture project (a programme which annually designates a city to receive special support for its cultural efforts), in recent years cultural tourism has contributed to the shift in the museum's role in cultural life. Many of these institutions now see themselves as centres of such activity. In addition to this change in self-perception, museum display practices have also evolved. For fashion collections this evolution has been away from a mainly object-based emphasis on chronologies and stylistic analysis towards a more interdisciplinary methodology, which includes questions of meaning and interpretation (Styles 1998: 387). This opinion is echoed by dress historian Lou Taylor who writes about the diversity of new theoretical viewpoints, ' ... there is no doubt of the positive excitement and innovation to be found within the crosscurrents now whirling through dress history/ dress studies ...' (Taylor 2002: 273). The British government echoed this outlook in a consultation paper on the future role of museums, in which it stressed the importance of making objects accessible in a manner that is interpretative as well as informative (Department of Culture, Media and Sport 2005: 20; 41).[1]

For fashion collections, displaying clothes in the context of a city tradition engages with these new methods and approaches to fashion history in a way that can be compelling and approachable for the visitor. The precedent for this type of display has been set in both European and North American institutions. Local museums in particular have long used dress to explore regional social history. More recently, larger museums in major metropolitan areas have investigated city traditions with exhibitions such as *London Fashion* in 2001 at the Museum at the Fashion Institute of Technology (FIT); *Belgian Fashion: Antwerp Style* again at FIT in the same year; and *The London Look: fashion from street to catwalk* in 2005 at the Museum of London. Founded long before these recent displays are several museums whose purpose is specifically to chronicle their city's history, with fashion forming an important part of their collections. The Museum of London and the Museum of the

City of New York are two examples. Antwerp's Mode Museum (MoMu), which opened in 2002, is an influential recent arrival since it represents itself specifically as the champion and archive of Antwerp's avant-garde fashion production.

Although the Victoria and Albert Museum (V&A) holds Britain's national collection of dress and is located in a capital city in the heart of one of fashion's important urban centres, historically it has remained aloof from engaging with fashion in the context of city traditions. The Museum's major fashion exhibitions have tended to be chronologies (*Cecil Beaton: a fashion anthology*, 1972; *Fashion 1900–1939*, 1976) or monographs (*Ferragamo*, 1988; *Pierre Cardin*, 1991; *Versace*, 2002; *Vivienne Westwood*, 2004). The Museum's more recent experiments with other kinds of methodologies include *Street Style* (1995); *Cutting Edge* (1997); *Radical Fashion* (2001–2); and *Spectres* (2004–5). Despite these forays into non-traditional modes of presentation the V&A has not engaged directly in city-specific fashion projects, until now.

After a nine-month closure the V&A reopened its popular dress gallery with all new content in 2005. The Museum retired a strictly chronological fashion-through-the-ages display that had been on view for almost a quarter-century. Two goals motivated this dramatically simplified display: the need to preserve rare early garments and the importance of reopening the gallery as quickly as possible.[2] At the basis for the new arrangement of roughly 60 per cent of the gallery are a quintet of themes: the suit for men, the suit for women, the 'dress, dressing up, undress' and sportswear. The remainder of the gallery displays twentieth-century and contemporary women's fashion in relation to major metropolitan centres: Paris, London, Milan, Tokyo and New York.

Practicality determined the decision to structure part of the gallery around cities. This geographical framework helped systematize the display of modern fashion while capitalizing on the strengths of the collection and staff specialities. It also provides visitors with an efficient, comprehensible structure for visiting and appre-ciating the exhibit. Though this methodology risks oversimplification, many viewers – and indeed designers and their clients – do think of fashion in terms of specific city cultures and traditions.

As the curator responsible for the city sections, I selected designs that repres-ented key elements of a city's high fashion culture. Constrained by a lack of space, a single garment had to illustrate each designer's *oeuvre* while forming part of a rough, post-war chronology. A further challenge was the difficulty of representing New York's tremendous design contributions while working with a collection that, since its inception, has emphasized London and Paris: of the V&A's roughly 85,000 textiles and fashion objects only 1,200, or 1.5 per cent, were designed in the United States.

The V&A has rarely displayed its few but fine examples of American fashion. When the Museum's fashion gallery underwent its last major redisplay in 1984 it reopened with no examples of American fashion, except for Charles James, who designed both in London and New York. Yet the V&A's small group of American designs is outstanding, in particular, because in 1974 the Museum acquired, with the help of fashion photographer Cecil Beaton, over 400 examples of twentieth-century high fashion, haute couture and accessories of the highest quality from Paris, London and New York. The American designers included in the Beaton acquisition were: Adolpho, Adrian, Hattie Carnegie, Bonnie Cashin, James Galanos, Charles James, Anne Klein and Norman Norell. Despite this influx of compelling American material, at the 1984 reopening – a decade after the Beaton acquisition – New York designers were overlooked.

Another display challenge was that New York's fashion culture – its designers, their clients and the city's fashion press – does not represent that of the whole of the United States. An investigation of New York fashion leaves out the counter-cultural movements of San Francisco and the red-carpet influence of Los Angeles. Also excluded from this discourse are other well-dressed American cities like Boston, Chicago and Philadelphia, with their own fashion traditions and wealthy, fashion-preoccupied patrons. New York supplanted these important American fashion centres by the mid nineteenth century when steam power made the Hudson River navigable (Milbank 1989: 10). The city's manufacturers, importers and retailers soon made it America's fashion capital. And although by the end of the twentieth century Los Angeles had the highest concentration of garment production in the United States, New York continues to be the preferred design headquarters for emerging American designers as well as many major fashion brands. Even American high street giants like Gap and Limited Brands, whose head offices are in San Francisco and Cleveland respectively, have separate design offices in New York.

Leaving behind the comfort of chronology for a much more interpretative approach was difficult. Consequently, the Museum's fashion curators debated how best to present the collection and pondered scores of possible selections, each choice fraught with potential error. In the worldwide network of major galleries the V&A's fashion archive and the displays that draw from it are internationally significant. The V&A welcomes roughly two and a half million visitors annually and over the past decade over 735,000 people attended the Museum's five major fashion exhibitions.[3] With such visitor numbers, clearly curatorial choice – the process of selection and omission – can shape popular understanding and can contribute to the creation or perpetuation of mythologies.

Also problematic is the fact that the V&A's holdings of New York-designed fashion are strong on sportswear and ready-to-wear and less representative of that city's eveningwear and haute couture. Hence the V&A's presentation of New York's fashion history is skewed towards the informality of daywear. Constrained by the collection, the story told is one in which New York designers continued to satisfy America's enthusiasm for innovation while catering to their desire to maintain practicality and comfort (Milbank 1989:13). As the following account (ordered chronologically by the date of the designs) will show, curating the gallery's city segments involved inevitable compromise. It also required an examination of the relationship between major metropolises and the mythologizing of fashion.

Charles James (1906–78)

Important to a chronicle of New York fashion are the couture designs of Charles James. While James is perhaps best remembered for his extravagant eveningwear (his so-called Clover dress of 1953 is composed of thirty pattern pieces and layers of fabric (Martin 1997: 53)), he was also capable of stunning simplicity. The Museum does have examples of James's elaborate eveningwear but the garment representing him in the gallery is a late 1930s coat, which is the model of restraint (Figure 5.1). The Museum acquired the coat in 1978. It came with two Charles James evening bodices, one James evening dress and several accessories from Miss Philippa Barnes

Figure 5.1 Charles James, coat, *c.*1938, Victoria and Albert Museum Collection: no. T.291-1978. Photograph courtesy V&A Imaging, Peter Kelleher.

of West Malling, Kent and formed part of the Beaton collection. Regrettably there exists no information about the donor in the papers relating to the acquisition. I chose the coat for expedience: it was one of the few James pieces that needed no conservation in order to be displayed.

Though one might argue that the British-born James sits uncertainly as a New York designer, he lived in the city more or less continuously from 1940 until his death in 1978. James designed the coat in 1937, a few years before settling in New York. Made from black wool the sombre garment has tapered sleeves, a shaped waist and falls just below the knee. It also features a double-layered, standing collar achieved by inventive folds across the bodice. The coat is fastened by a single hook at the neck and one at the waist. Its sobriety is emphasized by the collar's monastic white lining. The coat's short skirt and fine details would have made it appropriate for a daytime city appointment. Its inventive but precise cut and trim silhouette – hallmarks of many of the New York designers on display – support the late fashion historian and curator Richard Martin's reference to James's coats and capes as 'one of his greatest achievements' (Martin 1997: 14).

Claire McCardell (1905–58)

Claire McCardell was another inventive, mid-century New York designer crucial to include. A graduate of New York's Parsons School of Design, McCardell designed from 1928 until her early death from cancer in 1958. Her stylish but affordable ready-to-wear and sportswear arguably had a greater impact on American fashion than the designs of someone like James, designing couture for a small, elite client list.

A 1955 hostess dress epitomizes McCardell's practical, casual elegance (Figure 5.2). McCardell's family donated the dress in 1978, along with two day dresses, a bathing costume and a skirt and jumper ensemble. In a letter to the V&A, her children Phyllis and Adrian McCardell wrote, 'We are pleased to give four Claire McCardell dresses to the Museum for its Costume Collections. These dresses were forwarded to you by the Fashion Institute of Technology. The only restriction is that these dresses can never be sold. If the Museum should decide to dispose of these garments they must be given to either the Met or F.I.T.' These are the only examples of this designer's work in our collection.

Though McCardell designed the dress for evening she intended it to be worn in the less formal setting of the home; thus the fabric is a fairly unglamorous, utilitarian wool. The classic sheath silhouette masterfully conceals the inclusion of side pockets, a functional detail typical of McCardell. The designer supposedly insisted on pockets in every garment, for beyond their use for carrying things, pockets offered a lady 'a place to put one's hands so as not to feel ill at ease or vulnerable' (Yohannan and Nolf 1998: 51). The dress's wrap waist, tied with a long sash is another McCardellism, as

Figure 5.2 Claire McCardell, hostess dress, 1955, V&A: T.77-1978. Photograph courtesy V&A Imaging, Peter Kelleher.

she herself called her signature design elements. Emphasizing the waist, the bright red sash of red wool crepe adds a splash of electric colour to the dress's subdued hues of moss green, navy and black. This bold use of colour was a recurring feature in McCardell's 1950s designs (Lee 1975: 291). The year McCardell designed this dress *Time* magazine featured her as a cover story (2 May 1955). The accompanying article praised the designer as a catalyst in the evolution of American fashion.

Geoffrey Beene (1927–2004)

Another New York design luminary was Geoffrey Beene. During his forty-year career he dressed generations of New York women. At the time of his death in 2004 Beene was still designing for private clients, whose wardrobes depended on him. Beene began his own label in the 1960s with the simple sheath and A-line dresses that were then in vogue. By the 1970s Beene departed from the stiff construction of this early work to design clothes with a relaxed fit, such as flowing pyjamas and tubular dresses. Beene also delighted in experimenting with fabrics both sumptuous and pedestrian, what journalist Beth Cullerton referred to as 'an unlikely marriage between rich and humble' (Cullerton 1995: 52). Unfortunately, with so few Beene examples, the V&A is unable to represent his later work and the breadth of his talent.

The Beene design on display dates from 1969. It is a day dress of plain navy wool with a three-button closure (Figure 5.3). Its smart, sombre style would have been appropriate for a dressy city event. The garment illustrates Beene's career-long avoidance of the waist as a horizontal line in favour of swirling the fabric around the body (Martin 1998: 85). The white leather-covered buttons are the dress's only decoration. In selecting an ensemble to represent Beene, there were only two designs to choose from. Since both are day dresses from the 1960s regrettably the Museum's choice does not represent the whimsy often found in Beene's eveningwear.

Figure 5.3 Geoffrey Beene coat, *c*.1960, V&A: T.112-1989. Photograph courtesy V&A Imaging, Peter Kelleher.

Though the acquisition records do not describe the circumstances of the donation or who wore the dress, the curator's justification for the acquisition is germane, 'Geoffrey Beene is an influential designer with an international reputation. His clothes are distinctive and are recognized for their impeccable construction and finish. Mrs Mendes (the curator) has been looking for examples of top American designers for the collection, as our collection is poorly represented by them.'[4]

Bonnie Cashin (1915–2000)

While Beene's sense of fun added humour to eveningwear Bonnie Cashin's blithe informality invigorated mid-century American sportswear. Though Cashin worked in New York for most of her thirty-year career, she was born in California and spent six years there designing costumes for film. Cashin's West Coast years informed an aesthetic that borrowed easily from other cultures and traditions. A southern Californian dash infused Cashin's clothes, which fit the indeterminate dress code – neither formal nor informal – that emerged in 1960s America.

Cecil Beaton might well have been referring to Cashin's designs when he wrote in 1971, 'Today everyone is allowed to put on what they like – anything goes, except boredom.' (Ginsberg 1971: 7) Cashin's talent lay in creating coordinated yet comfortable ensembles appropriate for many social settings and activities. Beaton secured a 1971 tan suede trouser suit from Cashin for the V&A as part of the 1974 acquisition. The outfit's slightly rustic quality would have been fashionable at an informal daytime city or suburban event in the early 1970s. With a blue wool jersey hooded top, relaxed silhouette and coordinated blue leather trim the light-hearted effect is characteristic Cashin (Figure 5.4). The jacket's shape is a reference to Japanese happi coats, a kind of Pacific Rim globalism long before such ideas were current (Martin 1998: 86). Cashin rendered it in casual suede with vaguely Native American accents. The trousers are flatteringly pegged and the top is informally sleeveless. The suit is one of five Cashin designs in the V&A, four of which were gifts of the designer via the Beaton collection. I chose this ensemble over others because it combines so many of Cashin's design hallmarks. Also, it is notable that the outfit features trousers at a time when they were just beginning to be universally accepted on women.

Halston (1932–90)

In contrast to the youthful playfulness of Cashin's creations, the fashions of Roy Halston Frowick (Halston) brought a sexually charged glamour to 1970s' New York. During that decade Halston was an important figure in the city's fashion culture and became one of its celebrities. Halston was associated with New York's landmark

Figure 5.4 Bonnie Cashin ensemble, 1971, V&A: T.80A, B-1974. Photograph courtesy V&A Imaging, Peter Kelleher.

department stores; he was a regular at the city's society events and nightclubs; and his clientele included high-profile, glamorous society women.

Starting out as a milliner, Halston sold hats from a boutique in Berdorf Goodman from 1958 to 1968. He left to start his own clothing business, selling his designs through stores around the country and from a shop within Bloomingdale's. Halston created sophisticated styles for both day and evening that flattered a slim, lithe figure. His eveningwear, as well as his personal life, was linked with the legendary nightclub

Studio 54, which opened in New York in 1977. In the 1980s after a legal dispute Halston lost control of his design name and stopped designing commercially.

Halston's society clients included Mrs Betsy Kaiser, the donor of the emerald-green evening dress on display (Figure 5.5, far right). Mrs Kaiser donated this early 1970s design in 1989, along with a pair of coordinating, impossibly high sandals. At the same time she also donated several outfits by other American designers. Mrs Kaiser was born Betsy Pickering. She was a successful fashion model in the 1950s for the Ford modelling agency, which employed her while she was still a student at Sarah Lawrence College. Remaining a well-dressed New Yorker, with residences in both Manhattan and Palm Beach, Mrs Kaiser donated parts of her wardrobe to the Metropolitan Museum's Costume Institute, including a number of Halston designs. Harold Koda of the Costume Institute referred her to the V&A. According to the acquisition file, at the time of her V&A donation, Mrs Kaiser was moving house. She dropped the clothing off at the Museum when she came to London to attend the Henley Regatta.

The V&A's collection contains only two Halstons, both donated by Mrs Kaiser. The dress I chose exemplifies Halston's effortless, urbane style and includes several of his signature design elements: the dress accentuates the figure, features a halter-

Figure 5.5 Display case of New York Fashion at the Victoria and Albert Museum London. Halston evening dress (far right), *c.*1975, V&A: T.314&A-1989. Arnold Scaasi evening pyjamas (second from right), 1994, V&A: T.74:1-2-1999. Zac Posen dress (far left), 2000, V&A: T.213-2004. Photograph courtesy V&A Imaging, Peter Kelleher.

neck and conveys an overt sexiness (the skirt is slit up to the top of the thigh, exposing the entire leg when the wearer walks). It is also a fine example of 1970s New York-designed eveningwear.

Donna Karan (1948–)

While Halston's work is often associated with New York nightlife, Donna Karan's is inextricably linked with the workplace. She and the other members of the so-called American Trinity of Karan, Lauren and Klein are all included for two reasons: first, because of their dominance of late twentieth-century New York ready-to-wear; second, because each designer promoted a recognizable wardrobe for their vision of the modern woman. Having worked for over fifteen years with American sportswear designer Anne Klein, Karan was well positioned to launch her own company in 1985. Karan described her motivation as a desire 'to simplify our way of life, how we dress, be able to travel, do things, be in the world' (Sischy 2000). When she first began designing her own label it quickly became clear to Karan that she was designing for the working woman (Milbank 1989: 285). Her thoughtfully designed systems of separate pieces unite powerful chic with comfortable fit, a desirable combination for workplace wardrobes. A day dress from the mid 1980s represents the designer in the V&A's fashion gallery (Figure 5.6).

The family of the late Baroness Birk donated the dress to the V&A upon the Baroness's death in 1997. Baroness Birk was a life peer and working woman with a family. Born in 1919, she began her career as a journalist and went on to become a founder and associate editor of the woman's magazine *Nova* in the 1960s. She became involved in politics, serving in Parliament from 1967 to 1997 as an MP for Finchley, London. Her offices included posts in the Department of the Environment (1974–9), and the Privy Council Office (1979). In addition to the dress on display the family also donated two other Karan dresses (one black and one navy), as well as a black and white Sonia Rykiel ensemble of cotton jersey from the late the 1980s and an early 1970s Valentino leather jacket. As a donation, these pieces come together in a fractured but suggestive picture of one working woman's wardrobe: dark colours, functional pieces that are stylish but far from trendy, worn by a woman who required clothes that complemented her role in public life.

I chose the dress for display because it sums up much of Karan's design ethos: it is a sturdy, versatile garment that can be worn, as magazine copy might put it, 'from day to evening.' It is black, the near uniform colour of the late twentieth-century working New York woman. The skirt falls slightly below the knee with a flatteringly asymmetrical neckline and hemline. Karan softened the waist with a sarong-like drape across the midriff. These figure-enhancing features appealed to a varied clientele, including sophisticated older women such as Baroness Birk who, when she bought the dress in the mid 1980s, would have been around seventy.

Figure 5.6 Donna Karan dress, *c.*1985, V&A: T.98-1998. Photograph courtesy
V&A Imaging, Peter Kelleher.

It is intriguing that a British establishment figure such as Baroness Birk turned
to Karan as a designer. For Karan, perhaps more than any of her peers, promoted
her clothing as intimately linked with New York City life. Karan's advertising
campaigns have juxtaposed her clothes with images of New York taxis, the city's
skyline and the Statue of Liberty. These images enticed customers by associating
Karan's designs with a romantic, idealized Manhattan. In expressing her views about
the city's appeal Karan said, 'Everybody wants a piece of New York. New York is
the hub ... New York means being international' (Sischy 1998: 14).

Ralph Lauren (1939–)

Offering a very different sartorial vision to Karan's designs for city living, Ralph Lauren's clothes and their marketing, particularly in the 1980s, dealt in a nostalgic interpretation of an English country wardrobe. McDowell suggests that this strategy resulted from an awareness that a customer's loyalty comes from identification 'not with the man alone but with a way of life' (McDowell 2003: 79). By mid decade Ralph Lauren had been designing under his own label for fifteen years and had stores across the US and Europe.

A 1997 gift by Londoner Jill Ritblat included several quintessential Lauren outfits. The Ritblat donation was the largest individual gift of dress to the V&A. In the catalogue accompanying a display of the Ritblat collection, V&A curator Amy de la Haye wrote that the donation 'provides insight into the diverse social requirements of an elite social life' (1998: 7). Among Ritblat's Lauren ensembles was a wool skirt, cotton shirt with pie-crust collar, and pink wool, cable-knit jumper (Figure 5.7), which she bought at the designer's London shop on New Bond Street in 1981.

Figure 5.7 Ralph Lauren ensemble, *c*.1981, V&A: T.509:1-4-2000. Photograph courtesy V&A Imaging, Peter Kelleher.

In a recent interview Jill Ritblat described the experience of making a purchase in Lauren's retail establishment and provided compelling, descriptive details of the outfit's personal significance. She recalled the shop as 'part of his (Lauren's) superb marketing strategy promoting this dream image of nonchalant, fashionable class and inherited status. The shop was designed like a fashionable country house, with roaring log fires, leather armchairs, plants and fitting rooms like a country house dressing room. It even smelt divine – of a sort of woody potpourri.'[5]

Ritblat's specific memories of the outfit also indicate how English women of her social milieu were wearing Lauren at this time. She went on to say

> The concept of the clothes was a far away era of tweedy elegance. I bought the outfit because it fitted, indeed exemplified, the perfect English weekend. In fact the two sharpest memories I have of wearing this outfit were both weekends, probably both in the autumn of 1981. One was to arrive at and leave a very smart weekend shooting party in Hampshire, and the other was to go up to Bristol University with my husband, before we were married, to visit his daughter when she was a student there. This doesn't sound like a glamorous outing but it was special for a number of reasons, not least that he was young and dashing and drove us up in his Ferrari!

Though the outfit referenced Old World country elegance, Lauren reworked it with a twist. Ritblat said, 'What I liked was the way it combined a traditional English idea of comfort and luxury with the slightly eccentric, very un-English silver belt. The outfit doesn't look much now, but it was surprising and delightful, and I remember it made me feel cheerful when I wore it.'

Calvin Klein

In the same decade Calvin Klein was promoting an aesthetic altogether different from Lauren's countrified weekend wear. Klein's innovative, prescient vision of America's wardrobe needs resulted in quiet, minimalist clothes, which allowed the wearer to interpret them and make their own. Focusing on pared-down sportswear and versatile, interchangeable pieces, Klein built his design house into a fashion empire. The garment representing Klein's work in the fashion gallery is a sleeveless summer day dress of crisp, sharkskin suiting (Figure 5.8). Dating from 1986, the dress's simplicity exemplifies what Martin refers to as 'a Shaker-like harmony with fashion basics that prizes luxury but is never gaudy' (Martin 1998: 89). A full skirt falls to mid calf and is accented by a plaited belt. The subdued grey colour is characteristic Klein. Like much of Klein's daywear, it is a multi-purpose garment that allowed for effortless elegance in a variety of settings.

The dress was part of a large donation from Calvin Klein. Between 1996 and 1997 the company purged their archives and offered outfits to museums in the United States and in Europe. In a letter filed with the acquisition papers dated 1 May 1997, the archive staff wrote to the V&A:

Figure 5.8 Calvin Klein dress, 1986–7, V&A: T.236:1-2-1997. Photograph courtesy V&A Imaging, Peter Kelleher.

The Calvin Klein Archives project would like to consider the V&A for donations of Calvin Klein Collection apparel and accessories. We wish to increase the representation of Calvin Klein apparel and accessories in major twentieth-century costume collections both here in the US and abroad for future research, education and exhibition.

The V&A curator at the time, Amy de la Haye, went to New York in June 1997. A few weeks later her selection of approximately twenty-five daywear ensembles and a variety of accessories arrived at the V&A. From this wealth of choice I selected the daydress because it typifies Klein's understated luxury.

Arnold Scaasi (1935–)

A turbulent alternative to Klein's calm understatement are the dramatic designs of Arnold Scaasi. As a designer to singers, actresses and former First Lady Barbara Bush, Scaasi's unique contribution to New York's fashion culture was the lavish, moneyed confidence of his over-the-top eveningwear. Acknowledging Scaasi's opulence in the selection for display, the Museum also wished to honour the designer's generous donation of a number of garments upon his retirement in 1997.

Canadian-born Scaasi settled in New York in 1952 and began working with Charles James. Scaasi opened his own design house in 1957 and immediately established his signature style: theatrical eveningwear and a vivid colour palette. His bold creations, typified by the tropically coloured evening pyjamas chosen for the gallery (Figure 5.5, second from right), had renewed popularity in the opulent 1980s and into the 1990s. Scaasi designed the pyjamas in 1994. This was a decade in which he created slim-silhouetted clothes whose fabrics, textures and colours were the focal point (Scaasi 1996: 184). The pyjamas are made from turquoise and purple silk with a parakeet design and are covered entirely with clear sequins. Scaasi accented the waist with a purple silk sash and included a shawl trimmed with purple fringe. New Yorkers like the actress Mary Tyler Moore, the philanthropist Brooke Astor and socialite Blaine Trump commissioned similarly noticeable Scaasi eveningwear for the gala events that form the New York establishment's social calendar.

I chose the pyjamas from among the V&A's vivid Scaasi holdings because they illustrate the immoderate, impractical side of New York's eveningwear (its jump-suit like construction makes dressing and undressing needlessly complex). Also, Scaasi designed the garment at the end of his long, successful career.

Zac Posen (1980–)

Representing the most recent generation of high-profile New York designers is Zac Posen. The dominance of a handful of ready-to-wear empires at the end of the last century left little room in an already crowded New York fashion industry for new design visions. However, in the past few years the talents of young designers like Posen are finding critical and commercial success. At the time of writing Posen is the only designer of this new wave whose work is represented in the V&A, an unfortunate deficiency which the Museum is working to correct. Like many of these individuals, Posen started his company in the aftermath of the terrorist attacks of September 11, 2001. Posen said that paradoxically, the upheavals of the post-September 11 economy helped his fledgling company. Economic difficulties left many New York-area factories struggling and thus willing to work with young unknowns. This enabled Posen to manufacture his clothing locally, a factor he has described as critical to his design success.[6]

A native New Yorker, Posen enrolled in London's Central Saint Martins College of Art and Design (Saint Martins) fashion BA in 1999. While a student there Posen participated in 'Curvaceous', a thoughtful exhibition conceived by V&A curator Lucy Johnston in 2001. 'Curvaceous' displayed a selection of Saint Martins students' work, which took inspiration from nineteenth-century underwear in the V&A's archive. Posen's design referenced traditional corsetry, in particular its intricate fastenings. Posen's dress is composed of about fifty thin strips of brown leather. Each strip is fastened to the next entirely by hooks and eyes (the only seams in this dress are at the shoulders). Thus the dress's shape can be adjusted as the wearer wishes. Posen said about his design at the time, 'My dress shows the progression of the changing silhouette from the bondage of Victorian life to women's emancipation from these confines' (Posen, *Curvaceous* label text). The dress came off display in time for the designer to include it in his first catwalk show as part of New York Fashion Week in February 2002. He then donated it to the V&A's permanent collection. This dress represents Posen in the fashion gallery (Figure 5.5, far left).

Posen sells his clothes across continents, the mainstream fashion press regularly features his work and his client list is celebrity-studded. Designing for an urban sophisticate with New York as her backdrop, Posen described his home city by saying, 'New York is a dramatic city. It's high drama, it's high energy. I don't think there is a place that runs faster. I think it's important to have the costumes to dress for that.' Posen has carried forward several elements of his student work. He is preoccupied with making clothing for a woman who is 'strong, intelligent and feminine'. Known particularly for his dresses, Posen also continues to include a sense of flirtation in his clothes, seen early on in the V&A dress's peek-a-boo hook and eye closures.

Yeohlee (1955–)

In contrast to Posen's sartorial flirtation, the clothes of Malay-born, New York-based designer Yeohlee Teng challenge the values of New York's high fashion and couture establishment (Bolton 2002: 106). Born in 1958, Yeohlee has been designing under her own label for over twenty-five years. Designing with an active, urban woman in mind, Yeohlee's innovation is a year-round, season-less wardrobe that allows a woman to dress once for the entire day (Bolton 2002: 107). Yeohlee's clothing is efficient and multi-functional: it can be layered, is often made from new textile technologies and can be worn for different levels of formality. She has donated several ensembles to the Museum.

Yeohlee uses simple shapes and modern fabrics to create clothing that is, in her words, architecture for the body. An Autumn–Winter 2000–1 ensemble of sleeveless top and trapezoidal skirt represents her work in the Museum's gallery (Figure 5.9). The outfit is typical of, as she calls them, her designs for modern living which by

Figure 5.9 Yeohlee Teng skirt and top, 2000, V&A: T.82:1-2-2001. Photograph courtesy V&A Imaging, Peter Kelleher.

their plain cut and a minimum of decoration allow for ease of movement. In the press release for this collection, 'Mind over Matterhorn,' Yeohlee wrote 'These clothes are yours and yours alone. Most importantly, it is that whether other people notice you or not, you are happy: with who you are, what you're doing and what you are wearing. It's the only Alp worth scaling.'

Conclusion

From Charles James's inventively simple coat to Yeohlee's architecture for the body, the V&A has attempted to represent twentieth- and twenty-first-century New York fashion design using examples from its permanent collection. But as this investigation has shown, New York's high fashion persona is complex, multifaceted and not easily characterized. Constrained by a limited collection and with room for only eleven designers the V&A's representation of New York Fashion reveals compromises and the occasional lack of provenance-related material. As a result, the Museum is working to build up its holdings of key pieces of American design and continues to strive to fulfil its obligation to gather ample provenance information at the time of donation.

Collectively, the outfits discussed represent over sixty years of New York fashion design. Predominantly smart daywear, in their pared-down construction and sensible details the clothes hint at the active lives led by the women they were designed for. The occasional burst of impractical glamour suggests, though does not adequately depict, the formal eveningwear that New York designers have created to keep pace with that city's demanding social calendar. Of the eleven ensembles, six were donated directly by the designers or their families, who sought to ensure their own posterity abroad and to benefit collections outside the United States. The remaining five were donated by private individuals: busy, well-travelled, urban women; among them models, politicians and socialites. Their sartorial choices suggest active, city-based lives requiring wardrobes both versatile and chic. Yet of these five wearer-donors, only one was a New Yorker, the rest were English. This is suggestive not only of the cosmopolitan lives of our donors but of the inevitable appeal of looking like you have shopped somewhere else. For when buying a Geoffrey Beene design or a Donna Karan dress these English donors were perhaps, to paraphrase Donna Karan, buying a piece of New York – or at least a piece of New York's fashion culture.

Notes

1. The consultation paper states, 'Museums must be able to communicate to the public how their collections came to be made, what techniques were used, why they are important and the meanings they had for their makers and users, and those they retain for society today.'

2. The original chronology was the result of careful research for details like hairstyle, accessories and posture and took years to complete. For the 2005 reopening the gallery closed for nine months only and curators did not include hairstyles or accessories in the display.

3. The visitor numbers for major exhibitions were: 2004, *Vivienne Westwood* 170,834; 2002, *Versace* 160,543; 2001, *Radical Fashion* 93,215; 1997, *The Cutting Edge* 230,836; 1995, *Streetstyle* 108,950.

4. The dress (T.112–1989) was donated by Mr R. Rummond. There is no indication in the file as to who wore the clothes.

5. All quotes from Jill Ritblat come from an email exchange with the author in May 2005.

6. All quotes from Zac Posen unless otherwise indicated come from an interview with the author in July 2005.

–6–

New Stars, New Fashions and the Female Audience
Cinema, Consumption and Cities 1953–1966
Pamela Church Gibson

'Thank you so much for inviting me – I've got a wonderful new evening dress with yards and yards of skirt that I've been simply longing to wear. I'll go and press it ready for tonight.'

Audrey Hepburn in *Sabrina Fair*, 1954

'Surely the vogue for asexuality can go no further than this weird hybrid with butchered hair?'

Contemporary review of *Sabrina Fair* (*Films and Filming*, 1 1954: 20)

This chapter forms part of a wider, long-term project examining the new relationship between cities, cinema and consumption in the post-war period when patterns of female spending power changed radically and, within cinema, women were positioned as the centre of new, different modes of visual spectacle. As the quotations above suggest, some of the new stars of the period were presented in such a way that they seemed to address the female audience directly, to offer them new, different ways of dressing and perhaps of behaving. Unlike their predecessors, and some of their contemporaries, they did not seem primarily configured to satisfy a male gaze or to act out fantasies of wife, mistress, girlfriend. Arguably, film and fashion have been interlinked in many ways since the first decade of the last century; but there are interesting shifts and changes in the relationship from the 1950s onwards, and in the diegetic presentation and iconic potency of the cinematic heroine. And during this period, the use of certain 'fashion capitals' as cinematic location, even as filmic presence, is new and notable. Pre-war cinema, particularly Hollywood cinema, was largely shot on studio sets, while in the post-war period there is, across a range of national cinemas, a move towards location shooting designed to provide a new sense of place and authenticity. Furthermore, these cities were often used as a space to display the new fashionability of the central female character.

Janet Wolff and Elizabeth Wilson have discussed the growing visibility of women in urban space, from the nineteenth century onwards, and the possibilities of a female equivalent of that male wanderer of the modern city, the flâneur (Wolff 1985, 1995; Wilson 1991). In the late twentieth century, the seeming occupation of physical city-spaces by fashionable women was increasingly represented in film. However, while many city films have placed women in urban space, their mobility has nonetheless been heavily proscribed. The heroine does not parade through cities as powerful flâneuse, but rather as nomad – a twentieth-century reconfiguration of Baudelaire's 'fugitive beauty' (1975 [1857]: 170). I select the word 'nomad' – used very differently by Rosi Braidotti (1997) – to suggest the new, seemingly free, cinematic heroine, who is, nevertheless, invariably disempowered by and through the narratives in which she appears. Here, the narratives work to emphasize the limitations of this freedom, and to recuperate these heroines firmly into the patriarchal system (showing that while they themselves may start to 'look', they do not cease to become themselves the object of a male gaze). Thus each woman in the films I have selected is, initially, able to roam the city with a freedom they did not formerly possess. All prove, however, to be temporary 'fugitives' rather than truly empowered female figures.

Every major city has its key cinematic moments, when it is celebrated as setting or even as 'star' in its own right. Each 'fashion city ' discussed here has had one or two significant 'fashion moments' on screen, when the tropes with which we associate that city are defined, refined or underlined – and its permanent position on the fashion map is, at the same time, secured. The moments I have selected – of particular importance in the cinematic configuring of these four cities and their subsequent 'identity' – are linked not only to the post-war reconstruction of the fashion atlas, but to the emergence of these new female stars, who were radically different from their Hollywood precursors, and, significantly, to the appearance of new, oppositional cinematic movements in Italy, France and England.

The 'moments' scrutinized here date from the early 1950s to the mid 1960s. This period is one of economic boom, and sees not only the end of post-war austerity but also the triumph of consumerism, with women to the fore. Yet it is not associated with social or personal freedom for women – rather, with the continued curtailment of the very real financial, social and even sexual freedoms some of them had experienced during the Second World War. Many of these moments are taken from films designed to showcase the particular persona of Audrey Hepburn, a star who seemed directly to address these women who were freed from drudgery, who possessed new financial powers – and who were nevertheless still constrained in so many ways. On screen – as in her own life – Hepburn crisscrossed countries, even continents. In herself, she forms an integral part of many of these cityscape-defining sequences. The iconic potency that Hepburn possessed during her cinematic career has not diminished with the passage of time – if anything, it has increased. Always the favourite of fashion designers and editors, she remains a favourite with audiences. Recent work within film studies (Moseley 2003, 2005) indicates that in her own lifetime she was primarily a 'woman's star'. While this is the case, fashion-literate men may now

Figure 6.1 Temporarily escaping from her royal duties, Princess Anne (Audrey Hepburn) obtains a new haircut, a fashionable image (she's costumed here by the house of Fontana) and explores the Eternal City, with Gregory Peck's American journalist as her guide. *Roman Holiday*, 1953 (USA) directed by William Wyler. © Getty Images.

also be included in her 'fan base'. A commemorative screening of her films at the National Film Theatre in 2004 was sold out.

Her public image was both cosmopolitan and somehow deraciné. She grew up in Holland under the Nazi occupation, running errands for the Resistance and hiding out in cellars; she trained as a dancer in England, worked as a fashion model, was chosen for small parts in films and then for the lead in *Roman Holiday* (1953) for which she won an Oscar (Figure 6.1). She was instantly lionized by Hollywood, but she never settled there; she made her own home in Switzerland. Despite the wide range of films in which she starred, she is associated by most with a handful of films made between 1953 and 1961. These are the most memorable in terms of costuming and styling, and are responsible for her enduring appeal to those interested or professionally involved in fashion. The kind of character Hepburn invariably portrayed was not just waiflike, but even, at times, childlike. She was invariably paired with male co-stars much older than herself (Gregory Peck, Fred Astaire, Humphrey Bogart, Cary Grant) and never once is she seen walking down the aisle in her entire screen career. Rachel Moseley (2005) has argued that the uncertainty of the endings in Hepburn's films, the lack of any firm romantic resolution, coupled with the Cinderella-like quality of her own life, are significant factors in her incredible – and sustained – popularity with women. She is always a single woman, seeking for something outside her present experience. And this is where she fits so neatly into patterns that can be detected in the changing relationship between women, cities, cinema and consumption within this period. For Hepburn looked as her female audience wanted to look – and she behaved as they wanted to behave. But whatever freedom she seemed to embody was also heavily circumscribed or curtailed by the workings of the cinematic narrative. Like her female audience, her freedom was primarily the freedom to present herself in different guises, to change her look, to experiment with dress – and she provided two very different modes of appearance, one spectacular and the other more subversive.

Hepburn was inevitably the object of a new sort of gaze, a new 'look' not to be confused with the Dior-inspired 'New Look' whose wasp waists and ballerina skirts she sported to such effect (Dior's 'New Look' of 1947, which influenced fashion well into the next decade, was enormously popular with Hollywood costume designers because of its inherently spectacular qualities). This look was not necessarily sexual, since it was so often a female gaze. But it was, with hindsight, perhaps only a temporary gratification or form of wish-fulfilment. It most certainly acted as invitation to imitation and to new modes of fashion-related consumption. Hepburn herself was the object of female emulation in a way that was radically new within mainstream cinema. She offered women an alternative way of looking and behaving in a cinematic landscape dominated by blonde, curvaceous, traditionally glamorous Hollywood stars like Marilyn Monroe – or voluptuous brunettes such as Sophia Loren. Her appeal to women was twofold, as an engaging and childlike temporary fugitive from routines and rules, and as an elegant clothes-horse who also possessed a more casual, affordable, off-duty, or pre-transformation, uniform of simple black tops, narrow trousers and flat shoes. She was also remarkable for popularizing the slim, boyish figure – which would endure on and off screen – in an era of big-breasted stars.

Rome is the first city used to display her persona and to be created as a post-war 'fashion capital'. Although it is, of course, Milan that is the centre of Italian fashion and home to Italian couture shows, it is not as photogenic a city as Rome, which had already been shaped as a setting for romance through popular song. And Hepburn's first starring role was a romantic comedy celebrating the 'Eternal City' and its style. *Roman Holiday* (William Wyler, USA, 1953) gave some their first sight of this fashion arena; for others, it crystallized their growing awareness of the virtues of Italian style and its particular importance for young people. Rome had become a popular holiday destination for those who could afford the possibilities offered by the wider availability of air travel. Flights abroad were still, however, confined to the relatively rich and would remain so until the arrival, much later, of low-cost flights for all. Film, therefore, can be seen to function as the poor person's 'air travel', transporting audiences not only to places they could not afford to visit, but also serving as a showcase for styles and fashions that they might not otherwise see. The teenage narrator of Colin MacInnes's *Absolute Beginners* (1959) eloquently describes how, for the young and the excluded, flying 'abroad' represented the acme of glamour in the late 1950s:

> I reached the Buckingham Palace Road ... and the place where the Air Terminal stands opposite the coach station. And there on the one side were the glamour people setting off for foreign countries, mohair and linen suits, white air-liner vanity bags, dark sun-spectacles and pages of tickets packed to paradise, every nationality represented, and everyone equal in the sky-dominion of fast air-travel – and there, on the other side, were the peasant masses of the bus terminal shuffling along in their front-parlour curtain dresses and cut-price tweeds and their plastic mackintoshes ... (MacInnes 1959: 48–9)

Roman Holiday sets up the establishing shots of Rome which passed into the international cinematic lexicon – the Trevi fountain, the Coliseum, the Spanish Steps – and which were already the backbone of the itinerary followed by the new, select band of tourists (a word and mode of behaviour not yet debased) from Europe and America. But the film goes further – it makes the city a backdrop to the presentation of a new and, above all, youthful fashion heroine. This, after all, was the decade that saw the rise of teenage spending power. Hepburn plays Anne, the princess of a tiny Ruritania-like country, on a tedious state visit to Rome. She is confined not only by her royal role but by the stuffy, matronly gowns she must wear, stiff travesties of Dior's New Look. Seduced by the promised pleasures of the city streets beneath her window, the sights and sounds of the young Romans chatting, laughing and revving up their scooters, we see her contrive to escape for a night out. She finds in her elaborate wardrobe a plain blouse and full skirt, and climbs out of the palace window. She inadvertently gets very drunk and is rescued by Gregory Peck's dissolute American journalist. But the next morning, as she walks alone through the city streets, she seemingly transforms herself on screen from fuddy-duddy princess to gamine youth icon in a few cinematic minutes. We see her apparently getting, on screen, the famous urchin cut that thousands were to copy. Then, by rolling up her sleeves, putting on flat sandals and belting in her skirt, she appears to create the 'teenage' style that would soon be seen on high streets everywhere. In fact, this look was created for the film by the Italian design house of Fontana, who were to dress Ava Gardner in *The Barefoot Contessa* (1953) and provide a wedding dress for Lana Turner's second marriage that same year. But the audiences saw Audrey herself as the creator and embodiment of this look. And her pillion ride through Rome, perched behind Peck on a scooter, made this object of Italian style as desirable as the gleaming Gaggia espresso machines, now making their appearance in the new 'coffee bars' on British high streets (Hebdige 1988: 77–115)

The fact that Audrey's transformation is not only central to the story, but takes place *on screen* is vital to her popularity. Achieved through dress and styling, seemingly effortless and self-directed, it would occur in virtually every film she was to make. Here it is eventually reversed – for she must renounce Peck and return to her royal duties. The 'Cinderella' theme of transformation through costume is, of course, a cinematic staple and central to many films targeted primarily at a female audience – from *Now Voyager* (1938) to *Pretty Woman* (1990). But where Julia Roberts, even in 1990, needs guidance from her rich lover and a helpful hotel manager, Hepburn is usually able to control her own costume changes, to know what she wants and what will suit her. As the admiring Roman hairdresser tells her after she has persuaded him to chop off all her long hair, 'Now you look – what is the word? Cool.'

The infrastructure of Italian fashion had survived the Second World War, the defeat and occupation of Italy. There were no vast factories to be destroyed – only very small, family-owned firms, with a number of loyal craftsmen and outworkers. An awareness of the allure of Italian men's wear pre-dated the release of this film – the only choice for the truly discerning man, it was to be adopted by the 'modernists' of the late 1950s, the elder brothers of the style-conscious 'mods' of the 1960s (Chenoune 1995). But *Roman Holiday* not only launched Hepburn's career and innumerable imitations of her haircut and make-up – it made of Rome an acknowledged capital of women's fashion as well as the locale for romance and source of the more stylish man's inspiration.

A different Rome would appear six years later, on the cusp of the decade, a film which criticized Italian mores of the 1950s and prefigured the changing attitudes to sexual behaviour that would help to characterize the so-called 'swinging sixties'. This contrasting perception of the city was created from within rather than without, through the lens of an Italian director rather than that of a romantically minded American. Federico Fellini's most famous film *La Dolce Vita* (1959) is remembered for many things. It caused a tremendous scandal in Italy and enraged the Vatican with its depiction of the decadence of Roman society. It created the term 'paparazzi', now so familiar, in an era becoming increasingly obsessed with celebrity. For its anti-hero, Marcello, is a journalist, who spies on the rich and famous, with the assistance of his photographer friend, Paparazzo. The film also marked a definite shift within Italian cinema – it was released in the same year as Michelangelo Antonioni's *L'Avventura*. Both directors had been associated with Italian neo-realism, the new movement that dominated the post-war years. Here, they turned the innovative techniques they had learned in their radical portrayals of proletarian or rural life to studies of urban bourgeois anomie (Marcus 1986; Bondanella 1990).

Designers and fashion photographers often cite, in interview or biography, their admiration for *La Dolce Vita*. It is usually represented on postcards, in publicity material and in fashion images which reference the film by the iconic moment in which Anita Ekberg – as Hollywood glamour personified – frolics in the Trevi fountain, bursting out of a revealing black evening dress. But the true purveyors of Italian style, and those responsible for its real fashion legacy, are the figures of Marcello (Mastroianni), the cynical, frustrated novelist, and the stylish, equally amoral Magdalena, played by Anouk Aimée. The film not only looks backward to the elegance characteristic of the 1950s, but at the same time forward to the social and sartorial upheavals of the next decade. In terms of male attire, the young 'modernists' mentioned earlier were already wearing the short 'Roman' jacket with its narrow lapels and two back vents. Their outfits are meticulously described in *Absolute Beginners* (MacInnes 1959) and set disdainfully against not only the mainstream English men's wear of the time, drab, ill-fitting and redolent of 'demob' suits, but the other forms of subcultural dress currently to be seen on the streets, namely the 'traditionalists', bearded and scruffy, and the remaining 'Teddy boys', whose style was no longer subversive or confrontational. Some of Marcello's sartorial trademarks in this film were copied at high street level. His conspicuous cufflinks, the white tie worn over a black shirt and under a white jacket, all these filtered through into the wardrobe of young British men. Jacqueline Reich (2001) has described this very process in some detail, examining the reaction of British audiences, while Dick Hebdige (1988) has analysed the overall impact of Italian style on young men of the period.

But the overall portrayal of women is perhaps the most interesting aspect of the film here. Ekberg plays Sylvia, a voluptuous Hollywood star, who arrives in Rome and at her press conference confidently provides sassy, sexually provocative replies, based directly on remarks made to reporters by Marilyn Monroe. However, when she wanders the deserted streets of Rome at night with Marcello in attendance, she is seen as highly vulnerable, despite her triumphant splashing in the fountain, which the cold light of day shows to be hollow, even risible. She seems most truly animated when she finds a stray kitten, which she tries to rescue. By contrast Magdalena, the bored, pampered socialite, surely an Italian precursor of the 'It-girls' of today, is notable not only for her simple, elegant clothes but for her independent, even predatory behaviour. The first scene of the film is set in a fashionable nightclub, which she has visited at the behest of a boyfriend who, it is clear from a brief allusion, has treated her badly. She finds it stifling and swiftly leaves, taking the very willing Marcello. Her understated black dress, oversized dark glasses and the small flat bag slung on a chain over her shoulder mean that she makes the other women there look fussy and over-accessorized. She leads Marcello to her car, striding purposefully, even swinging her arms like a man. She drives him through the theatrically deserted stage set that the film makes of Rome – and later she initiates casual sex with him. At party after party, Magdalena appears – stunningly but simply dressed, always alone – and finds some man to gratify her whims and wishes. Yet like Marcello she is presented as unhappy, drifting, ultimately self-destructive. However both of them nevertheless personify the notion of 'cool', now so important to so many in Europe and America (MacAdams 2001). Both wear large dark glasses, day and night – which became another fashionable imperative. Interestingly, Hepburn herself had already done this, though in an unmemorable film, *Love in the Afternoon* (1957).

The Fontana sisters, again, provided the women's clothes for *La Dolce Vita* – their designs were so remarkable that, today, Dolce è Gabbana cite this film as a major influence on their work. The fashions we see vary. Magdalena's simple black dresses and the more bohemian outfits seen in the famous 'orgy' sequence are new and innovative, yet the Roman socialites who play themselves in the film wear more traditional Italian couture. The primary appeal of the film, in fashion terms, seems to be the presentation of new ways of dressing and behaving – so that here there is a link with the Rome found by Hepburn's visiting princess in the earlier film.

For many, Paris would seem to be the unchallenged fashion capital of the world. Yet, immediately after the Second World War, it had to fight off a fierce challenge from New York to keep that position – since through the Marshall Plan the Americans were paying for the post-war reconstruction of European economies (Steele 1997a; Veillon 2000). Dior's New Look of 1947 – a lasting influence and used memorably by Hollywood costume designers – helped them consolidate their former role as arbiters of global style. In her next film, Audrey Hepburn – again – was transformed on screen to create one of the best arguments for the continued supremacy of Parisian couture. The heroine of *Sabrina Fair* (1954) is a chauffeur's daughter who falls in love with the wayward younger son of her rich employers. She is consequently packed off to Paris to learn cordon bleu cookery – but she also learns how to 'be in the world, and of the world' as she tells her father. This process involves the skills of self-transformation, so that when she returns home she is almost unrecognizable. She herself suggested, that for the post-Paris scenes, she should wear clothes designed by a genuine couturier – and so began her lifetime collaboration and friendship with Hubert de Givenchy (see Givenchy's Introduction in Clark Keogh 1999). She announced, as their collaboration developed, 'I depend upon Givenchy as American women depend upon their psychiatrist' (Paris 1997: 252–3). Although the film is set mainly on Long Island, it is her Parisian wardrobe that enables her to bewitch both brothers – and to make the women of Manhattan high society look frumpy. She showed American – and other – audiences that Paris had an undeniable right to its position. She also reminds us again that she can control her own shape-shifting, dressing down on screen, in bohemian black turtleneck and trousers, for a confrontation with the elder brother.

Her next film was actually set, for the most part, in Paris – and showed off the city as synonymous with style. Interestingly, however, leading French directors of the pre-war period did not, themselves, do this. Instead, Jean Vigo and Jean Renoir displayed a fascination with the streets, the proletariat, the middle classes, even the criminal underworld. Renoir only depicted the elegant bourgeoisie in order to subject them to criticism. His most famous film, *La règle du jeu* (1939), portrays events during a high-society country house weekend. The women are dressed here by Chanel – but they are not there to be admired. There is of course another Parisian woman – the bohemian – who pre-dates the pre-war Left Bank of Hemingway, let alone that of the post-war existentialists. She can be traced back to the stories of Offenbach, which inspired Puccini's opera *La Bohème*. A particular style for the bohemians – black turtlenecks and uncoiffed, long hair for both sexes – emerged in Paris in the post-war years, moving from the Left Bank to Greenwich Village, and then to London's Soho. The stylish chanteuse Juliet Greco – glimpsed briefly in Cocteau's film *Orphée*, in black turtleneck (and heavy eyeliner) became an alternative fashion icon, despite Koenig's assertion that her black sweater was 'antifashion' (Koenig 1973: 198). Hepburn cannily turned this look into a mainstream fashion statement, smartening it and wearing it both on screen and off. Yet the tidying up of the bohemian black did not detract from its anti-fashion appeal – in all these films there is at least one scene where Hepburn reverts to her simple black, putting aside her new couture trappings and showing that she herself is in complete control of her appearance. Consequently she could function simultaneously as conventional fashion icon and champion of anti-fashion, showing women how they might move between the two styles, subverting the first role by reminding us of the potency of anti-fashion.

Her famous ballet shoes became so popular that famous shoe designer Salvatore Ferragamo created an expensive version, christening it the 'Audrey' pump, which is still manufactured. Indeed, the house of Ferragamo are aware of the debt they owe the star, and mindful, too, of her unchanged popularity. Consequently, in 1999, the Museo Salvatore Ferragamo, in Florence, held an exhibition commemorating Hepburn's characteristic style. Most of the exhibits were garments lent posthumously from her personal wardrobe, and the catalogue reminds us forcefully that the two different styles we see on the screen – the Givenchy gowns and the simple, pared-down day outfits of pants, T-shirts and turtlenecks – were an accurate reflection of her own taste (Ricci 1999). There is no discrepancy between the created on-screen image and the personal style of the woman in question.

The film *Funny Face* (1955) is a musical that provides a charitable picture of the fashion industry, with Hepburn as an intellectually aspiring bookshop assistant, Jo, discovered by a top photographer and whisked off to Paris to model a new collection by a top American magazine, *Quality* (Figure 6.2). Real-life photographer Richard Avedon acted as 'Visual Consultant', and took all the photographs seen on screen. Here, Jo does need some initial help, for she regards fashion as trivial and only agrees to go to Paris so that she can meet the philosopher she idolizes. The photographer Avery (Fred Astaire) discovers her, and the French couturier (Givenchy under a pseudonym) selects her outfits for her. However, the efforts of the magazine team to change her hairstyle and to pluck her eyebrows are firmly rejected. The thick eyebrows were as much a part of the signature Hepburn look – and as much of a lasting fashion legacy – as the urchin haircut and the blunt fringe. When the lights go up and we see Jo walking towards us down the showroom catwalk in the first of her couture outfits, a floor-length evening gown and sequinned cape, the editor asks her 'How do you feel?' Jo's reply is 'I feel wonderful – but I don't feel

Figure 6.2 Taken to Paris as unwilling fashion model, the bookshop assistant and aspiring intellectual, Jo (Audrey Hepburn), seeks out Bohemian Paris and Left Bank life – her outfit shows the pre-transformation Audrey, whose black turtlenecks and narrow pants constituted an image just as iconic as that created for her later in the film by Hubert de Givenchy. *Funny Face*, 1955 (USA) directed by Stanley Donen. © Getty Images.

like ME.' However, by the end of the fashion shoot in its different Parisian locations, Jo becomes so confident that she can create one of the images herself, not requiring instructions from Astaire/Avedon as in the previous photographs. She emerges from behind the statue of the 'Winged Victory' in the Louvre and advances down the staircase with her arms upraised, the cape of her evening outfit billowing out to echo the shape of the statue behind her. 'You've outgrown me', Astaire/Avedon tells her admiringly. This shoot is based upon what had now become the established tourist itinerary – the Louvre, the Arc de Triomphe, the Flower Market, a boat trip down the Seine with a barge standing in for a bateau mouche. Jo also sees bohemian Paris for herself; and discovers that her favourite philosopher is a lecherous old man surrounded by sycophants. So she becomes absorbed into the world of fashion, and ends in the arms of Astaire: she has not really 'outgrown' him in terms of the cinematic narrative, but ends up both romantically and professionally attached to him in some unresolved way.

So 'chic Paris' is configured forever through the transformations of an actress in – though not of – Hollywood cinema. But bohemian Paris was soon to create its own cinematic space – and an equally compelling image of a complementary fashion city. The French New Wave swept across the sands to swamp the Cannes Film Festivals of the late 1950s; it was created by a group of young men who wrote, at first, for *Cahiers du Cinéma* and then began to make their own, deliberatively alternative films. Low-budget location shooting, lack of continuous narrative, extra-long takes and unexpected jump cuts characterized these new films. *À bout de souffle* (1959), the first film made by Jean-Luc Godard has unexpectedly become a fashionista's favourite. It stars little-known American, Jean Seberg, as Patricia, studying at the Sorbonne, and the young Jean-Paul Belmondo as a petty criminal. After a bungled theft and unintentional murder, he drives into Paris and, shot through the car window, we see Notre Dame and the bridges over the Seine – but presented to a jazz accompaniment. He finds Patricia on the Champs-Elysées, still a chic boulevard, before the later arrival of the car showrooms and fast-food outlets. She is wandering up and down – selling the *New York Herald Tribune* – and wears a simple white T-shirt bearing its logo over black leggings. Her hair is even shorter than Hepburn's – perhaps she might be seen as a precursor of the 'waif' style of the 1990s.

This particular sequence, shot in one long continuous take, where Belmondo joins her and they stroll up and down as he expresses his feelings for her, is an iconic moment – not only in cinema, but within fashion imagery. Later, she subverts designer Paris by wearing a Dior dress to interview an American writer arriving at the airport. Despite the white gloves, her close-cropped hair and flat pumps appropriate the dress for 'alternative' style, rescuing it from the oppressiveness of couture. Patricia is a student, a traveller, she has career aspirations. But she is portrayed as shallow and treacherous. She depends on her parents for money – and it may be the reward money that leads her to betray her lover to the police. She watches as he lies dying in the gutter after an attempt to outrun the gendarmerie – and the last shot of the film shows us her face, puzzled but not overly distressed, as she tries to work out the precise meaning of the particular insult that formed his last utterance.

Seberg's contemporary, Brigitte Bardot, had already become the symbol of freedom for young French women. She too had subverted the power of couture not only through her championing of ready-to-wear clothes on and off screen, but through her creation of a radically new form of fashion She wore blue jeans or simple dresses, and her long, dishevelled bleached-blonde hair was copied then as today. But although she began her career modelling in Paris for *Elle*, she is forever seen as linked to her adopted home of St Tropez. We visualize her barefoot and bikini-clad on a beach, rather than strolling along a boulevard.

New York, which had cheekily challenged Paris in 1945, would eventually gain its own fashion power – and arguably this was achieved in the very early 1960s through two iconic women. One was Jacqueline Kennedy and the other the star whose style she clearly emulated – Audrey Hepburn once again. *Breakfast at Tiffany's* in 1961 put New York firmly on the fashion map and at the same time set up the cinematic tropes that would afterwards always represent Manhattan. The yellow cabs, Fifth Avenue, the Greenwich Village brownstones, the crowded sidewalks, all these formed the setting for the film. The credit titles show us the workings of Baudelaire's 'pouvoir empreinté' or 'borrowed power' (Baudelaire 1975) with one particular, memorable shot through the window of Tiffany's, across the rows of diamonds, to Audrey-as-Holly Golightly (Figure 6.3). She stands outside in the dawn light, sipping her Italian cappuccino and nibbling her French croissant, sporting Paris-couture-with-a-twist, huge dark glasses and floor-length dress, her black, blonde-streaked hair piled high. The first scene shows the familiar on-screen transformation – Holly is asleep in bed, wearing a man's dress shirt as nightdress. But when awoken, a swift dash into

Figure 6.3 The nomadic Holly Golightly (Hepburn) stands on the sidewalk of Fifth Avenue at dawn, gowned by Givenchy, and sips her coffee while she gazes through the window of Tiffany's at the diamonds on display – whose borrowed power arguably augments her allure. *Breakfast at Tiffany's*, 1961 (USA) directed by Blake Edwards. © Getty Images

the bathroom and a hunt round the chaotic flat enable her to accomplish a complete volte-face in moments. When she asks the hero 'How do I look?' he can only reply, truthfully, 'Amazing.'

Holly Golightly is surely the first true urban nomad to be seen on screen. She keeps her ballet slippers, cat food and champagne in the fridge, lives out of packing cases and survives financially on the lavish tips that she earns as a high-class call girl. It turns out that she was not christened 'Holiday Golightly' but 'Lulamae Barnes' and is in fact an impoverished orphan from the Deep South – a truly perfect transformation. Holly's other source of income is the money she is paid to visit an old man, a mafioso, imprisoned in Sing Sing. But it seems that the innocent weekly 'weather reports' she brings back are, in fact, enabling the gangster to continue his work while behind bars, and this precipitates the film's dénouement. In the 1958 novella by Truman Capote on which the film is based, she flees New York and abandons the obviously gay narrator – she disappears to Brazil and is last heard of travelling on a horse through Africa. But this is a cusp-of-decade Hollywood film – 1950s morality and 1960s expectations mean that a happy ending is needed. Wearing her Givenchy trench coat, standing rain-soaked in an alleyway, she is persuaded to stay in New York and in the embrace of George Peppard. The film involves various 'zany' exploits that would come to be endemic in 1960s cinema – the two shoplift in the five-and-dime and invade the august floor space of Tiffany's, persuading the fruity-voiced English salesman (played for authenticity by English character actor David Tomlinson) to engrave a keyring from a cracker so that Holly can at last have something from her beloved Tiffany's. The shop represents not material wealth but the emotional security she craves. She explains to the narrator that she visits Tiffany's regularly to stand outside and be 'calm', that the 'quiet grandeur' and 'simplicity' of the place make her feel that 'nothing bad could ever happen there' – words from the original novella, which George Axelrod, who adapted it for the screen, carefully incorporated into the dialogue.

Manhattan as it is now represented within the cinema, on television and within fashion imagery was first delineated in this film, and became newly synonymous with chic. Although Hollywood films of the 1920s and 1930s are often set in New York, they were invariably shot in studios on the West Coast, with a minimum of location shooting. The link between Manhattan and elegant women depends upon interior, studio-based shots of apartments, hotels, restaurants, department stores and bars. But the streets of the city are a site of masculine activity and occupation. Gangsters conduct their gun battles; the heroes of musicals can dance along the pavements and – in *On the Town* (1947) – on the roof of the Empire State Building. Women are not seen on the sidewalks or roaming the city and, apart from the location shooting on the skyscraper, there is little attempt to give an authentic sense of place.

Interestingly, Capote was very unhappy with the choice of the elegant Hepburn to play the heroine of his novella. He wanted Marilyn Monroe – and, had his wish been granted, Manhattan would not have been synonymous with this quirky version of couture. Monroe would have brought Hollywood opulence onto its streets – after all, she is synonymous with its glamour. She might have worn gowns designed by costumier Jean-Louis, who for her famous appearance in New York, at Madison Square Garden, where she sang 'Happy Birthday' to President Kennedy, dressed her in a transparent, clinging sequin sheath. Certainly, the cinematic 'fashion moment' created by the opening shots of the film, the juxtaposition of Hepburn's quirky elegance with the streets of Manhattan at daybreak, would not have entered the collective consciousness in the same way, nor provided such a gift for the cinematic 'image banks' so frequently ransacked by fashion editors, stylists and photographers.

Kennedy's wife, Jacqueline, based her early signature style in the public arena around the clothes designed for her by American Oleg Cassini. Yet the inspiration for these is surely derived – though this has never been acknowledged – from Hepburn's key Givenchy outfits. The simple shift dresses, boxy jackets, collarless coats and pillbox hats were all seen on Hepburn on screen before they were hijacked by Cassini and Mrs Kennedy. 'Jackie' herself was drawn to Givenchy's designs – for her famous, triumphant trip to Paris in 1961, she selected a long black Givenchy evening gown, which she wore to the main reception at the Palace of Versailles (Bowles 2001). She also wore another of his floor-length dresses at a private function in the White House the following Christmas, when she did not feel obliged to promote American designers (Bowles 2001). These clothes can be seen in Bowles's catalogue for the exhibition mounted at the Metropolitan Museum of Art in 2001 to commemorate 'Jackie Kennedy: The White House Years'. The very fact that the exhibition was conceived and presented in this most prestigious of settings shows the continuing lure of this period in her life, and the style that is always linked to it.

In 1965, her life changed completely when she married shipping billionaire Aristotle Onassis. This second swathe of publicity – showing a life spent on luxurious yachts, at jet-set gatherings and doing little but shop and sunbathe – spawned a new 'Jackie Style' (Clarke Keogh 2001). She famously adopted simpler outfits – paparazzi shots from this period invariably show her in Capri pants, T-shirts and outsize dark glasses. Yet this style, too, had been previously modelled both on screen and off by Audrey Hepburn. However, this second incarnation – the 'Jackie O' look, as it was christened by fashion writers who still use the term – is, nevertheless, seen as something Jacqueline herself created, and her image helped to strengthen New York's power and influence as fashion centre.

London is the final stage in this journey; in the 1960s it was for a short while the epicentre of the 'youthquake', world leader of popular musical taste and arbiter of world fashion. It also poses problems in its cinematic treatment of the 'fashion moment' that London was enjoying. For the cinema of the period does not, contrary to popular supposition – and indeed critical wisdom – cheerfully celebrate 'Swinging London' (see, most recently, Luckett 2000 and Brunsdon 2004). On the contrary, the texts of the period are dark, problematic and worryingly punitive of female transgression. Furthermore, very little is seen of the West End and the films most certainly do not – as is commonly assumed – use settings taken from the 1966 map, published in *Time* magazine, of 'Swinging London' landmarks.

These 'swinging sixties' films, in fact, show us dystopian visions of the city – with lesser-known London locations as backcloths. *The Knack* (1965) is set in the suburbs, *Alfie* (1966) shows us Notting Hill (then deeply unfashionable), while *Georgy Girl* (1966) is located in Maida Vale and much of *Blow-Up* (1966) is filmed in Brockwell Park, despite its use of a mews flat belonging to a real-life photographer. These films may give audiences the odd glimpse of familiar, tourist-type London landmarks – the Albert Hall in *The Knack*, Trafalgar Square in *Darling* (1965) and *The Ipcress File* (1965) – but what is interesting is their persistent refusal to celebrate Chelsea or the West End, to use fashionable locations and to show off recognizable and 'trendy' clubs, bars or restaurants. Only *Smashing Time* (1967), a very feeble parody of 'Swinging London', which was both commercially disastrous and critically savaged, has sequences set in Carnaby Street, a recording studio and the Post Office Tower's revolving restaurant-in-the-sky.

Nevertheless, the British New Wave of the early 1960s, with its male-centred narratives set in the North, was certainly followed by films set in London, with a woman at the centre of the narrative. And these, inevitably and sometimes consciously, showed off the fashions of London in the 1960s, often using clothes by new young designers. But invariably the heroines of these films headed back to the provinces, or drifted off elsewhere. Furthermore, unlike the Audrey Hepburn films, transformation through dress was often linked to moral decline. Actresses like Rita Tushingham and Julie Christie usually wore simple ready-to-wear clothes, easily available for a female audience intent on emulation – though it must be stressed that, at a time when many women were skilled home dressmakers and paper patterns often quite sophisticated, Hepburn's elegant gowns did not function merely as fantasy. Most of the British women Rachel Moseley interviewed, all of an age to have formed her fan base when the films were first released in this country, described in detail their attempts to make their own versions of Hepburn's designer dresses (Moseley 2003).

But in the new British films, when the indigenous stars don expensive, exclusive clothes, it is either as temporary masquerade or, disturbingly, as an indication that the character is dubious and mercenary, or rapidly deteriorating in some way. Charlotte Rampling as Meredith in *Georgy Girl* is dressed throughout by new design duo Tuffin and Foale – and Meredith, unlike the frumpy heroine, is shallow, selfish and spoilt. So, too, is the fashion model Christie plays in *Darling*, whose successful career and increasingly duplicitous private life are mirrored by the changes in her wardrobe. Her chain-store skirts and sweaters are replaced by expensive coats and dresses. It seems that, in the New British Cinema, the heroine should look more like the young girls sitting in the audience than the traditional models then to be found in the pages of *Vogue* magazine. Again, there are exceptions – new British star, Susannah York, playing a boutique owner and designer in the unsuccessful comedy-thriller *Kaleidoscope* (1966) wears expensive-looking clothes created for her by Foale and Tuffin. But neither these outfits nor the presence of new Hollywood star Warren Beatty could salvage a disastrous film – indeed, it seems that the most innovative films of the period were those where the cast, director and scriptwriter were home-grown.

This is underlined by Audrey Hepburn's own, perhaps unwise, attempt to move with the times, to abandon her personal style and to appear instead as a 'Swinging Londoner'. In *Two for the Road* (1966) she wore outfits designed for her by Mary Quant, Paco Rabanne, and, once again, Foale and Tuffin. Here she plays a married woman who is heading, it seems, for the divorce courts – and who sets out on a catastrophic holiday to salvage her future. The film was obviously intended to create a new, younger fan base – she was made up to look like a London 'dolly bird' with overly pale lips and heavy false eyelashes, while her hairstyle was changed to reflect the ubiquitous Sassoon-inspired bobs and fringes. Like the fictional holiday, the film's reception was problematic, and for the remainder of her career, Hepburn returned to her own more classic style. She could, it seems, be 'alternative' in her simple bohemian black, but audiences did not want her to abandon this for the 'trendy' miniskirts, vinyl shorts and baker-boy caps that she wore in this one attempt to reflect the new London. But the puritanical attitude of these new British films towards expensive clothes and over-coiffed hair was, in fact, a true reflection of this London 'fashion moment' of the mid 1960s. London fashion was youth-driven and truly youthful-looking. The stars of these films, with their tousled hair and casual clothes, were pictured not only in the new teenage magazines but in the august pages of a changed *Vogue*.

The quintessential London girl and first British superstar, Julie Christie, made her name in *Billy Liar* (1963), a film which links the New Wave to the London tranche of films through the movements of the character she plays, Liz. An English urban nomad, Liz has made her escape from the Northern city where the hero remains imprisoned in his tedious job, dreaming of his own flight to London and even a life with Liz, but unable to make the break. On her arrival back in Leeds, having hitched a ride home in a lorry, Liz/Christie established her persona indelibly, and ensured her lasting stardom, with a four-minute canter through the city centre. She skips along, swinging her shoulder bag, jumps over puddles and pulls faces at herself in the plate-glass window of a chain store – she challenges and plays with the oppressive nineteenth-century industrial city around her, claiming the urban space for herself and oblivious of others. Contemporary newspaper reviews of the film saw her as embodying the new zeitgeist, both in this sequence and in the closing moments, when she succeeds in catching the last train to London that the hapless Billy contrives to miss. Alexander Walker went so far as to claim that 'British cinema caught the train south with Julie Christie' (Walker 1974).

But – significantly – her on-screen freedom was circumscribed by her cinematic relocation in the capital. When she subsequently starred in the London-based *Darling* (1965), her freedom was curtailed and her wings clipped. The narrative ensured that Christie's character was punished for her wilful behaviour. *Blow-Up* (1967) showed the fashion industry as meretricious and misogynistic; *Performance* (1969) featured a drug-addled, washed-up rock star – played by Mick Jagger – living a hermit-like existence in a basement flat. Perhaps it is not difficult to see why London, having created the sexually available, seemingly passive 'dolly bird', should next see on its streets demonstrations supporting the women's movement (both Radner 2001 and Breward 2004 provide detailed descriptions of the emergence of the 'dolly bird 'and her impact on fashion imagery.)

In these fashion capitals, then, a pattern can be discerned around the creation and configuration of women – as consumer and as consumed. Its later trajectory continues to deploy the images set up here – which remain the visual shorthand for these cities in subsequent films, and in addition make of them global centres for fashion consumption. Meanwhile, the Hepburn image continues to act as a principal fashion referent, showing evidence of a reluctance to relinquish it and move on. Indeed, it is so potent that it has been borrowed and re-presented endlessly – taken from cinema, first for reconfiguration in fashion magazines and then to appear on television. In the 1990s, the US television series *Sex and the City* showed off an updated take on Holly Golightly's Manhattan – its narrator Carrie Bradshaw a modern variant of the earlier heroine. Carrie possesses very little apart from her wonderful clothes and her sixty-odd pairs of Manolo Blahnik shoes, yet she somehow contrives to live as she does on the money she earns by writing a column about sex for a newspaper. Carrie is a modern waif – even now, a woman's freedom in the city seems dependent on the 'pouvoir empreinté' of her glitzy habitat. The series ends with the rescue of the damsel-in-distress, and her rejection of Cartier diamonds in favour of a five-and-dime nameplate necklace she bought for herself in New York – yet both proffered lifestyles depend on a man's protection and salary. This suggests that despite fifty years of social change, for many women 'freedom ' is still both illusory and problematic. In fact, many of the successful 'rom-coms' and 'chick flicks' that Hollywood has offered up to a receptive female audience since the huge box-office success of *Pretty Woman* in 1990 have the same fairy-tale quality as the early Hepburn vehicles. The Cinderella story retains its potency- the audience is, simply, more knowing.

But the real cinematic legacy of the very different films presented here for consideration is their symbolic potency. These films contain particular representations of different 'fashion cities' that have, it seems, become permanent components of visual culture. Lastly, this new focus in the post-war period on the inherently cinematic qualities of Rome, Paris, New York and London linked these cities indelibly to particular images of women's changing role within urban space. And these images, seemingly fixed in the popular psyche, show us women in the city at that particular historical moment when changes were under way but their independence was still fragile and circumscribed, their power linked inextricably to their new patterns of consumption and their 'fashionability'. Perhaps Hepburn's androgynous image, so appealing to women, and her dual role as fashion icon and anti-fashion champion, have retained their appeal precisely because of their subversive potential. For women are still aware of the limits on their ability to roam alone – the real fun of the flânerie still eludes them.

Part III
Re-fabricating the Urban Order

–7–

How New York Stole Modern Fashion
Norma Rantisi

The year was 1973. The occasion was a fashion show at Versailles, an event organized by New York fashion publicist Eleanor Lambert as a benefit for the palace. Five American designers, including Bill Blass, Oscar de La Renta, Anne Klein, Stephen Burrows and Halston, were brought to France to show alongside French designers Yves Saint Laurent, Pierre Cardin, Hubert de Givenchy, Emanuel Ungaro and Marc Bohan at Christian Dior. What no one expected, however, was that the American designers would outshine the reigning stars of French (and at that time, world) fashion. But the French themselves conceded defeat. Cardin claimed the Americans were 'excellent' and Ungaro cried out 'genius'. The headlines in the New York Times read 'Fashion at Versailles: French Were Good, Americans Were Great' and several observers indicated that the Americans had stolen the show (McColl 2001).

The event marked a symbolic turning point in world fashion history. France's hegemony as a fashion centre, with Paris as its capital, was not only being challenged but slowly reversed by the ascendance of American fashion and the rise of New York as a new fashion world capital. By the late 1990s, New York-based designers Marc Jacobs and Michael Kors were given creative control at French fashion houses Louis Vuitton and Céline. As in the case of Tom Ford at Gucci, the objective was to infuse American sensibility into the European luxury market, at a time when fashion was becoming a more commercialized and global enterprise. New York always had a specialization in mass markets given its origins in ready-to-wear production. Now that fashion was becoming the 'business of commercializing art', New York's designers were well situated to ride the fashion wave.

But New York's transformation to a centre of fashion was neither an easy nor inevitable one. According to Christopher Breward, fashion represents 'clothing designed primarily for its expressive and decorative qualities, related closely to the current short-term dictates of the market, rather than for work or ceremonial functions' (1995: 15). This implies the need to strike a balance between art and industry. Yet, at the turn of the twentieth century, New York represented a manufacturing hub with little or no fashion design talent, where apparel firms were mass-producing Parisian styles for the many. How then was it able to cultivate its own design talent and to marry the commercial with the aesthetic? To be sure, part of New York's success can be attributed to 'historical accident' and to where the New York industry was situated in relation to broader socio-economic trends or to major political events, such as the Second World War. A closer examination, however, reveals that its success also lies in a set of local dynamics and in the ability of local apparel actors to anticipate or respond to new competitive pressures.

The development of a host of apparel-related institutions in the city – from design schools to buying offices to trade associations – has been critical in enabling manufacturers to acquire the knowledge, skills and resources needed to adapt and stay attuned to shifts in consumer preferences (Rantisi 2004a). The spatial concentration of these key institutions in the heart of Manhattan is also a key part of the story. Many economic geographers and sociologists have highlighted the significance of physical proximity for the development of social networks and an open exchange of information (Storper 1997; Scott 2000a). And the fact that New York's Garment District is so centrally located within the city means that manufacturers benefit from proximity to a range of cultural activities, from retail districts to museums to Broadway, not to mention the nightclubs and street culture, all of which serve as significant sources of aesthetic inspiration (Rantisi 2004b). The diverse cultural and economic fabric of the broader urban setting serves as a base for the development of major fashion houses *as well as* a location where 'high fashion reinvigorates and renews itself, as it bumps up against the rawness of the real city' (Gilbert 2000: 13).

The story of New York fashion is thus a story of both an *industry* and a *place* and of the dialectic between the two. In this chapter, I recount this story by tracing the evolution of the Garment District and the broader New York fashion economy. I show how the District, as a proximate network of social and economic relations (i.e. a 'cultural industry'), was able to nurture a local design community and by extension, a distinct New York aesthetic that could stand apart from – and pose a formidable challenge to – Paris (Figure 7.1). The story of New York fashion however is not just a rosy tale. At the dawn of the twenty-first century, the industry faces new challenges in retaining New York's status as a fashion world city. The chapter will conclude with some reflections on these challenges, and particularly, on the imminent decline of the Garment District as the spatial anchor for the industry.

The Rise of the Garment District as Industry and Place

The rise of the Garment District in its present location can be dated back to the early twentieth century and occurred in response to a number of related developments. Through much of the mid-to-late nineteenth century, the apparel industry was situated on the Lower East Side of Manhattan, which was a port of arrival for immigrants. At this location, the retailers and wholesalers who established the industry (many of whom were German Jewish immigrants) could easily tap into a readily available labour pool, often constituted by kinsfolk (Waldinger 1986). However, after later waves of immigration, the Lower East Side was no longer viable as a manufacturing

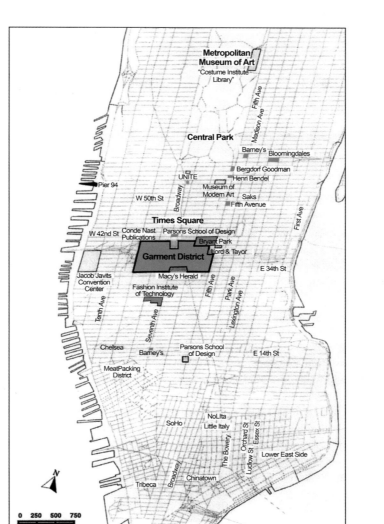

Figure 7.1 The fashion landscape of New York City.

and wholesaling district for a significant share of apparel producers. Due to overcrowded housing settlements and the expansion of government and financial activities there, elite and middle-class residents moved northward in search of more elegant residential locations. Retailers were quick to pursue their clients, and manufacturers, in turn, followed their market.

A new geography for the industry was also prompted by the general surge in the demand and supply for ready-to-wear apparel. Recent immigrants were feeding the apparel-making machine from the consumption as well as the production end, as US cities were undergoing a process of rapid urbanization and industrialization. The changing social and economic status of women was also integral to the rise in demand, as growing numbers were entering the workforce and had less time for custom-made fittings or making their own clothes. Due to its port and favourable location along the Hudson River, New York became the transportation hub for the US Eastern seaboard, making it a natural trading centre for the rest of the country and the main beneficiary of this heightened demand (Helfgott 1959; Green 1997).

On the supply side, the rise of ready-to-wear and the supplanting of home-made production were accelerated by the invention of Howe's sewing machine, which mechanized part of the production process, and by innovations in fabrics that were more amenable to machine production. The development of a range of retail formats, from the department store to mail-order catalogues, allowed consumers far and near, elite or non-elite, readily to purchase the new wares and to keep the fashion cycle in motion (Braham 1997; Scranton 1998).

As a consequence of these developments, wholesalers and manufacturers needed larger spaces to coordinate the production process and newer spaces in which to display their expanding commodity lines to local and out-of-town buyers. Proximity to transport nodes was also significant as the market was no longer a local one and employees were increasingly dispersed across Manhattan and the boroughs. The construction of Penn Railroad Station (in 1910) as well as the availability of spacious loft buildings made Midtown Manhattan an appealing site.

The spatial contours of the District within the Midtown area however were dictated by other political-economic factors. The northward push of retailers from Lower Manhattan resulted in the establishment of a retail district along Fifth Avenue in the eastern half of the Midtown section. In catering to the new elite residents of the area, department store and boutique owners sought to construct a centre of leisure and project an image of refinement. The merchants were concerned that an influx of manufacturers and loft-style buildings would disrupt this idyllic picture, so they formed a Fifth Avenue Merchants Association and pressured the City to pass a zoning ordinance in 1916 to restrict industrial uses in the area (Jackson 1995). In response, manufacturers congregated in the western half of the Midtown area to benefit from the Midtown amenities and remain close to the stores, creating a space of production adjacent to – though separate from – the pre-eminent space of consumption in the city.

The Garment District is usually demarcated as the area bordered by 40th street to the north, 34th to the south, Fifth Avenue to the east and Ninth Avenue to the west (Figure 7.2). Over time, as more manufacturers congregated there, support services, such as textile representatives, trim and button suppliers and lending institutions ('factors'), emerged to serve the new apparel cluster and to solidify its reputation

Figure 7.2 New York, fashion capital of the world. Street advertising *c*.2003. Photograph: Norma Rantisi.

and character as a distinct quarter. Seventh Avenue, which ran through the centre of the District, became home to fancy showrooms, signifying the power and influence that apparel would command in the local economy.

The rise of the New York Garment District in the urban landscape (and the popular imagination) was not only associated with a concentration of related apparel activities within a shared space of production. The District (or 'Seventh Avenue', as it was dubbed by industry insiders) came to represent a symbolic anchor for a broader nexus of institutions in the city to support and mediate apparel production and consumption. On the production side, for example, the International Garment Workers Union (later called UNITE) developed in response to the poor working conditions of immigrant garment workers in the early 1900s and the consequent workers' strikes. The union was instrumental in negotiating the Protocol of Peace in 1910, which led to the establishment of the Department of Labour and set the foundation for 'collective bargaining between management and labour' (Green 1997). The trade journal *Women's Wear Daily* (*WWD*), now the leading source of information on market trends, was instigated in 1910 mainly to report on the workers' strikes and played an important role in keeping industry insiders abreast of the latest developments in the trade (Waldinger 1986). Apparel design and production programmes were established at the Pratt Institute (in 1888) and the Parsons School of Design (in 1906) to qualify a new cadre of recruits for the bourgeoning industry.

On the consumption side, resident buying offices in the District marketed New York apparel to retailers, by serving as liaisons between local manufacturers and out-of-town buyers. The New-York based fashion magazines *Vogue* and *Harper's Bazaar* aroused an interest on the part of the broader population. With the aid of fashion photography by the late 1920s, fashion advertisements in these magazines and in the popular press, more generally, were critical in cultivating a homogeneous (or 'mass') consumer market across the USA that could sustain large volumes of ready-to-wear production (Ewen 1976; Martin 1995a; Goldberg 2001). As former editor Edna Chase stated, the intention of *Vogue* was to show the women in the rest of the USA 'what the smart women of New York were buying' (Chase and Chase 1954: 40). New York's vibrant retail scene added to the excitement and buzz of consuming apparel, with trademarks such as Macy's, Lord and Taylor, Bloomingdale's and Bergdorf Goodman making shopping a pleasurable experience rather than necessity for out-of-town buyers as well as consumers (Goldman 1949).

Together, these institutions along with the apparel-related services that emerged in the early twentieth century constituted an 'industry', encompassing a chain of interconnected activities that traced the apparel product from manufacture to distribution to consumption. The geographic proximity of these activities within and around the District was critical to the industry's success, as it served to reduce transport and transaction costs and to allow for high turnover in production. By the early 1920s, New York's position as the centre for apparel in the country was unrivalled. The city had a particular strength in women's wear, which was more labour intensive than men's wear and relied on a fast turnaround, and for which New York constituted 80 per cent of the national share of the product value (Richards 1951, Helfgott 1959).

Despite the successes, however, a critical element of the local industry was still lacking – the *conception* of the product. New York mastered the manufacture, distribution and marketing of products but the inspiration for the styles was Paris. Parisian designers and fashion figured centrally in local design school instruction, in the pages of the fashion magazines and in the window displays of local department stores. Retail buyers and manufacturers would regularly send representatives to the fashion shows in Paris to purchase samples or sketch the designs (Lee 1975; De Marly 1980; Ewing 1992). For their part, the American general public endorsed this view through their consumption practices, favouring products with 'made in Paris' labels (whether real or fake), and for the wealthier clientele, by making trips to France to shop in the boutiques (Richards 1922; Roshco 1963). Guidebooks for Americans were instrumental in reinforcing the Paris–fashion link. In the symbolic ordering of world cities, Paris was clearly at the pinnacle of the fashion hierarchy (Gilbert 2000).

Paris's supremacy over New York at this time could be attributed to the distinct organization of each city's respective industry, *haute couture* and *ready-to-wear*. In Paris, haute couture represented an elite industry, made up of a select group of couturiers adhering to a set of conditions pertaining to design, production and marketing. The use of the 'haute couture' label by fashion houses was regulated by a commission, the Chambre Syndicale de la Haute Couture, which advocated on behalf of couture houses with respect to intellectual property rights, labour issues, foreign relations, advertising and the coordination of the fashion shows. The Chambre also assisted identifying financial backers for the designers, and this support and validation enabled its members to take risks and create exclusive designs (De Marly 1980, Ewing 1992). Although the first couture house in Paris was formally introduced by Charles Worth in the mid 1800s, the significance of fashion as a marker of distinction was popularized by the French court at Versailles as early as the eighteenth century. As Green (1997) has suggested, the emphasis in Paris has always been on differentiation, rather than imitation.

In New York, ready-to-wear was born in the late 1800s, in an era of industrialization, to serve the immediate, functional needs of the masses. The emphasis was on cost-efficient, volume (re)production. Consequently, the institutions that emerged in the Garment District supported the commercial imperatives of the industry. In contrast to Paris, New York lacked an infrastructure to nurture and promote artistic creation and to validate 'design' (and by extension, 'the designer') as a production strategy. By the early 1900s, apparel had already become big business for the local economy. The challenge that remained was building on the existing industrial base to attain a distinctive fashion identity by reorienting the city's 'space of production' to allow for social and cultural influences. Such an opportunity, however, arose in the 1930s and 1940s. The next section reviews a series of events that coincided in this period, offering the industry the prospects for a 'cultural turn' and for the rise of new institutions that could mediate the aesthetic and the commercial.

The Institutionalization of New York Fashion

Economic geographers have offered critical insight into the processes that give rise to cultural products, namely, goods or services that are valued for their aesthetic or symbolic attributes relative to their utilitarian ones (e.g. Scott 1996, 2000a). In particular, these scholars have drawn attention to the urban basis of cultural production, highlighting the significance of an array of cultural and economic activities for promoting aesthetic innovation and for the development of networks among cultural institutions to facilitate the exchange of information and ideas. In the early 1900s, New York City had not yet made its mark as a cultural centre. As

Guilbaut (1983) notes, the USA was becoming a major industrial and financial player on the global scene with New York City as its primary centre, but Paris was not only the reigning fashion capital, but more generally, the world cultural capital, as home to renowned artists, such as Matisse. Like the fashion magazines, other New York cultural institutions, such as the Gallery of Modern Art and the Museum of Modern Art, tended to privilege Parisian works and talent in the 1920s and 1930s.

However, New York's economic advantage would soon translate into greater demand on the part of an expanding bourgeois class for local amenities, amenities that would embody US values of 'liberal democracy' (Guilbaut 1983). While not yet on the international radar, New York did bear witness to the development of a thriving music and performing arts scene at the turn of the twentieth century. Vaudeville, Broadway and some of the major music houses (under the umbrella of Tin Pan Alley) would feed off the creative and vibrant energy that came with the rise of industry and urbanization in Manhattan. And by the 1930s, a local band of avant-garde artists, seeking to break with Parisian hegemony, started to garner attention (both negative and positive) from local press and exhibitors. The influx of European exiles, many of whom were artists and intellectuals escaping fascist regimes, added to the cultural blend by importing 'Old World' experiences and skills in ways that would mesh with 'New World' dictates (Guilbaut 1983; Scott and Rutkoff 2001).

New York's status as an arts centre was slowly coming into being and gaining legitimacy. The city's status as a cultural centre was reinforced through the establishment of landmark institutions, such as the Guggenheim Museum, Carnegie Hall and the Lincoln Center for Performing Arts. New York apparel would both benefit from and contribute to this emerging cultural matrix. Local cultural institutions and 'industries' (particularly in popular music, theatre and cinema) served as significant sources of inspiration but were also consumers of fashion. For example, the New York high-end ready-to-wear designer Norman Norell began his career designing clothes for Broadway and the movies. In the 1930s the Costume Institute was established by a local theatre group, a testament to the links between the performing arts and fashion. It became increasingly common to see fashion publicized alongside modern art in magazines, such as *Harper's Bazaar* (Chase and Chase 1954; Guilbaut 1983). As Entwistle notes, a fashion system entails more than the provision of 'garments for wear', it 'endows garments with beauty and desirability, sometimes making direct contact with art' (2000: 43). New York's cultural base was a central part of the fashion system that was emerging, one that would endow apparel with aesthetic value.

Although New York fashion's coming of age could be attributed in part to the city's wider cultural transformation, it was also conditioned by industry-specific developments. As the industry was maturing, a new generation of talent was emerging from local design programmes and this generation profited from the convergence of a new supply of resources (material and economic) and new demands arising from changing social conditions. The development of fabrics (such as rayon) and the innovative uses and combinations of traditional fabrics produced materials that were not only amenable to machine production but could be used in the construction of more casual ready-to-wear styles. Such styles were in demand as increasing numbers of women were entering the workforce. These women were engaged in a broader range of activities (work and leisure), and had less time for custom-made fittings, prompting the continued rise of ready-to-wear, and within ready-to-wear, a distinctive modern fashion called 'sportswear' (Milbank 1989; Ewing 1992). Claire McCardell, who was trained at the Parsons School of Design, has been credited as one of the first sportswear designers, redefining American fashion by introducing beautiful yet comfortable garments, which were *not* inspired by Paris (Yohannan and Nolf 1998). These simple, wearable styles gained broad acceptance because they resonated with new social roles but also, more generally, with values of democracy and with a view of dress as a means of blurring rather than marking social distinctions (Green 1997).

However, the broader recognition and acceptance of this burgeoning New York talent demanded the support of local buyers, fashion editors and journalists, who mediated consumption trends. With the industry's continued expansion, this support came as social ties were forged between key actors in the Garment District. In February 1931, a group of leading women in the industry, including *Vogue* editor Edna Woolman Chase, Helena Rubinstein, Elizabeth Arden, Dorothy Shaver and Eleanor Lambert, held the first meeting of the Fashion Group (later known as Fashion Group International). This association represented all facets of the industry, including designers, textile manufacturers, retailers, fashion press and fashion educators and focused on apparel and fashion-related commodities, such as home furnishing, accessories and cosmetics. The stated objectives of the group were to promote the exchange of information and to enhance the careers of women in the industry. Shortly after its establishment, group members acted on these objectives. The association sponsored lectures on merchandising and advertising and established an annual fashion show, and by 1932, prominent group member Dorothy Shaver, then vice-president of Lord and Taylor, started naming American designers, such as McCardell, in her store ads (Milbank 1989). Local talent also benefited from the annual openings at the Costume Institute, which became the industry's biggest social event, linking designers with style promoters and other cultural elites (Chase and Chase 1954).

These initial efforts to promote local talent were hastened by the onset of the Second World War and the closure of Paris as a result of the Nazi occupation in 1940. Magazines, retail buyers and Seventh Avenue manufacturers could no longer turn to Paris for inspiration or for models. Thus, the focus shifted inward. Necessity demanded that a new source of talent be nurtured to fill the void, so industry elites took on the task of bolstering this new source. On the production end, the Fashion Group's fabric division brought fabric manufacturers and designers together to develop materials that could be used to produce quality garments (Fashion Group Records, Box 73, f.8, 1940). And there was the establishment of the Fashion Institute of Technology in 1944 by industry and union leaders, which ensured a supply of specialized labour (Scranton 1998). Industry actors also recognized the need to validate new styles that were being produced. Fashion publicist Eleanor Lambert started to organize semi-annual press weeks and fashion journalists started profiling American designers and their designs in publications such as *The New York Times* and *The New Yorker*. The Garment Retailers of America promoted local talent by underwriting New York fashion shows and Coty, the cosmetics company, instituted an annual Council of Fashion Critics award (Milbank 1989). Even the established magazines started providing coverage to high-end ready-to-wear designers, with *Vogue* featuring the designs of Norman Norell and Pauline Trigere (Meyer 1976).

To be sure, Paris still had the cachet of world fashion capital. After the war was over, it quickly regained its status and presence in the fashion press. By 1947, *Vogue* editor Carmela Snow was praising Parisian styles and crediting courtier Christian Dior with having reinstated French fashion with his 'New Look'. Retail buyers and manufacturers were flocking back to Paris for inspiration. However, Paris was no longer the exclusive source of media attention, as fashion magazines and newspapers were providing increased coverage of the collections presented by New York department stores, fashion houses and wholesale manufacturers. In a speech to the Fashion Group, Dorothy Shaver went so far as to state 'American designers have simplified lines without making them stark. They have created comfort and freedom without sacrificing smartness ... Is it surprising that French couture no longer reigns supreme in the fashion world and must share its throne with our designers?' (Fashion Group International Records, Box 76, f. 5, 1952)

By the post-war period, the new institutions and networks in New York laid the foundation for a set of industry relations that could produce and endorse uniquely local designs. While the 1950s witnessed the rise of other regional apparel centres in the USA, such as Los Angeles, no other city could compete with New York's specialized fashion services and its status as publishing centre for the country. New York also had the status of cultural capital, and its museums, theatres and department stores became a favoured destination for both local and European high society after the war. As New York was becoming synonymous with style, the industry was establishing its place within the international fashion circuit.

Branding the American Designer (or 'How Calvin Got his Groove On')

The rebirth of New York ready-to-wear as 'fashion' occurred at a unique time when the post-war economic boom had created a surge in consumer demand. The growth of a middle class with new suburban homes and disposable incomes meant that markets existed for high volume, consumer goods; and apparel manufacturers, who now had merchandising *and* design capabilities, were well positioned to fill such markets. But this production wave did not last. By the 1960s, mass markets were saturated. Supply exceeded demand, which had become increasingly segmented. The rise of social movements (e.g. feminism and identity politics) and the advent of subcultures such as the 'youthquake', which was grounded in both fashion and music, gave birth to alternative styles and to new sources of fashion direction. These trends, coupled with the rising incomes of the middle class, meant that the survival of ready-to-wear apparel firms would lie with their capability to cater to and manage the increasing 'individualization' of market demand, a capability that rested with their style innovators – the fashion designers.

Up until the 1960s, however, American fashion designers lacked financial and managerial independence and did not share equally in the gains that accrued to apparel manufacturers from the new-found recognition of American sportswear. Designers were the employees of apparel firms and specialty shops and were generally relegated to the backroom, with few opportunities to meet the buyers or clients. They also lacked their own identity and their own labels. In contrast to Paris, where designers were viewed as the pivotal element of the fashion system, the 'stars', New York designers were viewed as a subsidiary element. To quote Bill Blass: 'we were the help' (Gandee 1999: 537).

The new economic context of the 1960s altered this trend. Designers, such as Blass and Ralph Lauren, started opening their own operations and capitalizing on their roles as fashion originators to distinguish themselves as well as their products to cater to new markets demands. As the mass-market system reached its limits, image and symbolic forms had become important mediums by which to differentiate fashion, so designers would contribute to the image-building process by publicizing their lifestyles. In the 1970s, figures such as Calvin Klein, would feed into the cult of personality by appearing at public events and providing interviews for magazines (Agins 1999). Calvin Klein was also notorious for regularly socializing with other fashion designers and celebrities at local nightclubs, such as Studio 54. One of the most innovative strategies that designers such as Klein employed to promote their image was moving their labels from the inside of their jeans to the outside. By the 1980s and 1990s, popular marketing tools included brand logos (such as CK or DKNY), multiple-page advertisements in the established magazines such as *Vogue* (at a price of no less than $6,000 per page), and public ads, such as billboards in New York's Times Square.

The rise of new markets clearly placed a primacy on marketing for the industry, and as Angela McRobbie (1998) has noted, this primacy is reflected in the rise of image-makers to support the creation of symbolic attributes and discourses. For New York fashion, this entailed a reorientation of mass-market institutions that privileged the homogenization of tastes, such as fashion magazines and retailers. Indeed, in line with the growing individualization of demand, the 1980s and 1990s saw the proliferation of niche-marketing magazines, which catered to a particular set of clientele, such as plus-size women, African-Americans or teens. Lifestyle magazines, such as *In Style,* also gained popularity by featuring fashion *on* or *alongside* high profile stars, and more established magazines, such as *Vogue*, *Elle* and *Harper's Bazaar* have now adopted this strategy, replacing the supermodels on their front covers with well-known celebrities (Kuczynski 1999).

The retail sector has also undergone a process of restructuring to adapt to new competitive pressures. For example, designer boutiques, which house the designer's entire collection and which are now commonplace in major retail stores, were first introduced in the 1970s when Ralph Lauren convinced Bloomingdale's to provide him with his own department so that he could promote a particular lifestyle (Agins 1999). This early version of lifestyle merchandising has now been extended through the development of the flagship store, whereby the designer decides on the content and layout of their collections as well the interior and exterior architecture of the space (Moore 2000). Since the 1980s, young designers have increasingly opted to locate their retail/design spaces outside of the established retail and garment districts, in sites such as the Lower East Side, where a distinctive atmosphere could play into their efforts to differentiate themselves and their designs (Rantisi 2002).

Another significant image-maker for the industry is the Council of Fashion Designers of America (CFDA), an honorary society of high-end designers, which was established in 1962. Since its inception, the CFDA has advocated on behalf of designers and promoted their occupation as an 'art', like that of other cultural industries. In their efforts to validate local talent, they also sponsor an annual fashion award. In 1993, the CFDA established an institution which, along with the magazines, would become the industry's most important marketing tool for the industry, the 'Seventh on Sixth' Fashion Show. Situated in Bryant Park, just northeast of the Garment District, this biannual show coordinates the presentations of the high-end, ready-to-wear lines and parallels the shows in Paris, London and Milan. As the director of the CFDA has stated, a centralized showing is significant because it creates excitement and buzz for New York designers and increases media coverage both locally and internationally (personal interview 2000).

Hence, with a reorientation of New York's fashion institutions to accommodate the rise of the designer as producer *and* marketer of fashion, established high-end ready-to-wear lines, such as Donna Karan and Calvin Klein, have now become globally competitive brands. The demands for their minimalist styles continue to surge in Europe and Asia and have also spilled over into a demand for American talent, as European houses from Gucci to Louis Vuitton have hired US designers in the last decade to develop their ready-to-wear lines (personal interviews 1999; Hirschberg 2001). As indicated by a local designer, the rise of globalization and telecommunications had led to a blurring of fashion and commerce and 'since American fashion was business-oriented to begin with, New York designers have new found respect and credibility' (personal interview 2000).

The ascendance of New York ready-to-wear and the ready-to-wear designers within the global fashion hierarchy however has posed a serious threat to couture in Paris in the last several decades. As women increasingly favour comfortable and casual styles that can suit their varied lifestyles, the demand for luxury good has been on the wane. In 1929, there were ninety-one couture houses in Paris, but today, there are less than a dozen (Reynolds 2003). In the 1960s, couturiers sought to generate sales by selling their name (and the cachet of their couture products) to licensees specializing in the production of other products, such as perfumes. However, the ability of designers to control the quality and image that was projected in these licensed products has remained difficult (Agins 1999). By the 1970s, couturiers such as Yves Saint Laurent started experimenting with their own ready-to-wear lines, based on their couture concepts, and in 1973, the Chambre du prêt-à-porter des couturiers et des createurs de mode was established to support and promote these emerging lines. Yet, the smooth transition to ready-to-wear has been inhibited by the lack of wholesale distributors and large-scale retailers, and the limited local expertise in manufacturing and merchandising skills demanded by higher volume production (Ewing 1992; Agins 1999; Scott 2000b). Thus, it is not too surprising that Paris has sought to hire American and British designers in recent years.

Living on the Edge of the Art–Commerce Balance: Can New York Maintain its Status as World Fashion Capital?

In an era of globalization, New York fashion has fared well due to the emergence of an institutional infrastructure (or 'fashion system') that has enabled local producers to balance aesthetic attributes with commercial imperatives. Designers have been able to draw on a range of local cultural institutions for sources of inspiration and on a well-established set of production intermediaries for the commercialization of their designs (Rantisi 2004b). However, the ability of the industry to retain this edge in the face of competitive pressures proves daunting. In recent years, globalization has brought new constraints, as cost remains a significant element in capitalist competition, translating into the privileging of commercial imperatives on the part of key industry actors. In the 1980s and 1990s, for example, the industry witnessed a wave of mergers and consolidation within the retail sector. By 1999, the top six department stores controlled 90 per cent of national apparel sales (WWD 1999). Fashion magazines and trade publications have experienced their own set of mergers (Kuczynski 1999). The increasing hierarchy that now characterizes industry relations creates a context in which only the most established fashion houses can afford magazine ads or can access retail buyers. New talent is increasingly locked out of opportunities that their predecessors in the 1930s had for establishing ties with key industry elites, who serve as the gatekeepers to consumer markets (see also McRobbie 2002).

The privileging of commercial imperatives is also evident in the evolution of the Garment District as a space of production. Since the 1970s, the District has faced the loss of manufacturing jobs due to rising labour and real estate costs, as apparel firms have increasingly outsourced production needs to overseas producers. Although the union negotiated a special zoning amendment to protect manufacturing in the District, there has been limited enforcement. The activities that have remained are primarily the value-added activities of design and marketing (e.g. the showrooms), with limited production for samples and the manufacture of garments with a fast turnaround. (Much of the production that now remains in the city is centered in Lower Manhattan (particularly Chinatown) and in the outer borough of Brooklyn.) In 1993, the city established the Fashion Center Business Improvement District (BID), which has helped to clean and beautify the District and project its identity as a centre for fashion production. The revitalization of the District, however, has made it a more appealing location for new uses, such as high-tech firms or advertising agencies, from which real estate owners can extract higher rents.

At a time when 'fast fashion' is becoming the new production paradigm for apparel (Segre Reinach 2005a) – a paradigm reliant on the flexible coordination and communication between retail, design, and production – the aforementioned trends which prefigure the dissolution of the District threaten to compromise the competitive advantage of New York firms. The history of New York fashion illustrates that it was the coming together of industrial and cultural activities that allowed for the dynamism, versatility and innovation of New York designs. Now more than ever, the ability to achieve a balance between art and industry demands the integrity of the District as an industry *and* a place.

–8–

Milan

The City of Prêt-à-Porter in a World of Fast Fashion
Simona Segre Reinach

In this chapter I will analyse the shifting profile of Milan as a fashion city, and its possible evolution within the new global scenario.[1] In so doing, I will raise some issues that reveal the present transnational character of fashion. Foremost among these, the 'Chinese textile problem' has been a dominating theme of the Italian media in the last two years, reaching its peak in January 2005 when, with the end of the quota system of the 'Textile Agreement', many different reactions arose. The discourse in fact can be reduced to two main opposing views. Either China is considered as a threat to fight with taxes and new quotas to protect Italian fashion from 'Chinese invasion', or it is considered as an opportunity to sell more fashion brands to the emerging Chinese market. In both cases what is missing is the appreciation that 'made in Italy' is not a given, but a fluctuating concept in a very unstable picture. One of the elements of the picture is the fall of the primacy of the prêt-à-porter production regime. The assimilation of 'made in Italy' with prêt-à-porter needs therefore to be revisited in the light of the new emerging cultures of fashion, of which 'fast fashion' seems to fit most closely with the present-day culture of appearances and with the very pace of transnational industry. Milan, being the city that hosted the rise of modern prêt-à-porter, is especially sensitive to this crisis.

From Italian Style to Made in Milan

Italian prêt-à-porter, which reached the peak of its success in the 1980s, is not a phenomenon that appeared from nowhere, so to speak. As White suggests in an important text devoted to the renaissance of Italian fashion (2000: 1–7), it has its roots in the post-war period, especially between 1945 and 1964, when, also thanks to American funding, the textile-clothing industry started up again at full capacity. Yet while it is right to speak of continuity regarding the capacity to produce clothing (Italian ready-to-wear certainly did not appear out of the blue, but was the outcome of textile and industrial development), in terms of the significance which fashion was to assume in Italian culture and economics, it was a radically new phenomenon. In the early 1970s, a turning point took place in the history of modern fashion and

Milan was at the very centre of this process that gave rise to the prêt-à-porter of the fashion designers, a fashion system that was to enjoy international commercial and media success.

Onto a highly developed Italian textile tradition, with specific artisan competences scattered in various geographic areas, was grafted the art direction of the fashion designers who later became entrepreneur-designers – unlike the dressmakers and couturiers who preceded them – an expression of that merging between design and industry which marks Italian prêt-à-porter. The new Italian term *stilista* (literally 'stylist') also indicates the assertion of a different fashion culture and underlines the dramatic change that prêt-à-porter represents in relation to Italian Style. The characterization of Milan as a capital of international fashion took place in a brief, intense period: between 1972 (the year when several fashion creators abandoned the Florence fashion shows) and 1978, when men's ready-to-wear fashion also chose Milan, and when Modit, the board of regulation of the fashion shows, was founded by Beppe Modenese.[2] In 1972, however, twenty years after the first Florentine show, Milan was already the centre of a great deal of business exchange in the fashion sector because, from both the geographical and cultural points of view, the Lombard city appeared more suited than the Tuscan capital to support the development of fashion. *Milanovendemoda*, the trade fair organized by agents and representatives of the clothing industry with the aim of intensifying relations with the many buyers already active in the city, had been taking place since 1969. The main textile associations were formed or strengthened in those years: IdeaComo, the union of silk producers, was founded in 1974, and Federtessile (which groups together ten textile associations) in 1975. Between 1970 and 1975, as if silently called to fulfil a mission, the future fashion designers started to flock to Milan, following different projects, but with the same perception of the widespread effervescence in the city. With the creation of Modit in 1978, the mechanism of the fashion shows was regulated and the role of Milan as the capital of ready-to-wear fashion was sanctioned. From then on the leading shows were held in Milan, in the tightly packed schedule handled by Modit, and from 1990 by Momi-Modamilano.

Milan's role in fashion should not be taken for granted. The fact is that between the 1970s and 1980s Milan did not become the capital of fashion, as is often claimed, but the capital of prêt-à-porter. It is commonly believed that what we do and think in one place could not be done or thought in another. We should then fully understand what kind of fashion ready-to-wear is, the cultural and geographic *humus* in which it sprang up and flourished, and the extent to which one depends on the other and what transformations for fashion and for the city lie on the horizon.

Economic, cultural and geographical factors, as well as a certain spirit of the times, make up the main ingredients for the success of both Italian ready-to-wear and Milan as a fashion city. Milanese fashion had in actual fact been the product of an atmosphere of an 'opening up' to cross-disciplinary influences and a sense of cosmopolitanism, which from the 1960s onwards many Milanese professional exponents of journalism, photography, art and culture had contributed to creating. The presence of design was an essential part of this atmosphere: Milan was the city of design long before it became the city of fashion. Milanese design was a forerunner of what was to become the fashion phenomenon on a wider scale. The concept combined the creative skills, experimentation with new materials and the industrial infrastructure necessary to start up the economy, and all of these preconditions joined together under the name and direction of the reinvigorated profession of the designer. It is no coincidence that today, in 2005, the endangered Milan fashion industry is looking again at design, as an example of a sector that has been able to evolve and shape its own destiny rather than simply react to events.

Swift to make its mark and appreciated by intellectuals (a new factor not wholly unconnected to its success, despite the negative period the city and the country were going through in the years of political terrorism (1969–81) and the oil and industrial crises), fashion in Milan metabolized and provided a new driving force for the economy (Foot 2001). Ahead of other Italian cities, Milan was also able to combine the strengths of the manufacturing industry and the service industry. On the one hand, the city stood at the centre of an archipelago of specialized areas, the industrial districts, of which it is to a certain extent the capital. The industrial districts, on which the Italian prêt-à-porter system rests, are highly specialized, often vertically organized production areas: for example, Como for silk, Biella for wool, Carpi for knitwear, Castelgoffredo for hosiery, and the Italian Marches for footwear. On the other hand, Milan was also the leading Italian centre for communications: commercial TV channels started up in Milan, the editorial staffs of the leading fashion press were in Milan, as were the numerous advertising agencies and PR studios.[3]

Milan in the 1980s

In the 1980s, once it had recovered from the recession, and also thanks to the spirit of the fashion industry (as Gastel wrote, 'Fashion is the most fashionable thing there is' (1995: 164)), Milan became 'Milano da bere' (literally, 'drunken Milan', from an advertising slogan for Ramazzotti), an affluent, dynamic city, rich in events to be consumed at will, all marked by fashion and the world revolving around it, from Versace's supermodels, to the fashion shows and celebrity events linked to them. Milanese ready-to-wear became a stable phenomenon conferring a specific physiognomy on the city. This was also visible in the real estate acquisitions made by the fashion designers. Many *palazzi* of the old Milanese families changed hands in a few years. For example: the building in Via Borgonuovo belonging to Franco Marinotti (Snia-Viscosa) and the Riva cotton manufacturers became Giorgio Armani's headquarters. Palazzo Rizzoli in Via Gesù was transformed with the contribution of the architect Renzo Mongiardino into Gianni Versace's headquarters. The Missoni family acquired a six-storey palazzo in Via Durini. And, after the historic palazzi in the city centre (which, with the store windows of the luxury stores, formed the by-then-celebrated 'Fashion District'), in the following decade it was to be the turn of the former industrial areas outside the city centre to become the focus of restyling by the fashion designers, when entire districts such as Porta Genova, the Bovisa and Porta Vittoria were upgraded thanks to the interest of fashion entrepreneurs in those areas.

In the 1980s the fashion show dominated the Milan stage. Trussardi transformed his catwalks into shows of great impact, taking place in unusual locations such as the La Scala opera house, Piazza del Duomo, the Brera Art Gallery, the Central Station and San Siro horse race track. Apart from their actual participation, the impression in the 1980s was that large parts of the city and its citizens were intimately involved in fashion culture, which was itself entwined with the worlds of advertising, the television studios and the Socialist Party. In that decade the relationship between design and fashion grew even closer: *Memphis* and radical architecture included fashion in their creative horizon. And, from the mid 1980s, with the ongoing economic growth, the financial aspect of fashion was also strengthened. Milan's role became international, thanks to the export of designer label garments and in general to the success Italian designers were enjoying in Europe and in the United States (in 1982 *Time Magazine* dedicated its cover to Armani, the first fashion designer after Christian Dior to be awarded the honour), especially in New York. As the fashion critic Suzy Menkes wrote:

> Perhaps only in Milan, the heartland of modern design, could a tailor have envisaged making factory-line slipcovers for the human frame – reminiscent of the beige calico shrouds that are placed over basic chairs at every Armani event. (2003: 68)

The Armani story is in many ways a parable of Milanese ready-to-wear with the contract with Gft (1978) sealing the new relationship between fashion design and industry, restraint and rigour as hallmarks of the designer, and the huge billboards in Via Dell'Orso for Emporio Armani as the symbol of the democratic spread of fashion. Armani, born in 1934, is part of the first generation of fashion creators who made their name in the new fashion city of Milan. Stefano Dolce and Domenico Gabbana are representatives of the second. It is singular that they are still described by journalists as the 'young designers', although they are now over forty and other, much younger creators are on the scene. The 'young' label is probably still applied to Dolce and Gabbana as the last followers of the original model of Milan prêt-à-porter, whose features we may sum up thus: a heroic debut with 'a summons to show' (in this specific case, a phone call from Beppe Modenese, president of the Italian Chamber of Fashion); business skills (they financed the first show themselves and then immediately founded the firm); segmentation of their product into first lines, second lines, jeans, perfumes and licences; spectacular promotional strategies; and the use of endorsers from the star system. Their high-profile advertising presence at strategic points in the city, like the airport, has helped to lock their identity with the city (Figure 8.1).

Milan in the 1990s

The New Yorker argued that if Armani could be considered the Volkswagen of Milan, Miuccia Prada was its Mercedes. The city of Milan in the 1990s – the decade when Prada reached success – was very different from the one that had generated the fashion designers and the 'young' fashion designers. It was difficult to see this at the time, but today it seems obvious. Miuccia Prada (whose story is similar to that of many former Milanese girls from a good middle-class background) had little in common with the biographies of the first fashion designers, such as Armani, Versace, Krizia, Missoni and Coveri. First, she was not a fashion designer, at least not in the sense of knowing how to cut, sew and make a dress. As the British newspaper *The Observer* commented recently:

Figure 8.1 Dolce & Gabbana advertisement at Milano Malpensa Airport, September 2005. Photograph: Simona Segre Reinach.

Miuccia Prada doesn't sew, embroider or knit. I never saw her sketch a skirt or a shoe, nor is she likely to pick up a pair of scissors and cut out a dress.... She is not that kind of designer. Instead she surrounds herself with talented people whose job is to translate her themes, concepts and especially her taste into clothes that bear the Prada name. (16 May 2004)

Second, her success as a designer did not start in Milan – a city that on the contrary opposed her, and where the leading fashion press deserted her first shows – but in New York. After her New York 'certification', she won over her home town. Only after having made their name in the United States, did Miuccia Prada and her husband Patrizio Bertelli also make their mark in Milan. And, in Foot's shrewd observation, the fact that the most celebrated luxury producer in the world needed to start with the New York shows to make her name may be seen 'as a symptom of a slow decline in the central role of Milan within the world fashion industry' (2001: 154). That said, Miuccia Prada has surfed the wave of the crisis in prêt-à-porter, which she had astutely anticipated, even though it was still in the distance. At the end of the age of the democratization of fashion and the heroic times of the 'summons to show', Prada presented herself as a producer of elite, cerebral luxury.[4]

Year 2000: the Transformation of Prêt-à-Porter

Since the close of the twentieth century, many things are changing in fashion. Italian ready-to-wear is struggling in the twists and turns of the de-location of production, Chinese competition, counterfeiting and the fluctuating meanings of the idea of 'Made in Italy'. The 'democratic' model on which ready-to-wear was based – namely, fashion accessible through the trickle down of brands (first lines, second lines, young lines, fragrances, licences, etc.) – is gradually being replaced by a polarized orientation: extreme luxury, the almost unique item, on the one hand, presented in stores of great style and, on the other, fast fashion, the fashion of Zara, Mango, H&M and many others. Fast fashion is not based on a vertical, integrated production system, as Italian prêt-à-porter originally was. The garments may be made anywhere, wherever convenient, in China or Eastern Europe. The expiry of the Multifibre Agreement, on 1 January 2005, which liberalized the entry of Chinese textile products into global markets, as I have said above, represents a further difficulty for the leadership of Italian fashion. The culture of appearances is being transformed, consumers are not content with complete, linear lifestyles, such as Armani's sobriety or Versace's glamour, presented at regular seasonal intervals. The provisional, changing identities of new consumers favour the fast, fragmented proposals of the new fashion. From research I am currently undertaking on the relationship between Italy and China and their textile and fashion industries (Segre Reinach 2005a) I have learned that Italy still represents a model for China, at least as far as style and branding is concerned, but in many ways it is really China's vision of fashion that is at the vanguard. China is more attuned to fast fashion, just as Italy is by definition the home of prêt-à-porter.

Beyond Prêt-à-Porter and the Future of Milan

Milan is the capital of prêt-à-porter, one of several possible fashion systems that have dominated the modern history of Western clothing, its manufacture and consumption, so far. Ready-to-wear is a production and cultural model that reached its highest peak and success in business and communications in Milan. The evolution of the culture (and production) of clothing apparel, increasingly transnational, is however changing the privileged role of Milan in fashion's world order. The transformation of fashion cannot but leave its mark on Milan. The result is widely visible in its streets. The international luxury brands continue to open new stores in the prestige locations in the city centre, such as Louis Vuitton in Galleria Vittorio Emanuele and Ralph Lauren in Via Montenapoleone, the first monobrand store in Italy. At the same time, however, the same streets are dotted with new fast fashion stores, the Scandinavian H&M (taking the place of Fiorucci) and the Spanish Zara (in Corso Vittorio Emanuele).

Is Milan aware of this transformation? And how is it equipping itself to remain one of the capitals of style? Signs of change may be seen at the institutional level. The new Florence Fashion Centre is collaborating with Sistema Moda and Milan to deal with the crisis in the trade and set up a joint project for the relaunch of 'Made in Italy', with greater collaboration between the city of Rome, the home of high fashion, Florence, with its Pitti Uomo, Pitti Filati and Pitti Bimbo events, and Milan, where the prêt-à-porter fashion shows take place. The idea is to integrate the Italian know-how, which preceded the rise of Milan, and to enhance the whole image of 'Made in Italy', not just the ready-to-wear with which Milan is linked. On this subject Mario Boselli, President of the National Chamber of Fashion, states: 'In France, fashion is only Paris, but in Italy it is Milan, Florence and also Rome. It is an integrated process in which each part works together with the others and gives its contribution to the whole system' (quoted in *Women's Wear Daily*, 2 March 2001). Giovanni Bozzetti, Milan City Councillor for Fashion, shares this view: 'I see in our future a nation which plays a compact game, each with its own speciality – Milan for ready to wear, Rome for high fashion, Florence for menswear, Naples for tailoring' (*Milano è la Moda*, ClassEditori, 2004: 137.)

The traditional rivalry between Paris and Milan – which in the 1980s had led several fashion designers to 'choose' one or the other, seems to be fading, faced with Asian competition that is much closer to the new successful fast fashion system. Significantly Gft, Gruppo Finanaziario Tessile (one of the largest textile companies that had a primary role in the history of Italian ready-to-wear) has announced that by

2010 it will move completely to China. In response to such trends and to promote better European cooperation, a protocol agreement was signed (in Milan, since Lombardy with its 200,000 workers, is confirmed as the leading textile concentration in Europe) between Mario Boselli, president of the Italian Chamber of Fashion, and Didier Grumbach, president of the *Féderation Française de la Couture*, 'for a joint strategy regarding processes and changes to avoid being overwhelmed by [competition from the East]' (*Corriere Economia,* 13 December 2004: 26). In October 2005 a new textile association was also founded in Milan, with the aim of relaunching the Italian textile industry. The association, called *Milano Unica* is based in Milan and brings together in the city many different Italian textile exhibitions, IdeaBiella (wool), IdeaComo (silk), Moda In (textile and accessories) and Shirt Avenue. It is clear then that Milan aims at preserving its fashion leadership.

On 2 May 2005, at Palazzo Mezzanotte, in Piazza degli Affari, Milan, a two-day meeting was held, entitled *'Milano di moda:* First strategic conference on fashion' also described by the press as the 'Convocation of the States General of Fashion'. Guests were the historical protagonists of Milanese ready-to-wear – such as Ottavio and Rosita Missoni, Dolce and Gabbana, Mariuccia Mandelli, Laura Biagiotti, Roberto Cavalli, the forerunners of ready-to-wear, like Elio Fiorucci, the exponents of the National Chamber of Fashion, various major luxury companies, and the main universities in Milan. One message emerged loud and clear: 'only by changing everything can we win back our leadership', by which they admitted, perhaps officially for the first time, having lost it. That 'everything' to be changed merged in a criticism of the symbolic and structural centre of ready-to-wear, the fashion show, whose model goes back to 1951 and which appears, for many speakers, wholly inadequate to tackle the new market. The timing and presentation of models must change. No longer should shows last one week, but fewer concentrated days, four at most, to give journalists and buyers the time to travel between the increasingly numerous fashion weeks in the different cities throughout the world. And above all, the garments on the catwalks ought to be those of the current season, as happens in the 'design week', another significant event in the cultural and business life of Milan, and not those for the following season, so as not to give time for fast fashion protagonists (and the Chinese) to copy the models. As the Italian press recorded:

> Santo Versace and Gaetano Mazzotto are throwing down the challenge against the decline of a system which has made Milan great and which today seems endangered by Paris and New York. 'Today the addressees of the fashion shows are no longer the experts in the field', Versace explains, 'but consumers throughout the world. That is why it would be appropriate to present the season's collections in Milan and not those which will be on the market six months later'. Marzotto continues, 'in this way we forestall the imitators and counterfeiters of all kinds who will have less time and more difficulty in their falsifications'. (Giorgio Lonardi, *Corriere della Sera,* 4 May 2005)

It is significant that no representative of systems other than ready-to-wear was present at the conference; there was no fast fashion company, no 'Chinese competitor' apart from an entrepreneur from Prato (the Italian city that hosts one of the largest Chinese communities in Europe and where there are a few very successful and entirely Chinese-owned fast fashion companies) invited more as an orientalist curiosity than as a witness of the new transnational phase of fashion. Moreover, among the 'rival' cities, only Paris and New York were mentioned, as if the geographical and cultural context had remained stationary since the 1980s. Milan still *means* fashion, argued Stefano Zecchi, Councillor for Fashion in the Milan City Council in his paper to the meeting, but the question we must ask is whether it is still *in* fashion.

In this atmosphere we must also interpret the decision, after years of postponement, polemics and indecision, to officially start the construction of a *Città della Moda* (Fashion City), a project advanced by Nicola Trussardi in the 1980s when ready-to-wear was still in its heyday, and which has never been achieved. It is a polyvalent structure (designed by the architect Cesar Pelli) in the Repubblica-Garibaldi district, to be built on a 100,000-square-metre area intended for residential and business development and for offices, including a fashion museum that, believe it or not, still does not exist in Milan (Figure 8.2). The project finally took off in 2004 and will be completed by 2009. The fashion city: 'will become an excellent place to represent

Figure 8.2 Architects' model of 'La città della moda'.

the vocations and traditions of Italy and Milan where the creativity expressed by fashion, design, communications and culture may merge' (Brochure *'La Città della Moda'*, July 2004). The *Città della Moda* (costing €680 million and financed by Hines Estate) will, according to the Lombardia Governor, 'help to relaunch the city', though his optimism is tempered by one of his officials' 'hope that the fashion designers will not hamper the project' (*'La Città della Moda'*, July 2004). These two statements capture perfectly the present hopes and fears of the city. Will the old fashion system, that still monopolizes Milanese fashion culture, understand the changes that the transnational textile industry is undergoing and give Milan a chance to adjust?

In fact, despite the recent changes, Milan continues to be an ideal city for clothes shopping, due to the range, quality and variety of products on offer. Alongside boutiques, flagship stores, restored *palazzi* and the *maisons* of the great fashion designers – which still constitute the most visible part, but are probably destined to become future archaeological remains – we may glimpse a new network of shops and artistic-craft-business activities, which greatly remind us of the shape of Milan in the 1960s and 1970s, with its innovative stores such as Fiorucci, Gulp, Cose, La Drogheria Solferino and the creative atmosphere of the beginnings of prêt-à-porter. We may draw here on the memories of Beppe Modenese, who in an interview with Minnie Gastel recalled that:

> in 1978 for Modit we had invited to the fair the St. Andrews restaurant, the Einaudi bookshop, Renato Cardazzo's Galleria del Naviglio, the jeweller Luisa de Gresy, and I had also organised a small cinema which projected clips of fashion films. There were beautiful cafés, avenues of flowers … fashion helped to open up frontiers in a social sense. And from the point of view of image, it changed the mentality of Milanese shopkeepers who started to modify their stores in an innovative fashion. Unfortunately the ace card then has taken a negative turn: they flattered themselves that Milan had the finest fashion stores, jewels and luxury goods. But I miss the grocers, the bars, the flower shops, the stores which make the city come alive every day, but which have disappeared. (Gastel 2003)

Little tailors and dressmakers' shops, craft shops, new interpretations of luxury and commercial initiatives of various kinds are again flourishing in the city, standing apart from both the mass-production of the colossal flagship stores, and that of the new giants of fast fashion. As Gilbert writes, 'relatively small, independent designers and retailers may sustain a viable independent fashion culture, often within distinctive districts of the city' (2000: 13).

In the Isola district, to give an example of the new creativity, which seems to be once more arising in the city, there is the so-called *Stecca degli Artigiani*. This is built on a former industrial area (Siemens-Electra) abandoned in the 1960s and 1970s and then relaunched in the 1980s by the Milan City Council to host various artisan and artistic workshops. Another example is the former Braun Boveri factory – occupied by artists in the mid 1980s – now the official headquarters of a Centre for Contemporary Art. I like to think of this district – one of the many where this transformation is beginning to be seen – as a metaphor for a possible future for Milan. A future upgrading as a vital shopping city (and not just for tourists), in continuity with its history as a Hanseatic city, as Aldo Bonomi (2004) describes it, where the experience of fashion may live alongside the newly emerging expressions of creativity. And perhaps it is no coincidence that the inhabitants of this neighbour-hood, bordering on the Garibaldi district where the colossal 'City of Fashion' will arise, have demonstrated against the enactment of the plan, fearing that the new initiative – seen by many inhabitants of the area as a barefaced colonization by a prêt-à-porter singing its swan song – will destroy the authentic substratum of this district (Figure 8.3). But what the inhabitants of the Isola perhaps do not see is that here Milan is already in the future, where boutiques like Agata Ruiz de la Prada's in Via Maroncelli stand alongside new dressmakers' and independent stores of various kinds.

Fashion is an important part of the show of urban life and its experiential aspect, as Gilbert (2000: 11) argues, is closely linked to the vitality and the quality of the

Figure 8.3 Hands off the Isola! Women protesting against the proposed construction of 'La città della moda' in the Isola District of Milan, July 2004. Photograph: Simona Segre Reinach.

place where purchases are made. As Diego Della Valle, Chief Executive of Tod's states, 'a brand must eschew look-alike stores across the world and offer products specific to various cities' (Michault 2004). But in Milan in particular, the designer fashion seems more intractable about transforming, about measuring up to the changed scenario, almost oppressed by the weight of its glorious past. The transition from a culture exclusively linked to prêt-à-porter to a more articulate, complex interaction of the global and the local is the key point on which the future of Milan as capital of style depends. For this reason, in Milan creativity currently no longer seems to exhaust itself in fashion, which in the last few years has been perceived as more than a significant experience, almost as an incursion on the life of the city.

Prêt-à-porter today is being criticized and deconsecrated. 'Fashion Weak' is the title of a recent happening made by an independent group of young Milanese activists during one of the last official fashion weeks, to protest against the imposition of fashion on reluctant Milanese citizens – the exact opposite of what happened in the 1980s. The 'Fashion Weak' happening, we must however point out, was organized in one of the most prestigious fashion schools in Milan. So, if it is true that fashion cannot be denied as an essential feature of the city, especially in Milan, where it is consubstantial, it is equally true that Milan must find a new role in the increasingly wider transnational network of fashion capitals, and start to offer experience and not just products: a shopping city able to communicate first of all the essence of itself and its continuing vitality.

Notes

1. This essay is dedicated to the memory of Guido Vergani. I also wish to thank Djurdja Bartlett who provided constructive comments and suggestions.
2. The shows organized by Giovanni Battista Giorgini in Florence in 1951 marked the end of the monopoly of the French fashion designers and the start of Italian Style. They were attended by an international public including the leading American buyers. Among those abandoning Florence in the early 1970s were Walter Albini, considered the founder of Italian prêt-à-porter, Ken Scott and the Cadette brand. In 1974 women's fashion definitively left Florence.
3. Berlusconi's first private channel, TeleMilano, started broadcasting outside Lombardy in 1978. Starting in 1974 as a cable TV in a building in the Milan02 housing estate, in 1980 it became Canale5. In Berlusconi's portfolio, Canale5 was joined by Italia1 in 1982 and Retequattro was acquired by Fininvest in 1984.
4. For example, Prada eschews the 'second line' concept. Its Miu Miu is a completely different line from Prada.

–9–

Mapping Moscow Fashion

Spaces and Spectacles of Consumption

Olga Vainshtein
(translation by Charles Rougle)

When Walter Benjamin travelled to Moscow in 1926–7, he remarked on what seemed to him to be the spontaneous quality of street trade.[1] He paid particular attention to the production of traditional toys, small wooden trinkets painted in bright colours. Indeed, an equally spontaneous market for food and everyday goods existed all over the city. Much as today, anything could be bought or sold on the open streets of the revolutionary capital. This phantasmagoria of 'wild' commerce revealed to the attentive observer one of Moscow's secret lives where the symbiosis between town and country played itself out. Behind the gates of the walled metropolis one could find signs of country life with hens, vegetable plots and babushkas in flowered shawls.

Many nuances of Moscow life captured by Benjamin are relevant today for understanding the urban landscape, particularly through street commerce. Presently the glamorous spectacle of capitalism masks what is otherwise a deeply rooted system of traditional Russian trade. Even now in gigantic open markets permanently anchored on the outskirts of town one can buy anything from marinated cabbage to woollen socks to the latest bootleg computer games and music discs. The flea markets that so intrigued Benjamin continue to recycle history as young clubbers buy Soviet kitsch as articles of retro-chic. The amazing variety of goods in Muscovite markets has long reflected the city's status as imperial, and later, federal capital. When Benjamin's communist lover, Asya Lacis, urged him to buy her an Eskimo coat, he refused at great pain, as it would have consumed all the funds he had for his trip. But Lacis made it clear that such articles were the stuff of city dreams; however austere her revolutionary politics, exotic clothes were still a mark of luxury. This imperial matrix remains a deeply ingrained force amidst today's ongoing restructuring of retailing.

Mapping Moscow fashion implies examining the multivalent shifts in fashion geography, the dynamics of newly emerging and disappearing spectacles of consumption. The contemporary fashion landscape in Moscow envelops quite a few distinctive fashion cultures, representing competing economic models. These various economic sites symbolically reflect different stages of Russian history; overlapping in space, they create a heterogeneous cityscape, interweaving local fashion cultures. The process of inevitable globalization, however, does not exclude the tensions between divergent fashion cultures. Yet on a broader scale one can trace the persistence of certain collective patterns of consumption through periods of political change. Indeed, for even the most avant-garde urban consumers the experience of Moscow's shopping routes displays a surprisingly conservative 'memory of place'.

The main established sites of consumption figuring in this chapter are urban markets, central department stores, fashion streets and new fashion districts, created by the competing corporations in Moscow. The street markets represent the traditional mode of commerce, going back to the most ancient periods of Russian history. The department stores, which started to appear in the nineteenth century, represent the advent of capitalist modernity. After 1917, in spite of the recurrent lack of everyday goods, department stores continued functioning through the Soviet period and fashion streets, such as Kuznetsky Most remained familiar shopping routes. From the beginning of perestroika in 1985, some pre-Revolutionary forms of trade such as street markets gained new popularity, quickly transforming urban space. This transitional period from socialism to capitalism brought dramatic changes. The growing social contrasts were meaningfully performed through the spatial restructuring of the city centre; the new 'luxury streets' squeezed out the traditional urban markets from the centre of Moscow and totally transformed the old department stores. This chapter aims to show, through a series of case studies, how these changing spatial configurations of Moscow fashion cultures reflect longer histories and current concerns.

Our first case study will be focused on the traditional spaces of Muscovite commerce. Moscow has long been known as the 'calico capital' of Russia. In 1917 textiles – especially cotton, but also wool and silk – were the largest single industry in the city, employing over 43 per cent, or two of every five factory workers (Geinike, Elagin, Efimova and Shits 1991 [1917]: 6–7). The most important textile factories were located in Lefortovo and Zamoskvorechie, and the largest silk factory was in Khamovniki. The principal commercial district was always the territory of the ancient 'White City' in the centre of Moscow. For centuries the basic form of trade there was the street market, and the principal commercial space was in special rows of covered stalls. The Upper Row sprang up as early as the sixteenth century and was located between Nikolskaya street and Ilyinka on the site of the present GUM (State Department Store), while to the south of Varvarka was the Lower Row, which was torn down in 1930. Up until the mid nineteenth century, trade was concentrated near the Kremlin. The main Moscow bazaar was on Red Square, beyond which was the Middle Row in Kitay-Gorod. Pride of place there was held by rows of stalls named after the goods in which they dealt: Vetoshny (Rag – hence the present street name Vetoshny Pereulok), Shapochny (hat), Kaftanny (kaftan), Sukonny (cloth), Sitsevy (calico), and there was the Vshivy (flea) Row selling second-hand clothing. The Middle Row was situated between Ilyinka and Varvarka, where today the Gostiny Dvor shopping centre is situated. Many foreign merchants visited Moscow, and at times wholesale trade was in the form of barter for furs, a common export item.

Also figuring importantly in urban commerce were the temporary street markets. Most sprang up spontaneously around the city, although some of them – the largest – had permanent locations. Such was the Sukharevsky Market dating from the late eighteenth century, which originally dealt in foodstuffs and then in the nineteenth century in old books and antiques. During the early years of the New Economic Policy, a time of relative economic liberalization in the Soviet Union, there was a huge flea market there where one could buy almost anything. In 1925 it was cut back considerably and moved to a courtyard near the Forum movie theatre, and in 1930 it was closed down completely. The famous poet Osip Mandelstam wrote of the Sukharevsky Market: 'Evidently Sukharevka can't wait – she has already spread out her wares directly on the roadway: fan-shaped piles of books, toys, wooden spoons ... Trifles, uninteresting merchandise' (Mandelstam 2003: 9–10).

Walter Benjamin, whose *Moscow Diary* was referred to above, noted the fluid boundaries and dynamic spread of street markets throughout practically the entire downtown of the city. In 1926 his observant eye noted Russian peasant women who in the winter loaded baskets of apples, candy, nuts and sugar figurines onto sleighs, covering them with kerchiefs to shield them from the cold; Chinese selling paper flowers; sellers of colourful wooden toys and glass Christmas tree ornaments; even Mongols selling leather portfolios (Benjamin 1997: 28–9). On his strolls around Moscow with Asya Lacis he bought black and gold lacquered Palekh jewellery boxes, decorated wooden nesting eggs, Russian lace and 'knitted kerchiefs with designs Asya said the peasant women copied from frost patterns on windows' (Benjamin 1997: 25–6). Benjamin was especially impressed, of course, by the gigantic flea market on Sukharevka. He was bewitched by the sight of the alienated phantasmagoric life of the goods there: 'Here at the market the architectonic function of goods becomes apparent: rolls of cloth form pilasters and columns, while shoes and felt boots strung in a row above the stall form the roof of the kiosk' (Benjamin 1997: 101). He came to the insightful conclusion that this motley market life was intimately connected with the essence of Moscow's urban life: 'As I moved around the many squares and avenues of booths I realized the extent to which this predominant structure of markets and fairs defines significant expanses of the Moscow streets' (Benjamin 1997: 101).

Benjamin's observation applies equally well to other periods in the history of Moscow. Spontaneous 'natural' street commerce regularly erupted on the streets of the city. It became particularly active in times of economic crisis such as the 1920s, the Second World War and the first years of perestroika. During such historical upheavals Moscow seemed to return to its past and its ancient indigenous form of commerce. Thus during perestroika in the mid 1980s it was not unusual to see rows of vendors right in the centre of the city. On Tverskaya Street, in the street underpasses, everywhere people were standing and holding food and clothing and all sorts of things for sale – just as when Benjamin was strolling around the city. Osip Mandelstam's metaphor springs to mind: 'trade boils up from below as though born of the very soil' (Mandelstam 2003: 10).

Even now one can observe the vital force of this tradition in the local 'weekend fairs', organized in Moscow in spring and autumn by the special order of the city mayor. Traffic stops, and small streets are turned into festive markets with carnivalesque atmosphere (actors dressed in Russian folk costumes greeting the people and performing the old songs). These fairs are indeed the festivals of consumption for the poorest citizens, as everything sold there is quite inexpensive. Goods are brought from provincial Russian cities and include food, housewares and clothes. Clothes are mainly of Russian production, but basic Chinese and Korean wares are also represented. The prices are low due to the huge economic difference between the capital and small towns; Moscow still remains the third most expensive city in the world. Vendors pay almost nothing for their participation in the fair. For nostalgic observers these fairs provide an additional emotional bonus, giving the unique chance of 'travelling in time', as one can find there the simple Soviet things, typical of the socialist era, but no longer available in Moscow shops: basic warm underwear, unadorned linen tablecloths, zinc basins and cast-iron frying pans.

In literature this spontaneous street commerce was frequently associated with Asian bazaars, and Moscow itself with Eastern cities and countries. The relational identity of Moscow in this particular aspect was routinely contrasted with the rival city St Petersburg; strict and elegant St Petersburg was symbolized as a Western capital, 'the gates to Europe' while relaxed and feminine Moscow was the metaphorical Eastern capital of Russia.[2] Thus the hero of Ivan Bunin's story *Pure Monday* falls in love with a strange woman who for him comes to symbolize Moscow: 'He smelled the slightly heady odor of her hair and thought: Moscow, Astrakhan, Persia, India!' (Kanunikova 2003: 162). Many historians connect this 'Eastern face' of Moscow with the Mongol period in Russian history, and travellers invariably noted the Asian features in Old Moscow architecture, particularly the many-coloured domes of St Basil's Cathedral.

Essential features of the Oriental bazaar include obligatory haggling and the importance of rhetoric. Out of lively face-to-face interaction with vendors in the street markets arose a form of discourse referred to as 'the Muscovite "mot juste"' (*metkoe moskovskoe slovo*) – a special marketplace culture of proverbs and witty sayings. 'What are you looking for?' – asked a vendor, and a potential client replied: 'I am looking for my happiness.'[3] This variety of urban folklore has attracted considerable scholarly interest (Ivanov 1986).

A similar view of trade as a form of personal contact prevailed at all markets trading with clothes that began to appear in Moscow during the early perestroika years. Spatially these markets were structured very much as in Benjamin's descriptions:

enormous motley labyrinths in which all goods were jumbled together without the slightest indication of any kind of order. The first and most famous such market was the enormous Luzha[4] bazaar at the Luzhniki sports stadium, which featured mainly Turkish and Chinese clothing supplied by so called 'shuttle traders' (*chelnoki*), a perestroika neologism referring to individual vendors, mostly women, who at their own risk travelled to Turkey and China and brought back with them huge chequered bags full of cheap clothing. These sturdy oilcloth bags blocking the doorways of the subway trains soon became symbols of cheap goods. Thanks to the shuttle traders the problem of scarce mass-market clothing in the early perestroika years was solved, and the consumer-good markets seemed to have gained a firm foothold in the centre of the city. Innumerable kiosks, set up in the underpasses or near the subway stations, began at this time to sell miscellaneous items, clothing and food. These brightly illuminated outlets created the impression that a new order had arrived – it was not for nothing that the Soviet Union of the perestroika period was known as a 'kiosk civilization'. The most successful shuttle traders opened permanent kiosks in the centre of the city near the tube stations or in the underground crossings.

In only a few years, however, in the mid 1990s, the shuttle traders were beleaguered by taxes, and trips to Turkey for clothing declined sharply. The famous Luzha market was closed down completely, and the other markets gradually began to be squeezed out of the downtown district. Some moved to more distant locations, others such as the Savelovsky, Kon'kovo and Cherkizovsky Markets became established near the outlying subway stations, and some prospered beyond the city limits on the Moscow Ring Road. However, several city stadiums – Dynamo (a former mecca for obtaining footwear), the Central Army Stadium (specializing in the wholesale perfumery trade) and the Olympic stadium – have retained associations with cheap commerce. Even now after shuttle traders have had to leave their favourite 'sites of recreation', the stadiums still function as typical zones for sales and discount shops: the cultural memory of place cannot be easily erased.

The trade centres or malls that have sprung up since the late 1990s represent an intermediate form of commerce. These consist of glassed-in pavilions in which a multitude of small shops rent floor space. The owners of most of these little stores are successful shuttle traders who have managed to raise their businesses to a new level and acquired permanent business partners in Turkey, China and Italy. However, these shops are now losing out to major international brands such as Zara, Mango, Promod or Motivi, which also lease space in these centres.

Despite all the changes that have taken place in society, the street-market culture of personal interaction is still alive, albeit subliminally, and continues to influence consumption styles in the stores of Moscow. Shoppers (especially middle-aged or older) often adopt the lively and sensual style of the market by inertia – complaining about prices, asking the personal opinion of the sales clerk as they try on clothes, talking about themselves. They are losing the pleasure of embodied consumption; the impersonality of modern department stores often inhibits their purchases even when they have the money. Buying things directly from individual vendors retains the charm of forbidden fruit even for young and trendy consumers. Although they may themselves consider it bad form to shop for clothes at a market (or they do shop there but hide these 'sins' from their 'sophisticated' friends), they still value the element of personal communication and lively atmosphere of the place. In the area of fashion commerce this explains the popularity of such things as the 'showrooms' that have become popular in Moscow during the past three years. Often these are simply private multibrand shops in rented apartments whose owners deal with a list of trusted customers. Buying fashionable clothing in such a locale offers an opportunity for a confiding and amiable exchange of opinions between client and seller, thus restoring a subjective element to the transaction. Historically such showrooms date back to the culture of the black marketeers and speculators of the 1960s and 1970s. A *fartsovshchik* would buy clothing from foreign tourists and often sold it at home to clients they knew. Frequently clothing was brought in from abroad. The business was considered rather chic among the young people of the period, for many black marketeers read samizdat literature and were friends with dissidents and avant-garde artists. The secretive atmosphere and oppositional attitudes surrounding them made every purchase of clothing a personal adventure. This was a different, intimate and conspiratorial side of fashion commerce that contrasted with the openness of the street market.

Among the black marketeers there reigned a genuine cult of Western clothing, whose foreign origin was always underscored, and there was a fetish for things coming in from abroad. Vestiges of this attitude survive in one interesting form of contemporary fashion consumption, namely shopping tours. Most popular in Moscow are trips to Greece for fur coats – so called 'fur-trips'.[5] Most frequently these are three-day trips with visits to fur centres, for in Greece there are entire cities and regions that cater to Russian tourists. Many tourist agencies in Moscow offer such tours cheaply, since they can fill seats on charter flights. The 'fur-tour' travellers are usually lower-middle-class women for whom a fur coat, especially a mink coat, is a dream from youth and a status symbol. The striking number of women wearing fur coats in the Moscow subway is one consequence of this phenomenon. A more prestigious variant of the foreign clothes trip is the Milan shopping tour. This is something reserved for upper-middle-class women or fashion plates from the Moscow in-crowd. As a prêt-à-porter mecca when sales are on, Milan attracts Russian shoppers, for the glamorousness and sexuality of Italian brands such as Dolce and Gabbana, Gucci and Fendi has made them particularly popular in Moscow. Today Milan's popularity among trendy Russians has clearly eclipsed that of Paris, the traditional fashion utopia.

As for the ready-to-wear market, thus far Moscow obviously trails the fashion cities of the world. Many fashion-conscious middle-class Russian women shop abroad as much as possible, since even if the brands they want can be had in Moscow, the exorbitant downtown rents make them much more expensive. Some categories of consumers cannot buy clothes to their taste in Moscow at all. 'My dream is to find at least one shop in Moscow where I could buy elegant, inconspicuous and smart women's clothes' says book designer Irina Tarkhanova (Tarkhanova 2005), a complaint that is heard frequently among Moscow's artistic bohemians, who prefer an ascetic style with avant-garde elements and refuse to wear sporty or erotically glamorous clothes.

A few small stores, such as Koks in Maroseika or Lena Makashova's Shirpotreb in Sokolniki, cater to avant-garde tastes. They carry the products of Russian designers intended for the domestic market. They are all primarily oriented toward youth fashion and are located in the less expensive parts of the city. The 'Rock-kultura' shop selling clothes to fans of rock music is situated in Sadovaya ring. Such stores find it difficult to survive downtown. The talented designer Lena Kvadrat, for example, was forced to close her store Artpoint on the Arbat despite a devoted young clientele. Unable to pay the exorbitant rent there, she preferred to move her company to Austria, although her designs continue to be sewn in Russia. At present her store in Vienna is doing well. The bohemian vintage boutique Brocade, once located in Gostinny Dvor, was similarly obliged to close. The avant-garde youth fashion brand 'Alex' in Rozhdestvenka had to be relocated to Petersburg. For economic reasons, only the stores dealing in luxury goods can survive in central Moscow, a situation resulting from the relatively recent rapid march of the city toward capitalism.

Yet historically downtown is the area where fashion commerce, including rather democratic stores accessible to consumers of various income levels from among both the young and the middle class, has traditionally been located. As Yu. Veshninsky has demonstrated, the centre and the western region of Moscow have preserved their prestigious connotations through all the historical changes and this determined the high prices for land (Veshninsky 1998: 198–225). Calling this phenomenon 'Moscow West End', Veshninsky shows that it has always specialized in cultural production, being the region of scientific and educational institutions, entertainment and numerous clothes shops (on Moscow's cultural geography see Ilyin 2004: 131–95).

Kuznetsky Most: a Fashion Street through the Ages

Kuznetsky Most has long held a special place in Moscow's fashion topography. Originally there were many blacksmiths there (hence the name, which translates as 'Blacksmith's Bridge'). These were later moved to Petersburg and the Zamoskvorechie neighbourhood of Moscow, and part of the Kuznetsky quarter was given to Count Vorontsov. Vorontsov erected several buildings there that became occupied by shops dealing in cosmetics and luxury goods and later by hairdressers, confectioners and jewellers. Kuznetsky Most became a fashion street in a real sense in the latter half of the eighteenth century, when Catherine the Great issued an edict granting trade privileges to foreigners. It was then that French merchants began moving in. Thus the specific character of the street as a centre of fashionable commerce was established rather early. 'In the eighteenth century Kuznetsky Most was already being frequented by strolling dandies and elegantly dressed women who left behind enormous sums in the cash boxes of the enterprising Frenchmen and Frenchwomen.' (Geinike et al. 1991 [1917]: 37).

Most of the clientele for luxury goods were Russian nobles. Much like the Americans (Gilbert 2000: 18), Russian aristocrats regularly travelled to Paris to consume fashionable clothes, but also French urban culture, manners and lifestyle. This was the typical situation in nineteenth-century culture, when Russian fashion looked to France and ladies subscribed to fashion magazines from Paris. Thus the distinctive tendencies in the Russian cultural reception of France were already formed in that period. Moscow fashion has typically positioned itself as provincial in regard to Paris. This has translated into an exaggerated readiness to copy the latest trends, intensified by the fear of inevitable delay, and with the front lines often finding themselves to be fashion victims. The cult of Parisian things was based on the notion of superior craftsmanship and sophisticated French taste. However, popular Russian concepts of luxury visibly differed from those of the French. The difference had several implications: First, Moscow ladies demanded more conspicuous, instantly recognizable chic. The Parisian fashion sometimes seemed too restrained to them. Yet, at the same time, conservative Russian morals did not accept the signs of sexual liberation in Parisian fashion; in 1910, when the famous poetess Anna Akhmatova brought Paul Poiret dresses from Paris, it was a scandal, as they were to be worn without a corset. Finally, the dominant Russian concept of luxury implied a 'total look' in which the ensemble and all its details were colour-coordinated, whereas other parameters – the fabric, cut and style – were considered less important.

In the nineteenth century even the vocabulary of fashion consisted entirely of French and English words. At times this language became the subject of literary debates, and the position of writers on the use of foreign words often directly echoed both their own fashion preferences and their literary views. Those who favoured French fashion were regarded as Westernized advocates of freethinking cosmopolitanism and pernicious liberal ideas that were polluting the pure Russian language. The literary debate 'On the Old and New Style' repeatedly resorted to parallels between clothing and language. French fashion during this period was frequently associated with loose morals, hence the following passage from Griboedov's famous comedy *Woe from Wit* (1823–4):

> The French! With all their fashion shops and streets,
> Their books and writers and artists,
> They break our hearts; they make our money fly,
> I wonder why
> God will not save us from their needles, pins,
> Their bonnets, hats and all the other things. (Griboedov 1993)

These lines are spoken by the landowner Famusov, who is reprimanding his daughter Sophia for her love of French novels and fashion: 'You read those silly books at night. And that's the fruit of it' (Griboedov 1993). His thinking is typical of the later Slavophiles, who regarded the dominance of French fashion as indicating a lack of patriotism. In the eyes of most Muscovites, however, Paris was always the ideal capital city of fashion, the Mount Olympus of nobility and style, and Kuznetsky Most was a French embassy and oasis in downtown Moscow. This attitude was so deeply entrenched that it was only briefly shaken by the war with Napoleon in 1812.

Before Napoleon's army entered Moscow, the military commander of the city, Count Rastopchin, abolished French businesses. The merchants themselves, however, did not abandon Kuznetsky Most, and as the great fire of 1812 raged the invading French soldiers hastened there to protect their compatriots' fashion boutiques (Fedosiuk 1991: 61). When the French left, commerce resumed as before, and as early as 1814 the journal *Russkii vestnik* (*Russian Messenger*) was complaining that 'once again the rule of French fashion is firmly entrenched on Kuznetsky Most.' An 1826 Moscow guidebook declared:

> From the very beginning of this street, that is, from Lubyanka to Petrovka, you will see on either side an unbroken row of shops with different goods, above all couturiers … From early morning to late evening you will see a multitude of carriages here, nearly all of them loaded down with purchases. And the prices? Everything is three times its worth, but our fashion plates don't care: 'bought on Kuznetsky Most' lends everything a special charm. (quoted by Fedosiuk 1991: 62)

Thus it is not surprising that already by 1833 signs in French that had been banned in 1812 were everywhere, and once again the poets had ample reason to complain:

> The smiths on Blacksmiths Bridge left long ago
> It's now a motley corner of Paris
> That enserfs Russian ladies
> And levies on them quit-rent. (Viazemskii 1986: 350)

In the latter half of the nineteenth century English, German and Italian shops joined the French on Kuznetsky Most. Among the most important may be mentioned Louis Morais, Rallé, Datsiaro, Fulda, Brocard and Fabergé. These names were uttered one after another like a magic incantation or an alphabet of consumption (Slonov 2003 [1914]: 350–1). Not unexpectedly, it was in the neighbourhood of Kuznetsky Most that a new type of store – the passage or arcade – now began to spring up. As the feminist historian and cinema scholar Anne Friedberg has argued, passage through the new arcades of nineteenth-century Europe generated new subjective effects for men and women alike in changing urban landscapes (Friedberg 1994: 32–8). This new visual paradigm stood an excellent chance of also developing in the streets of the Russian capital. The first passage in Moscow was opened on Kuznetsky Most by General Tatishchev, it was followed in 1840 by the Golitsinsky Gallery between Petrovka and Neglinka. Behind the Maly Theatre in the nineteenth century were also the Golofteevsky Passage and the Aleksandrovsky Passage. The Solodovnikovsky Passage was named after its owners, but originally it was called Bon Marché by analogy with the famous Paris store. Close by on Pushechnaya street was the Dzhamgarovsky Passage.

The first department stores began to appear only at the end of the nineteenth century. The Scottish merchants Muir and Mirrielees opened their store in 1885. The State Universal Market or *GUM* rose alongside the Kremlin across Red Square between 1887 and 1893 (it comprised more than 1,000 shops). On Petrovka the Petrovsky Passage was completed in 1906 and later was transformed into a department store. Thus the evolution of new forms of retail fashion very much paralleled European trends. By the end of the nineteenth century banks and bookstores also began opening on Kuznetsky Most. Quite understandably, this historical parallelism with European tendencies was broken during the Russian Revolution. 'In the 1905 and 1907 Revolutions this entire bourgeois neighborhood remained a bastion of counter-revolution. After October 1917 foreign firms quickly disappeared from Kuznetsky Most' (Fedosiuk 1991: 63).

Yet despite all these changes Kuznetsky Most somehow managed to preserve its role as a street of fashion. Soviet clothing stores sprang up in place of the former stylish shops. The pre-revolutionary Lyamina shop was replaced by Leningradodezhda (Leningrad Clothing) and then by Torgsin (an abbreviation of the Russian '*Torgovlya s inostrantsami*' – Trade with Foreigners). Torgsin stores began appearing in Moscow in 1930. Carrying foreign goods but accessible to everyone, 'they were elegant, fashionable stores, unusual for Moscow that had become rather impoverished in the years of the First Five-Year Plan. They sold rare goods, which had not been seen for years, things, some of them even imported. People would say of a well-dressed woman that she probably bought everything at a Torgsin' (Fedosiuk 2004: 149).

The Torgsin grocery stores stocked delicacies; manufactured goods in others included clothing, fabrics, footwear and some second-hand goods. Torgsin purchasing centres were scattered throughout Moscow. The Torgsins used a system of vouchers, known in the parlance of the time as 'bonds' (*bony*), which could buy goods in exchange for valuables and silver. This system was subsequently employed in the well-known Beriezka stores, where beginning in the Brezhnev period fashionable goods could be purchased with vouchers and foreign currency. The cult of Western goods among *fartsovshchiks* was further promoted by the mythological desirability of Beriezka products. This fact testifies to the continuing functions of exotic goods as indicators of imperial luxury. The desire of Asya Lacis to possess an Eskimo coat is fully inscribed in this semiotic frame; by contrast, Russian everyday clothes are traditionally regarded as common, uninteresting and of little value.

The Torgsin on Kuznetsky Most was later replaced by the 'Goods for Women' (Tovary dlya zhenshchin) store, opposite which, in the building that had earlier housed the fashionable James Shanks, was the Svetlana shop. Thus the fashionable profile of the street was preserved on a broad scale, and it came as no surprise that the 'House of Fashion' (Dom Modeley), the one and only Soviet fashion mecca, should continue the tradition by making its home on Kuznetsky Most. Even before the end of the war, in 1944, it was opened by Soviet government decree at No. 14, a building dating from the early twentieth century designed by the famous architect Erikhson. Because of its location it immediately became known as 'the House of Fashion on Kuznetsky'. Thus was the former glory of the fashion street appropriated and exploited by the Soviet regime.

The first fashion show at the House took place in 1945. Among the participating creators of the collection was the elderly Russian designer Nadezhda Lamanova, whose career dated to before the Revolution. Previously No. 14 had housed the Mikhailov Furriery and a small skinnery, the only industrial enterprise on Kuznetsky Most. When the House of Fashion moved in, the luxurious interior décor of the building, including its decorative mouldings, marble staircases, and carved doors with gilded doorknobs, was preserved. Here in this bourgeois setting fashion shows were held three times daily, some of them open to the public and others closed to all but the Party elite and privileged clients: cosmonauts, actors, writers and so on. During the perestroika years Raisa Gorbacheva was a regular customer. Here, for example, she ordered a custom-made sura coat.[6] As the flagship state-owned fashion enterprise, the House of Fashion was said to be 'all-union' in scope. In addition to organizing lectures and seminars on fashion, it developed clothing lines for some 300 Soviet garment factories. For many years Tatyana Osmerkina was the chief designer, and it was here that the well-known designer Slava Zaitsev began his career in the business.

The House of Fashion models enjoyed particular fame during the Soviet period (Sazheneva 2004). Regina Zbarskaya, Mila Romanovskaya, Valentina Yashina and Tatyana Soloviova were considered the most beautiful women in Moscow. They had a bohemian lifestyle and were courted by celebrities. Tatyana Soloviova (now Mikhalkova), for example, married the famous movie director Nikita Mikhalkov and now heads 'Russian Silhouette', a philanthropic contest for young designers. The models participated in Soviet fashion shows abroad, visiting Hollywood in the 1950s. Such trips were extremely rare at the time and were invariably under KGB surveillance. The biographies of many of these beauties were rather sensational. The most famous of them, the 'Soviet Sophia Loren' Regina Zbarskaya, repeatedly attempted to commit suicide, succeeding on the third try. Some of them later emigrated. Mila Romanovskaya, the blond with the Russian braid who modelled the famous 'Russia' dress, went abroad. She angered the Soviet authorities by posing for *Vogue* on Red Square in slacks with her back turned to portraits of the Party leaders. During the socialist period the House on Kuznetsky also served as a research centre boasting a large library on the history of fashion, and it regularly published journals containing patterns. The designers there collaborated with art historians from VIALEGPROM (the Institute of Light Industry), which was especially dedicated to fashion.

Unfortunately, neither VIALEGPROM nor the House of Fashion has survived. The former was closed in 2000, and a sauna and casino appeared in its place. The latter shut down in 2002 and the building was auctioned off. Its archive, library and clothing collection (including the famous 'Russia' dress) disappeared, probably forever. The only reminder of the old House of Fashion is a small memorial plaque on the building, which now houses the Podium Concept clothing store, a boutique carrying eighty-eight different popular Western brands. However, the prices there are meant mainly for the new Russians – T-shirts are $70 and up, jeans around $300. Customers are few, and the interior of the store is ostentatious and pompous. The latest gossip about the development of Kuznetsky Most suggests that Harvey Nichols, extremely popular among rich Russians in London, will soon occupy the big building of the Technical library next to Podium.

These changes reflect the characteristic tendencies in Moscow's fashion geography. State institutions of Soviet fashion such as the House of Fashion or VIALEGPROM have not survived at all. What remains in the centre of the city are for the most part expensive stores dealing in luxury goods whose price is driven up further by high rents. Stores with a cheaper range of goods are disappearing or moving away from downtown. The Svetlana store was reconstructed and transformed into yet another multibrand centre. A few years ago, the Natasha store on Pushkin Square also disappeared and was replaced by a Benetton shop. At present Kuznetsky Most is dominated by foreign boutiques – Valentino, Versace, Ferré, Fabergé and Men's Merit. This is reminiscent of the situation in the nineteenth century, when fashionable foreign shops dominated the district. Perhaps the opening of new fashionable stores on the street heralds a return to its origins as an island of tradition in a sea of change.

The example of Kuznetsky Most shows that 'the functions of place on the macro-level, that is, on the level of the city district, have essentially been preserved' (Kagan 2004: 253). As Mikaella Kagan's analysis indicates, this is characteristic of the nature of place in Moscow as a whole, which has been surprisingly conservative despite radical upheavals during the transition to socialism and the perestroika period: 'The city that was built over the course of centuries turned out to be much more stable. All projects for creating the "city of the future" proved to be utopias … it turned out to be significantly easier to change the function of place on the microlevel than on the macrolevel' (Kagan 2004: 253). As we have seen, despite the changes of individual stores and institutions typical of the transitional period from socialism to capitalism, the general function of Kuznetsky Most as a fashion street has been sustained.

On the macro-level, the role of downtown Moscow (the historical 'White City') as an area in which fashionable stores are concentrated also remains. Within the city centre, however, a differentiation is underway between streets and individual large stores, which reflects not only cultural traditions but also a new balance of forces in the fashion market. Present-day economic geography has resulted from a partitioning of the city among large corporations representing global brands in Russia. Thus Stoleshnikov Pereulok is dominated by fashionable boutiques belonging to the Jamilco corporation: Chaumet, Hermès, Burberry, Escada, Salvatore Ferragamo and Christian Dior. Headed by the Syrian businessman Haled Jamil, the corporation also owns flagship avant-garde fashion store James on Tverskaya Street, which carries designer clothes by Ann Demeulemeester, Martin Margiela, Yohji Yamamoto, Jean Paul Gaultier, Shirin Guild and Sir Paul Smith. The store is frequently the site of fashion photography exhibitions and fashion parties.

Another major player on the fashion retail market is the Bosco di Ciliegi corporation led by Mikhail Kusnirovich, which imports brands such as Kenzo, MaxMara, Marina Rinaldi, Mariella Burani, Moschino, Etro, Nina Ricci and Lacroix. Bosco di Ciliegi caters for upper middle-class clients. The corporation markets itself as an autonomous empire with its own currency, the 'boscar'. Prices in all of its stores are in boscars, which were formerly indexed to the dollar and now to the euro. The geographical expansion of Bosco di Ciliegi is also very visible in Petersburg, where the corporation has recently promoted the 'Bosco district' – a whole block of shops in Nevsky Prospect.

Bosco di Ciliegi dominates the Petrovsky Passage, one of the oldest Moscow department stores located next to Kuznetsky Most. There the corporation conducts many of its PR events – parties celebrating the opening of new boutiques, photography exhibitions, and fashion shows. It designed the uniform for the Russian Winter Olympics team in Salt Lake City, and now markets a line of sporting goods under the Bosco Sport brand. Mikhail Kusnirovich is well known among the beautiful people of the capital as the sponsor of the annual 'Cherry Forest' classical music festival, and his company also patronizes a number of theatrical productions. Such events are aimed to create the image of a culturally sophisticated corporation. The PR-strategy of this corporation is structured around the retro vision of a patriarchal respectable well-to-do family, restoring to today the 'good old times' of bourgeois Russia.

Kusnirovich's latest much-noted business deal was the acquisition of a majority interest in GUM (the Main Department Store) for 100 million dollars. The intermediate seller was the Moscow businessman Lev Khasis, famous for his masterful and lucrative transactions. GUM, located on the site of the former Upper Row on Red Square, has long been a symbol of Russian fashion (Figure 9.1). Built as a commercial arcade around a central fountain, it was always a pilgrim destination for shoppers from other parts of Russia and for foreign tourists. In the Soviet period the store featured a studio, organized fashion shows and published its own fashion magazine, and the stairways were lined by people looking for scarce goods. The famous 'special section 200' provided services only to important clients (like communist bosses and their wives). Now this section works for Bosco di Ciliegi privileged clients. Kusnirovich will probably use GUM as a pilot venture to attract new tenants.

The Crocus Corporation headed by Aras Agalarov is also rated highly among noticeable players on the Moscow luxury scene. Their most famous project is Crocus City Mall, the 'tropical park of boutiques' on the Moscow Ring Road. The company constantly buys new licences to sell luxury brands, but its special profile is organizing commercial exhibitions in the Crocus Expo. A recent event was the glamorous 'Millionaire fair-2005' – the annual exhibition of luxurious goods. Russia is home to 33 billionaires according to Forbes magazine[7] and 88,000 dollar millionaires, according to a report by Merrill Lynch investment bank and CapGemini consulting firm, so the idea was to show these clients what to buy and where. The prime concern of organizers was to stop the export of clients, to make the rich spend their money in Russia. How does Moscow fashion business respond to this challenge? Does it influence the local fashion geography? The final section of the chapter aims to provide some answers.

Mercury: a Case Study

In 1870, the famous Moscow patrons of the arts Pavel and Sergey Tretyakov purchased a parcel of land between Nikolskaya Street and Teatralny Proezd. There

Figure 9.1 The GUM department store in Moscow. © Alexander Vainshtein 2005.

between two arches they built a street that quickly filled with clothing stores and antique and jewellery shops. The Moscow Merchant Bank also relocated there. The street became a fashionable and popular upper-class gathering spot, and until 1917 boasted a concentration of stylish Moscow shops. During the Soviet period the stores were closed and the Proezd itself was merely an insignificant connecting street. In 2001 it was restored and soon became home to fashion houses such as Armani, Dolce and Gabbana, Prada, Gucci, Tod's and Roberto Cavalli; Tiffany and Co., Baccarat crystal, Frette linens and Graf print designs; and Bentley, Ferrari and Maserati dealerships (Figure 9.2).

Now all the stores in Tretyakovsky Proezd belong to Mercury, one of the most active retailers in luxury fashion (Figure 9.3). Named after the Roman god of commerce, it was founded in 1993 and is headed by Leonid Fridlyand and Leonid Strunin, businessmen who in 2002 were on *Time* magazine's list of 'the 25 most influential people in fashion'. They are considered among the most successful businessmen in Russia, and in Moscow circles are familiarly referred to by their nicknames as 'the Lenchiks.' Graduates of the Moscow Institute of Transport Engineering, they began their business career in 1993 with the Chopard boutique. Eight years later they opened the '2001 Street of Boutiques'. The turnover of certain brands in Tretyakovsky Proezd shops approaches 10 to 15 per cent of total world sales. Thus the Gucci boutique in Moscow is second only to the one in New York,

Figure 9.2 The gates of Tretyakovsky Proezd, Moscow's 'Street of Boutiques' © Alexander Vainshtein 2005.

Figure 9.3 Advertisement for Mercury fashion and luxury goods conglomerate in front of the Kremlin. © Alexander Vainshtein 2005.

and the Dolce and Gabbana store is second only to the flagship store in Milan. The Tretyakovsky Proezd Prada leads in sales per square metre.

Standing out among the rest is the Giorgio Armani boutique – the first Armani store in Moscow and Russia and with 685.5 square metres the largest Giorgio Armani in Europe. The three-storey building designed by Claudio Silvestrin, the architect of the Armani stores in Milan, Paris and Tokyo, conforms to the sparse, ascetic, unadorned Armani style and atmosphere. The interior is finished in cream-coloured stone that contrasts with the dark wooden furniture and brass clothes racks.

The scale of Mercury's PR campaigns is impressive. Its billboards are everywhere in downtown Moscow. Right near the Duma the shell of the demolished Hotel Moscow is adorned with a gigantic Mercury advertisement for golden Rolex watches evidently intended to make customers of the legislators. Even the ancient building of the Historical Museum and the Kremlin towers seem to be microscopic in the shade of this megaposter. Most of the glossies carry advertisements for goods sold in Mercury stores, not to mention the hidden advertising. Periodically Mercury launches huge PR campaigns (Koroleva and Zakharova 2001). Thus to mark the opening of the Tiffany and Co. boutique a charity concert was organized featuring Vanessa May, and recently with Rado watches Mercury co-sponsored the Kremlin Cup tennis tournament. Judging by the corporation's journal *Mercury* (which, incidentally, is published in Monte Carlo), the company has boldly assumed the role of mediator between Russia and global luxury brands. Its advertising rhetoric transmits the discourse of the powerful imperial capital. One ad shows a Lamborghini photographed against the background of Moscow University's Stalinist skyscraper, and the caption describes the joy of possession: 'Even the endless Moscow autumn reflected in the tinted glass of a Lamborghini will pass like a single sunny moment' (*Mercury* 15, Fall 2005).

Aspiring to the role of guardian of the national heritage, in its advertising campaign Mercury openly invokes tradition by attempting to impart historical colour and nobility to the image of Tretyakovsky Proezd. The architecture of the street deliberately echoes the Old Moscow style. Lancet arches reminiscent of the

Kremlin gates border the little street and give it a touch of decorative theatricality. Here and there are reminders of bygone times. Visible to the right of the entrance arch from the Metropol Hotel is a fragment of a landmark tower from old Kitay-gorod, and to the left is a tower restored in the 1990s. The reduction of the past to a representation organized as a decorative display is very visible here, confirming Georg Simmel's concept of ruins as symbols to fix our shaken identity in a rapidly transforming world (Simmel 1996: I, 232). But although all the boutiques there partake of this local colour to allude to cultural continuity and ancient national traditions, the obvious paradox is that not a single Russian brand is available in Tretyakovsky Proezd – everything on display there is foreign. Russian designers are rarely represented in the luxury clothing stores, and in downtown Moscow their names adorn very few fashion sites. This reflects the current reality, for most affluent clients are reluctant to pay enormous sums for Russian-designed clothes, which are hardly to be found at all among the assortments of Mercury, Jamilco, Bosco di Ciliegi, Crocus and other major retail corporations.

Ordinary Muscovites humorously refer to the street as the 'Tretyakov Gallery'. The play on words here is based not only on the Tretyakov surname, but also contains a subtle allusion: the goods displayed in the windows of the street can only be viewed like pictures in a museum, for they are obviously beyond the means of the average consumer. Most of the customers in this 'gallery', of course, are super-rich oligarchs, and it is to them that the goods are meant to appeal, consisting exclusively of luxury items that can serve as status symbols. 'We want our customers to feel like members of a kind of club,' says Nadezhda Pobedina, the coordinating architect of the complex. 'We tried to create an ensemble with large display windows and passages allowing easy movement from one boutique to another. We didn't have any fixed strategy, only the desire to create in Moscow something like the Via della Spiga' (Messana 2004: 26).

Whether or not the designers managed to clone the Via della Spiga is truly debatable, but the idea of creating a club has clearly been successful. The provocative luxury there is inaccessible to middle-class consumers and does not attract tourists, so in the daytime the shops in Tretyakovsky Proezd are usually empty. Their 'own' customers do not begin arriving until evening, and then the narrow little lane is often full of Mercedes and similar cars. Occasionally the entire street is sealed off in connection with some PR initiative, at which times invitations are sent out to loyal customers in the Moscow glamour set, and it really does function as a closed club. One such event, for example, was the 'Celebrity Award' contest in 2005, when the perennial heroine of the society columns Kseniya Sobchak (the Moscow 'It' girl, who admits her role model is Paris Hilton) won a diamond-studded Jacob and Co. watch. Photos of this beau monde appeared in the glamour magazines that regularly carry advertisements for Mercury products, in effect triggering a trickle-down effect. What is perhaps specific to Tretyakovsky Proezd here is that the geographic and cultural boundaries of this luxury territory coincide to create a perfect 'time-space compression', accompanied, however, in line with the arguments of David Harvey, by a typical crisis of representation (Harvey 1989: 262). Symbols of the imperial past, the social elite and luxury fashion function in a very compact space, forming a spectacular and implicitly dramatic landscape of consumption.

TsUM: Mercury's Experimental Ground

The Central Department Store, known by its Russian initials as TsUM, was founded by the Scottish entrepreneurs Archibald Mirrielees and Andrew Muir (Pitcher 1993) (Figure 9.4). They started off with a small wholesale shop on Kuznetsky Most specializing in women's hats and gloves, and in 1885 opened Moscow's first department store. Located near the Bolshoy Theatre, Muir and Mirrielees quickly became one of Moscow's largest and most profitable such enterprises. At first it operated on a wholesale basis, but it gradually became obvious that retail was more profitable, and a few years later the store switched over. Quickly gaining popularity, Muir and Mirrielees and was soon on a par with London stores such as Whiteley or Bon Marché in Paris. Following the commercial style of major West European department stores, it used set prices, and soon became famous for its catalogues (which were distributed for free throughout European Russia), luxury goods and special services. It even boasted a darkened room where women could observe the

Figure 9.4 The TsUM department store in Moscow. © Alexander Vainshtein 2005.

changing colours of their potential purchases under the gaslights of an imagined night-time street. Loyal customers included prominent figures such as the writer Anton Chekhov. Its commercial success was clouded in 1892 and 1900, however, by fires evidently started by envious rivals of the foreign firm and for a time business had to be conducted in neighbouring rented buildings.[8]

A new seven-storey building combining Gothic and Modern styles was erected on the site of the old one by the architect Roman Klein.[9] It was the first in Russia to use reinforced concrete, which was employed in the construction of multi-storey buildings in America. The store was not a skyscraper, but at that time seven storeys was considered tall, and because the walls could be made thinner, the new technology significantly increased floor space. Opened in 1908, by 1910 the new store had become the largest in Russia. By 1913 it boasted eighty departments selling not only fashionable women's couture and footwear, but also furniture, china, sporting goods, rugs and so on. Muir and Mirrielees' turnover and range of goods rivalled even Harrods. It featured innovations such as an information desk, a waiting room, a Moscow city information service and two customer elevators. The latter caused quite a sensation, for at that time elevators were extremely rare.

The opening of the new department store marked the peak of Muir and Mirrielees' glory. Besides the store on Teatralnaya square, it commissioned Klein to build the Furniture and Bronze Factory on Malaya Gruzinskaya (now the Rassvet Factory). After the 1917 Revolution, however, its fortunes began to decline. In December 1918 Izvestiia announced that the store had been nationalized and renamed 'Moskommuna – Department Store No. 1 of the Moscow Union of Trade Communities'. In January 1919, the last of the former directors Walter Philip, who had been working as an ordinary sales clerk for a token salary, was dismissed. It was also at this time that the sales personnel began to change. Two hundred members of the Communist Youth League came to work in the store, learning the rudiments of the business from former employees of Muir and Mirrielees. Renamed Mostorg in March 1922, it became one of the largest Soviet stores, and many factories produced goods exclusively for it. Eventually renamed TsUM, it became a typical Moscow department store, with queues of customers (enormously long ones for goods in short supply) and rude sales clerks. The clothing range catered to the unpampered consumer, for a significant percentage of shoppers came from other provincial Russian cities. Everybody enjoyed tasty ice cream in paper cups sold in TsUM, something people remember today with nostalgia. Moscow ladies visited TsUM mainly to buy small items, as in pleasant contrast to the overall meagre offerings the accessories department always carried a wide variety of buttons, zippers and other fasteners. As in the early days of Soviet egalitarian ideology, this commercial space was heralded for making international wares more available to middle-class consumers. Yet with the collapse of the Soviet Union, this egalitarianism has also vanished.

In 1992 TsUM was auctioned off, and in 2001 the successful banker Lev Khasis (the same person who had recently resold GUM to Bosco di Ciliegi) became head of the board of directors. During this intermediate period the store still catered to the middle class and was always crowded. In 2002, however, the situation changed radically when Khasis sold his controlling share of the stock to Mercury, which at the time had just opened the 'Street of Boutiques'. Mercury had planned to make TsUM more 'accessible' than Tretyakovsky Proezd, but the meaning of 'accessibility' differs significantly from the usual understanding of the concept. Thus Mercury's public relations agent Yana Stebleva declared that in contrast to Tretyakovsky Proezd, TsUM was intended for very different customers sharing only one thing in common, namely a decent monthly income by European standards – $1,000–6,000 (Lykova 2004). Only top managers in foreign-owned businesses in Moscow make that kind of money, however, whereas the average salary in the state sector of Russia as a whole is only $240.

Not surprisingly, after Mercury's very first reforms TsUM's customer base began to shrink significantly. Former shoppers coming upon $1,500 Tod's or Bottega Veneta handbags left the store in a state of shock. 'We are not permitted entry there any more', said A. Ju. Nurok, thus expressing the attitude of many Muscovites working in the state sector (Nurok 2005). Journalists tried in vain to comprehend what was going on. 'You speak of TsUM's "accessibility",' one of them asked Vittorio Radice, the man behind the future face of TsUM, 'The owners of Mercury told me the same thing last year before the renovated store opened, saying that TsUM would be more democratic than the Mercury shops on Tretyakovsky Proezd. But TsUM carries the very same luxury brands as they do. To whom is such a TsUM accessible?' (Gubskii 2005)

The final phase in restructuring the store began in 2005, when Mercury gave the project to the aforementioned Italian 'retail guru', Radice, making him the head of TsUM's board of consultants. He is also in charge of reorganizing Mercury's DLT store in St Petersburg, and his résumé includes the successful transformation of Selfridges on Oxford Street in London and the restructuring of the Shopper's Stop chain in Mumbai, India. In 2003–4 he was on the board of directors of the British company Marks and Spencer. His latest project is the reorganization of the famous La Rinascente in Milan. 'And now he is a shop czar in Moscow,' exulted the well-known fashion journalist Suzy Menkes (Menkes 2005), who always writes enthusiastically about the Lenchiks. It is not yet entirely clear, however, how Radice's ideas will go over in the Moscow context. His main concept – to return to department stores the powerful and positive energy of the traditional rural marketplace – worked excellently in Selfridges where he organized such events as 'Bollywood', a festival of Indian culture, at which shoppers were invited to sample Indian products and cuisine. In the Russian context, perhaps, this could incorporate the historic potential of street commerce. However, such a project is not likely to appeal to Moscow consumers. Rich ladies, as a rule, consider grocery shopping to be beneath them and send their drivers or maids to the market. They are more likely to associate a festive atmosphere in a store with sales or bonuses.

One indubitable success in this series of carnivalesque events was the 'War of the Goddesses' presented by the well-known Moscow transvestite conceptualist Vlad Mamyshev (a.k.a. Vladik Monroe), who did impersonations of Marilyn Monroe (his best-known role) and Elizabeth Taylor in what he called 'Vlad Monroe's personal cinematic museum'. The commercial was filmed in the new TsUM, and the two 'stars' gave previews of their eveningwear from fall and winter collections in Mercury stores. A more promising idea of Radice's, perhaps, is to bypass the buyers and allow the manufacturers to determine the range. Here he has recognized a very real problem in Moscow. In their attempt to cater to the female high-society and nightclub set, buyers mostly go for the glamorous and/or bohemian in a product line, rendering the overall profile of many brands practically unrecognizable. A case in point is Mango for young adults: because Moscow stores mainly stock the evening line, the space available for casual wear is significantly decreased. 'Minimalism is not for us,' explains head buyer and vice president of Mercury Alla Verber. 'When people walk into a store and don't see a particular item they immediately suspect that we are hiding it' (Goldstein Crowe 2005). It is precisely such a range that predominates in TsUM. Although among the most recent tone-setters there are brands such as Diane von Furstenberg, Laundry, and Armani Collezione, some encouraging attempts at change are already observable. The store now stocks British brands such as Matthew Williamson, Alexander McQueen and Luella. A 'Young Fashion' floor has just opened. However, no young shoppers are to be found there, not simply because only a young oligarch can afford a Harley Davidson, but also because the assortment is limited to the already familiar Prada Sport, Toy Go, Armani Jeans and the more democratic JLo by Jennifer Lopez. Potentially subversive brands, appealing to younger, more experimental consumers are excluded by the very concept of luxury retailing that caters to the establishment.

Mercury, however, has not limited its activities to reconstructing TsUM and the 'luxury street' in Tretyakovsky Proezd. Other prominent sites include the Moskva multibrand shop on Kutuzovsky Prospect and the Europa section of the Radisson SAS Slavjanskaya Hotel. One of the company's recent ambitious projects is the construction of a 'luxury village' in Barvikha. Barvikha, a village located on the legendary Rublevo-Uspensky Highway in the western outskirts of Moscow, has long been a prestigious area of country homes favoured by high government officials and the business elite. In recent years the new Russians living in Rublevka have become the heroes of mass culture in, for example, Oksana Robsky's series of popular novels devoted to them, or the recent TV series 'Rublevka live'. The block of shops in Barvikha is meant to become a 'rural' twin to Tretyakovsky Proezd. It is called Luxury Village and will cater to 'paysannes' who can conveniently shop for their diamond necklaces close to their villas. The geographic expansion of Mercury thus continues.

Mercury's fashion strategy fully reflects economic development in Russia, specifically the first, 'wild' stage of capitalism in which the focus is on ostentatious consumption of glamorous luxury goods. Alternative or subversive fashion ideas are not welcome. The capital-city and imperial discourse and the national heritage are employed exclusively to serve the PR image of the company as a kind of 'megabrand' or state within the state. In Russian society luxury clothing has long played an important compensatory role, often serving as a more significant part of the individual's image than other status symbols such as automobile, address or vacation destination. It shoulders almost the entire burden of the need to attain social distinction through acquisition. This concept quite neatly fits the current striving for glamour in contemporary Moscow. For the moment the performance of luxury fashion and the production of urban space in the historical centre is dominated by just such a discourse of triumphant consumerism. Dress thus continues to function as the principal indicator of affluence and success. This is a long familiar phenomenon consistent with the 'conspicuous consumption' that Thorstein Veblen regarded as symptomatic of the first developmental phase of capitalist society.

However, Moscow also remains a city of intense social contrasts, and the widening gap between rich and poor, characteristic of a transitional economy, is fully reflected in the structure of shopping routes. While the centre of the city is being transformed into the zone of luxury shopping, the traditional low-price urban markets are being pressed out into suburban areas. A 'civilization of kiosks' has spread all over the capital catering to the needs of the poor. Quality clothes shops for middle-class clients are still very rare. And although the rich routinely overpay in the more expensive boutiques, the psychological patterns of consumption in new luxury shops are largely defined by the Soviet past. Clients are wary that the 'new' collections are in fact of the past season and often question the authenticity of the famous brands. This suspicious attitude, going back to the culture of urban markets, is still typical for the consumers of luxury goods.

The partitioning of the city among mega-retail corporations echoes the 'wild privatization' in the energy sector of the Russian economy. Yet the transformative potential of globalization at this stage does not fully suppress the existence of competing local fashion cultures. The consumption of fashion in Moscow fully reflects the peculiarities of a transitional multifaceted economy with divergent developing sectors. The capitalist segment of the market is represented by the active politics of global brands in Moscow, while the system of state shops, reminiscent of the socialist past, is almost ruined and exists mainly in the small provincial towns. Flexible urban markets and kiosks, successfully integrating into capitalism, function by the laws of a Third World economy.

The transition to capitalism in Moscow's fashion market has thus been far from seamless. Disconnections between local fashion cultures had to be experienced both by rich and poor. The restructuring of urban space brought dramatic changes in the everyday life of ordinary people – young and old – who suddenly found themselves living in a different city, without their local shops. Most vulnerable groups – 'the ordinary practitioners of the city' (De Certeau 1988: 93) – had to abandon their habitual routes. These changes at the level of the pragmatic use of the city are perhaps not so visible, but they do matter.

The architects of the new 'luxury' zones successfully exploit the warm emotional atmosphere of the old historical districts. The persistence of urban experience in fashion streets like Kuznetsky Most strongly relies on conservative 'memories of place'. Even the newly reconstructed fashion districts like Tretyakovsky Proezd demonstrate this deep need to be reinscribed in national tradition, even in the form of gimmick. Moscow seems to be a suitable place for the production of new mythologies: its rich experience of political changes and intermediary East–West geographical position makes it an ideal experimental ground for various cultural games. The resulting uneasy balance might reflect postmodernism's romance of the palimpsest. But, as we know, the discourse of fashion implies temporality, irony and the imperative for change, and Moscow's fashion world is as much about the future as the past. No doubt a new Moscow Diary has yet to be written.

Notes

1. The author would like to thank Christopher Breward, David Gilbert, Bruce Grant and Nina Poussenkova for their helpful comments.
2. Other oppositions of the two cities are structured as Moscow/country life/feminine/ warmth – St Petersburg/urban life/masculine/coldness (Slonov 2003: 75–8).
3. A real conversation overheard at a Moscow street market, 10 October 2005.
4. This is a play on words: 'Luzha' means 'puddle, pool' in Russian, but it was derived as short from the historic name of sports stadium 'Luzhniki', which thus came to mean 'mess'.
5. 'Shoob-tour' is an unintended play on the more accessible 'shop-tour'.
6. Sura is a kind of naturally brown karakul.
7. *Forbes* magazine (No. 2, May 2004) also says that the majority of Russian millionaires live in Moscow and by this parameter this is the highest concentration of wealth in one city in the world.
8. An analogous recent example is the 'sudden' fire that destroyed Bauklotz, one of the first German-owned household goods stores in Moscow in 1993. History tends to repeat itself ... but Mercury was careful to insure the TsUM building and the surrounding construction site.
9. Klein also designed the Museum of the Visual Arts in Moscow.

–10–

Shaping the Fashion City

Master Plans and Pipe Dreams in the Post-War West End of London

Bronwen Edwards

In 1945, London was faced with the task of rebuilding not only its war-damaged fabric but also its position in the changed national and global map of fashionable consumption. The city was ripe for redevelopment and there were a large number of competing visions for its future, within which fashion held a precarious position. The priority of London's retailers and fashion houses concentrated in London's West End was to reopen for business. They valued the West End in its current form, cherishing the reputation that was built within this historic framework. Yet there were others who had plans for the city's built fabric, its street networks and its future identity. A new generation of architect-planners installed at County Hall dreamed of a modern, planned metropolis, where civic spaces would triumph over consumption practices. They wished to replace the tangle of congested streets, the West End's lifeblood, with efficient urban motorways. Property developers were also an increasing force in post-war rebuilding, ensuring a prominent role for the commercial in central London, where there was much money to be made. These men were much more interested in maximizing floor space in towering new offices, than in the fashionable consumption taking place in the ground floors of the West End's buildings. This was an area that had been built up piecemeal along the historic footprints of its streets, characterized by gradual change and the fluidity of its shopping routes. The West End *had* been subject to significant changes before: the building and rebuilding of Regent Street, for example (Hobhouse 1975: Rappaport 2002). However, the current proposals were potentially on a much more dramatic scale. This was surely a moment when London as a fashion city, in the sense that it had hitherto existed, was about to change.

This chapter is intended not only as an exploration of post-war London as a fashion city, but as a way of writing a new kind of planning history, which draws it closer to theories of the development of mass consumer society and accounts of metropolitan consumption (Breward 1999, 2004; Rappaport 2000). The history of the post-war metropolis has frequently been told in terms of the modernist vision and the new social agenda of housing, greenbelts and the New Town, which were indeed its initial stated priorities (Porter 1994; Mellor 1997; Matless 1998). It is an account that has charted the failure of modern state planning to fulfil these dreams in the post-war decades, and its eventual replacement with Thatcherite, profit-orientated development of the 1980s. This chapter argues, through a study of the fashionable consumption cultures of the West End, that there is a more nuanced story to be told about these efforts to reconstruct the face of the metropolis.

It is a planning history that is interested in the planning imagination as much as the planning process, and in the un-built as much as the built, responding to Mort's call to abandon the exclusive focus on planning process (2004). It is the foregrounding of the relationship between planning vision and the built fabric of the city that allows an examination of shifting attitudes towards fashionable consumption and appropriate urban aesthetics in the West End. The chapter uncovers the divergent visions for the post-war West End by identifying the tensions between urban planning, architecture and consumer culture that were played out on Britain's most famous shopping streets. It is a story of the 'problem' of the fashion city, specifically the difficulties that 'modernist' top-down planning had in dealing with ephemeral, fashionable and distinctively metropolitan cultures of consumption. It discusses planners' struggles to hide, to control and finally to accommodate those cultures, and to reconcile them with the other characteristics of the modern city: property, commerce, and the civic. It thus addresses a key absence in existing planning histories, which have inadequately addressed the issue of consumption in their studies of cities in an age of the growth of mass consumption and consumerist values. It also extends the recent theoretical work within architectural history beyond its preoccupation with the texts of Loos and Le Corbusier, and with the white-rendered surfaces of inter-war modernism (Wigley 1995), situating the examination of modernism's denied 'other' in the post-war urban shopping landscape, and embedding it in the materiality of London's architecture.

The planning of the West End is tracked chronologically, starting with the period of 'reconstructive modernism' between the 1940s and early 1960s, when state planners such as Patrick Abercrombie sought to reshape London. This was a time when the problem of fashionable consumption, and indeed the problem of the West End as a central hub, became apparent. By the late 1950s, however, London was experiencing a new era of self-consciously metropolitan master planning. Plans were concerned with specific shopping streets and hubs such as Oxford Street, Regent Street and Piccadilly Circus, which also had implications for the whole West End. This period was characterized by a highly vocal battle for London between planners and developers. There was an emerging presence of the consumer in the proposals, who, given the world's eyes were now on the 'Swinging London' of fashion, boutiques and consumerism, it was increasingly hard to ignore. However, it is shown that the planners still fundamentally misunderstood how London's fashionable consumption actually worked: its architectures, street cultures and networks. The chapter ends by identifying the rise of a new approach to urban planning by the early 1970s with schemes such as that for Covent Garden. This new approach took more account of historic textures, existing character and communities, and explicitly accommodated the small businesses that comprised an important part of London's West End. It also signalled a more fluid, permeable understanding of the city's fabric and systems, allowing for a more flexible framework for the cultures that it housed. In short, whilst the research initially suggests a story of a significant *absence* of the fashionable consumer in the planning of the post-war metropolis, in line with the silences of the existing narrative, the chapter in fact uncovers a shifting response of planners and architects between the 1940s and 1970s to the growth of mass consumer society, and particularly to its increasingly high profile and concentrated metropolitan expression in central London.

'Rebuilding Britain'

The war years had given London a new 'architecture of destruction' (*Architectural Review*, 7 July 1941: 25), an architecture of smoke, rubble and shards from blown-out display windows. This dismal urban landscape had been impressed on the public imagination by a barrage of press photographs of bombed streets and buildings. In *Vogue*, blitzed London provided the backdrop for a series of iconic photographs by Cecil Beaton, with fashion emerging defiant and purposeful like a phoenix from the ashes. *The Architectural Review*'s photographer captured a typical scene in Oxford Street, 'the pinnacled façade of a Victorian store smeared with black by flames the firemen are still playing on' (*Architectural Review*, 7 July 1941: 27). At Oxford Street's Bourne and Hollingsworth, retailers were photographed in the act of rescuing a mannequin from the shattered display window (Figure 10.1). Yet London's iconic shops and shopping streets, located in the fashionable heart of the West End, were all too often under-represented in the roll calls of lost buildings regularly published in the professional architectural periodical press. Compared with Wren and Hawksmoor churches, historic parliamentary, business and legal buildings, even the most famous stores lacked the required architectural gravitas, and were tainted with associations of femininity and fashionability, long problematic for the architectural establishment. Yet these places remained an emotive element of this architecture of destruction, symbolic of London's urban pleasures, proudly fashionable displays and the independent spirit of this nation of shopkeepers. This part of the West End had long been a well-established, successful and thriving hub of fashionable consumption, pulling visitors from all over the country and beyond (Breward 1999; Rappaport 2000; Edwards 2003, 2005). Photographs of the West End appeared frequently in the popular press during the war years, and found a place in subsequent popular mythologies of the city's spirit. Such images stirred deep passions about the vulnerable historic metropolis, but they were also a powerful impetus for change, as soon as there was an opportunity.

Figure 10.1 The damaged windows of Bourne and Hollingsworth, Oxford Street in September 1940, City of Westminster Archive, T138(32).

While the bomb damage sustained in the area was only partial, photographs like these also drew attention to a much longer-term decay. Oxford Street had long enjoyed a reputation as a 'ladies' paradise' (*London: A Combined Guidebook and Atlas* 1937: 114), with a concentrated stretch of famous shops including Selfridges, Bourne and Hollingsworth, Waring and Gillow, Peter Robinson, Marshall and Snelgrove, D. H. Evans and John Lewis, in addition to the many chain stores, small independent shops and cafes. Before the war it had been known as a modern, fashionable and spectacular street, where department store owners' tastes and architects' flair were given the freest reign by regulators. Yet central London had seen little comprehensive redevelopment in the inter-war period, and for several years after the war building licences were still enormously difficult to obtain. Seen with the eye of the architect, planner or developer, Oxford Street was a shabby patchwork of shops, ranging from florid Victorian department stores to the inter-war chains with their cheap-and-cheerful vitrolite façades. None of this looked fashionable any longer, and while there were obviously other priorities during wartime, there was now a clear sense that this was a city ready for a new set of clothes. By 1945, the pace was gathering: West End streets were peppered with hoardings and temporary shop buildings, pointing to the future. Many were anxious that the opportunity should not be lost.

Many commentators have drawn attention to the development of a new broadly based interest in the future of Britain, and specifically London, in the 1940s (Gold 1997; Mellor 1997; Matless 1998: 189–95; Bullock 2002; Mort 2004). The *Architectural Review* noted this new mood in 1941,

> Architecture and town-planning, which have languished for years in the shadows of public inertia and disregard, have suddenly, as one result of the destruction of parts of our congested cities, sprung to life and become the focus of intense public curiosity … the public inertia – not to say boredom – that has acted as a drag to the very idea of planning for a generation past in now replaced by a genuine willingness both to take thought for the future and to visualise a future involving changes of a quite drastic character. (*Architectural Review*, 7 July 1941: 2)

Many groups were working on the problem of planning the future London, including the radical MARS group (Korn and Samuely 1941), the professional body the Royal Institute of British Architects, and even the Royal Academy. Schemes were well publicized within the professional and popular press, and many were featured in the RIBA's high profile 'Rebuilding Britain' exhibition at the National Gallery in April 1943 ('Rebuilding Britain', *Architectural Review*, April 1943). It is clear that many of these plans were urban ideologies as much as reconstruction strategies. It is also clear that within this very public discourse, London's architecture and planning had become an important means of expressing fundamental ideas about the nature of the metropolis and hopes for its future.

It was Patrick Abercrombie's 1943 plan for London County Council that formed the most important basis for early post-war planning of central London (Forshaw and Abercrombie 1943). Its geography has generally been interpreted as one of decentralization and New Towns, with its consideration of central areas concentrated on the City, the East End and other severely bombed areas. Mort has argued nonetheless for the existence of a strong metropolitan grounding within the London County Council's thinking. Drawing on Harley's concept of a 'subliminal geography of policy' (Harley 1988: 289), he argues that 'the authors of the documents generated a plethora of meanings about the metropolitan environment that were often disproportionate to their enactment as actual schemes' (Mort 2004: 124). This study has rather identified a distinctly anti-metropolitan tone to the planning rhetoric in addition to the geography. Apart from vague talk of drawing up a development plan in the future, the West End was relatively unaffected by the proposals (Forshaw and Abercrombie 1943: 23), and read as an ideology of urban reconstruction the conceptual focus of the new city was *also* elsewhere: in the social and architectural vision of decentralized housing estates, landscaped green spaces, efficient transport systems, carefully segregated industrial zones and so on.

Indeed, it is odd that this mass of plans for the capital should adopt this tone. Certainly there was little sense of London's international distinctiveness, its role as a fashion or consumption centre, or as a place of pleasure. The approach to the city was grounded in notions of amenity, community and the civic. Miles and Miles have argued that Paton-Watson and Abercombie's comparable plan for Plymouth of 1943, which rebuilt the city around the ancient church and the new shopping centre, *enshrined* consumption within post-war planning theory and practice (Miles and Miles 2005: 15). Similarly, London was drawn as a series of residential, economic 'neighbourhoods' or 'villages' with their own local centres. However, these shopping precincts were intended to be efficient rather than pleasurable spaces, minimizing the walking time of the housewife. Matless has drawn attention to the gender ideology implicit in reconstructive planning, read through designs for Ongar Town Centre: 'New Town communities as a whole were designed to cater for the new-trad woman … Such civic images contain within them a domestic model, community and domesticity fitting in with one another to produce an orderly everyday life, and ironing of the social' (Matless 1998: 245). Such places simply did not accommodate the West End's practices of fashionable consumption. Neither did the 'precinct' model fit well with the centralized cultural and shopping hub that was the West End, which was intended as simply the top level in a hierarchy of local, regional and national shopping centres.

Abercrombie constructed a moral geography of the West End, which was particularly apparent in his 'Central London plan' (see Figure 10.2). This labelled particular West End activities and places as problematic, notably Soho's 'central slum' abutting the shopping streets, hinting at the gay culture, prostitution and immigrant communities hidden in these backstreets (Mort 2004: 143). But embedded in Abercrombie's social democratic planning, there was also a specifically anti-metropolitan message regarding consumption. It appears that official planners like Abercrombie were distinctly uncomfortable with the 'fashionable' consumer and repeatedly presented the West End as a problem rather than as a vibrant retail centre and source of pleasure: 'one of the worst planned and architecturally designed areas of London and in parts is a central slum clogging development and traffic flow' (Forshaw and Abercrombie 1943: 23). This echoed Mumford's seminal *The Culture of Cities* in which he denounced the 'princely ritual of conspicuous expenditure' of the metropolis and the image of a 'valuable life that can be satisfied only by a ruthless concentration of human interest upon pecuniary standards and pecuniary results: the clothes of the metropolis, the jewels of the metropolis, the dull expensive life of Park Avenue and the Kurfürstendamm, Piccadilly and the Champs-Elysées, become the goals of vulgar ambition' (Mumford 1940: 230, quoted in Hall 1963: 38)

This was understandable in terms of wartime and post-war austerity, but it was also a longer-term element of British master planning, drawing on deeply held beliefs about the incompatibility of fashion and femininity with modern thinking and design. The early twentieth-century theoretical work of Loos and Le Corbusier, with their denigration of decoration, fashion and all things feminine, cast a long shadow over architectural and planning thinking (Le Corbusier 1998; Loos 1998).

2. The plan below gives a diagrammatic analysis of the central area as existing with its zones for Government, business, shopping, law, press, university, and the surrounding residential communities

Plate VI, facing page 24
A. G. Ling

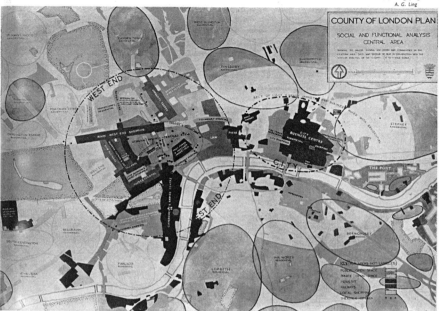

Figure 10.2 Abercrombie's 'moral geography' of the West End, Central London plan, J. H. Forshaw and P. Abercrombie (1943) *Country of London Plan*. London: MacMillan. Permission of City of London, London Metropolitan Archives.

It had fed a long-standing distrust of the taste of retailers and consumers alike, seen for example in the anti-consumerist debates over the reconstruction of Regent Street, finally completed in 1927 (Rappaport 2002). In short, whilst providing some rather desirable commissions, retail architecture had long been considered commercial, vulgar and popular, tainted by the feminized middle-class consumer culture that it served. Historians have now examined modernism's fraught relationship with its supposed feminine 'other', revealing the inherent tensions, inconsistencies and variety within Modernism (Colomina 1994; Wigley 1995; Reed 1996). Wigley, for example, has described inter-war modernism's denial of its own fetishization of the surface and close connections with the world of dress. Shopping cultures constituted just such an 'other', and during the early post-war years denial of it was apparent in plans for London. One problem was that while architects had an increasingly functional and spatialized approach to the design of buildings (see Gropius 1937), retailers still valued the traditional emphasis on 'façade', as an advertisement for the desirability and fashionability of the goods inside, and as a spectacular means of marking out their business within the street. But more serious issues were posed for retailers by the planners' desires to reduce the emphasis on fashionable consumption in the city.

Another issue was that the County of London plan divided London into a series of functional zones: for industry, community, traffic, business, etc., which didn't fit well with the functional complexity of the West End. Most importantly, this methodology created an artificial division between retail, which was conceptualized as local amenity primarily for domestic provisioning, and couture, which was positioned within 'industry', and lumped together with the sweatshops of Soho's rag trade, and with more obviously 'industrial' elements of the production industries. The West End of the mid twentieth century was a complex, interconnected cityscape that combined consumption and production. The small units for clothing production in the hinterland north of Oxford Street were closely linked with the fashionable clothing retailers situated on the nearby shopping streets.

Unlike Paris, it could be argued that London was a fashion city that seemed to be defined more overtly by its shopping, albeit very fashionable shopping, than by its couture. Yet it was difficult to extricate maps of shopping from those of dressmakers, tailors and couturiers, and all were grouped together in the itineraries of guidebooks and the shopping columns of fashionable magazines. The main arteries, Oxford Street, Regent Street and Piccadilly, housed most of the famous and prestigious stores, but their upper storeys were often rented to dressmakers, milliners and dress agencies. The West End's smaller streets such as Bond Street were home to the most exclusive shops, positioned cheek by jowl with London's fashion houses and small-scale dress designers. The distinction between salon and boutique was certainly not a clear one, as *Vogue* noted: 'there's a breath of Paris in the very word "boutique" – but London has translated it into something expressive of the personality and enterprise of her own Couture houses, several of whom have now opened these entrancing little shops in their salons' (*Vogue* January 1950: 68). The flavour of exclusivity and fashion also infused the West End's broader consumption cultures. There was also an intersecting neighbouring route of masculine consumption through the district, where consumption and production were again blurred: the traditional tailors, outfitters, bootmakers and hosiers of Savile Row, Jermyn Street and the Burlington Arcade, and the modern man's shops such as Simpson Piccadilly and Austin Reed of Regent Street, with their resident tailors and bales of cloth.

Metropolitan Master Planning

The plans of the late 1950s and 1960s represented a significant development from the early reconstruction plans in their abandonment of the preoccupation with the urban periphery and rediscovery of the metropolis. They were concerned with specific West End areas and streets, and the wider area that housed them. However, this concern with the metropolis was problematic as it reposed the difficult questions:

what should post-war London be like? What role should consumption be allowed to play?

In 1957, the developer Jack Cotton submitted plans for the Monico site on the north side of Piccadilly Circus. The controversy over this important metropolitan site instigated a series of ill-fated master plans for the Circus, many by eminent planner William Holford. The problem was that it was a hub of nation and empire, the site of popular gatherings on major national occasions, and one of the iconic spaces that represented London in the global imagination. Yet it was also a major traffic bottleneck and a centre of commercial office development. Equally important, although much less obvious in contemporary debates, was the Circus's position in the middle of London's most fashionable and successful shopping district, home to the major stores Swan and Edgar, and Lillywhites, and an important hub in the West End's network of shopping routes.

In 1961, the *Architect's Journal* published another set of proposals for a new raised 'shoppers way' above Oxford Street, linked to shops and offices at first floor level (*Architect's Journal,* 23 March 1961). The Buchanan report of 1963, *Traffic in Towns,* developed this idea in one of its principal case studies, designing a grid-like network of urban motorways and walkways in the area bounded by Oxford Street, Great Portland Street, Euston Road and Tottenham Court Road. A little later, plans were drawn up to transform Regent Street into a covered shopping arcade served by a raised tram system, with other traffic concealed beneath (*Aid to Pedestrian Movement* 1971). Such plans were not primarily about shopping. Indeed, their texts displayed a similar avoidance of fashionable consumption to that evident in Abercrombie's work. Much of this metropolitan planning was about creating new civic spaces, and defending them from the powerful influence of commercial developers and their architects (Levin 1959). But 'civic' had been perceptibly redefined from 1940s' understandings to encompass more explicitly pleasurable and metropolitan understanding of the city.

Holford's Piccadilly Circus, for example, was a place for people to meet each other, under the twinkling neon lights of advertising hoardings. The urban spaces depicted in *An Aid to Pedestrian Movement* (1971) were peopled by commuters and tourists, certainly, but also by shoppers. These were plans that worked on sites that abutted and overlapped with areas and streets with vibrant pre-existing consumer cultures and geographies, which it was becoming increasingly difficult to ignore. The review of the County of London Development Plan of 1960 acknowledged the concentration of London's shops in the central area, accounting for 8 per cent of total floor space (London County Council 1960, table 42) and a much higher proportion of street frontage: there was little sign of the predicted decentralization. Furthermore, the London County Council's planning directives of the period expressed a desire to retain the retail character of these parts of the West End (1951: 99; 1960: 149).

This was a time of comprehensive monolithic modernist vision, which invited permanent, directed change. (Figure 10.3) There was a strong desire to seize this

Figure 10.3 Fashion in the modern city. Woolmark Company Archive. Permission of London College of Fashion

rare opportunity to interrupt London's habitual pattern of uncoordinated, piecemeal change, adopting a policy of wholesale demolition. By 1963, Buchanan was already warning 'the opportunities which could have transformed Oxford Street into a first-class metropolitan shopping centre have been frittered away' (Buchanan 1963: 152). *An Aid to Pedestrian Movement* enthused that 'there is the prospect in the West End of London of very substantial redevelopment in the next two decades, extending from Covent Garden to Oxford Circus, having a degree of continuity and comprehensiveness that perhaps occurs only once in a century' (1971: 1).

This was at odds with the traditional expression of success in a street like Oxford Street, which when at its most prosperous worked through precisely such piecemeal methods. The frequent reinvention of shops through rebuilding, refacing or refitting, and the adoption of a succession of newly available architectural styles performed an important function in the West End, proclaiming a modernity and fashionability in tune with the consumption cultures of the area. In 1937, Harold Clunn had noted that 'in Oxford Street there is seemingly no end to rebuilding operations.' (1937: 497). Similarly, the *Financial Times* reported, 'The day cannot be far distant when the whole of Oxford Street will be modernised and rebuilt on the grand scale. Already the extreme West section is completely transformed and a series of great modern buildings occupies the whole stretch between Edgware Road and Orchard Street' (20 May 1936). This was not a method of urban transformation much valued by the post-war planners.

However, on another level, the fundamental willingness of the post-war plans to raze the city to the ground and start again emphasized the ephemerality, flexibility and consumability of the urban landscape, which was to relate in a very direct way to the new fashionable cultures of 1960s' 'Swinging London'. In 1942, Lionel Brett had expressed the common sentiment that 'the central shopping district east of Hyde Park' was 'unpleasant and worth replacing' (Brett 1942: 25). By the 1960s ideas about disposability were differently inflected, reflecting the new-wave ideas of architectural groups like Archigram (Sadler 2005). Theirs was a new, seductive architecture of the imagination, at once firmly metropolitan and fantastical. They spoke enthusiastically of throwaway buildings, of 'plug-in' and 'instant' cities, designing vibrant, disposable urban scenes full of fashionable young shoppers and Technicolor advertisements for consumer goods. Such visions were increasingly echoed in the graphic expression of the post-war plans, reflecting a significant shift in attitudes to the metropolis. As Peter Hall noted at the time, 'to argue ... that it is immoral to spend more on personal gratification, is surely reactionary, presumptuous, arrogant and quite irrelevant to planning' (Hall 1963: 38).

'Traffic in Towns': Shopping Routes and Urban Motorways

Post-war planners shared a belief that traffic chaos was much to blame for the problems of the central area. However, they also believed that they needed to plan positively for Britain's impending 'motor age'. The Buchanan report stated 'if we are to have any chance of living at peace with the motor car, we shall need a different sort of city' (Buchanan 1963: paragraph 35). This became one of the central principles of post-war planning, epitomized in special reports such as *Traffic in Towns* and *An Aid to Pedestrian Movement*, but also infusing the treatment of metropolitan spaces in Abercrombie's plan and shaping the designs for Oxford Street, Regent Street, Piccadilly Circus and later Covent Garden. This called for a new 'traffic architecture' (Buchanan 1963: 142), defined by movement, route and efficiency. Planners set about remaking central London as a series of efficient urban motorways and pedestrian decks. The issue for the West End as a hub of fashionable consumption was how far this comprehensive rethinking of the urban centre could accommodate the existing shopping arteries like Oxford Street, the meandering masculine shopping route running from Jermyn Street up to Savile Row, and the blossoming strings of boutiques in side streets like Carnaby Street, inconveniently placed within prime development sites.

A primary concern was the classification and segregation of different types of traffic, to rectify the problem of arteries like Oxford Street, where 'through', 'stopping' and 'pedestrian traffic' were combined into a confusing chaos (Forshaw and Abercrombie 1943: 4). For Abercrombie, the solution was one of ring roads, bypasses and precincts: 'the whole of central metropolitan London … is a precinct which needs protecting from traffic passing through it' (Forshaw and Abercrombie 1943: 10). Subsequently, planners became obsessed with the vertical segregation of vehicular and pedestrian traffic. Within such thinking, the crowds were lifted above the busy urban route ways of Oxford Street, Regent Street and Piccadilly Circus onto a raised deck system, 'the "new ground" level for city life, a platform from which the buildings would rise' (Buchanan 1963: 136).

The earlier plans were preoccupied with enabling traffic to move swiftly across the centre, with little thought that people might actually want to stop there. With their increasing interest in specific streets and hubs, later plans displayed a recognition of the routedness and experiential character of the West End. This culminated in *An Aid to Pedestrian Movement*, where a new raised monorail system was proposed, snaking around and through buildings, creating a new web of routes to connect the hubs within central London (Figure 10.4). There was more interest in flows and in the small journeys of the kind that constituted shopping trips. Explicit recognition of the importance of shopping routes was still often absent or muted in the text of the plans, reflecting the long tradition of denigration and denial noted earlier in the chapter. Yet consumption was a persistent subtext, particularly in cartographic plans and images, where journeys were increasingly being conducted by a hybrid shopper/pedestrian.

However, within this system, routes and movement were very much planned and controlled, in a way that did not allow for the ephemeral, shifting fashionable shopping cultures to be found yards away in Carnaby Street. Neither was there an understanding that 'bustle' and even 'congestion' might actually form the lifeblood of the retail centre. Buchanan found such chaos abhorrent: 'the effect of noise from traffic is particularly adverse … in Oxford Street, where conversation on the pavement is made difficult. And it is Oxford Street again which suffers most from the visual intrusion of the motor vehicle, where continuous streams of vehicles, moving and stationary, prevent the shopper from seeing across the street' (Buchanan 1963: 129). His concerns about the uncontrolled, hysterical West End street echoed the centuries-old discourses on feminine fashionable consumption in the city (Rappaport

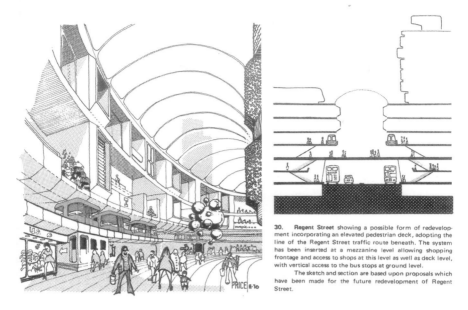

30.   Regent Street showing a possible form of redevelopment incorporating an elevated pedestrian deck, adopting the line of the Regent Street traffic route beneath. The system has been inserted at a mezzanine level allowing shopping frontage and access to shops at this level as well as deck level, with vertical access to the bus stops at ground level.
      The sketch and section are based upon proposals which have been made for the future redevelopment of Regent Street.

Figure 10.4 An 'aid to pedestrian movement' in Regent Street, *An Aid to Pedestrian Movement: A Report by a Working Party on The Introduction of a New Mode of Transport in Central London* (1971) London: Westminster City Council.

2002). But the West End's shopping cultures had long depended on a particular relationship between road, pavement and shop window, which was now being threatened not only by the traffic engineers but by a new way of thinking about retail architecture. In 1937, Gropius had predicted that 'the stores of tomorrow' would be tied differently into the structure of cities, their internal routes continuous with the streets, connected to each other with walkways, which *replaced* the shopping street as it had traditionally been understood. Retailers were resistant to this shift, and the developers who owned the sites had little interest in making new connections between their buildings and others. Both had yet to be persuaded that this would be the means of ensuring the central shopping area's survival in the post-war landscape of consumption.

'Such a city the planner improves at his peril': Rethinking the Shopping City

In April 1966, *Time* magazine published its special issue celebrating 'London – the Swinging City': a place of youth, pop cultures and fashion. The high profile rise of 'unplanned' yet dynamic consumer spaces such as the boutiques of Carnaby Street and Kings Road drew attention to the disparity between London's post-war planning visions and the version of the capital that was gaining prominence in the national and international imagination. In 1968, a comprehensive redevelopment plan was drawn up by Westminster, Camden and the Greater London Council, anticipating the closure of the Covent Garden fruit and vegetable markets (GLC et al. 1968). New housing, shopping, arts and entertainment structures were planned, providing a new metropolitan hub in the West End. It was the only element of the post-war metropolitan master planning discussed in this chapter that ever came into fruition, albeit partially, in the area.

The proposals were part of the same West End vision that had spawned the failed proposals for Oxford Street, Regent Street and Piccadilly Circus. They soon ran into entrenched opposition, stalled, were modified and then eventually enacted in very modified form. The Covent Garden scheme has often been seen to mark the demise of comprehensive master planning in metropolitan London and the rise of conservation and a new rhetoric of urban regeneration. The story has been told in terms of the failure of local government planning due to community opposition, political infighting, the fiscal crisis of the early 1970s and a change in broader public attitudes towards historic townscapes associated with the rise of the architectural conservation movement (Porter 1994; Bradley and Pevsner 2003). This study suggests, however, an alternative reading in which the proposals tell of a hugely significant evolution in understandings of the importance of fashionable consumption in London, building on the lessons learned over the post-war decades, connecting with revised attitudes to the townscape.

Certainly, it is significant that the proposals for Covent Garden retained and recast Charles Fowler's nineteenth-century Market House, and included a historic 'character route' running through the district from east to west. It seemed the planning community was finally heeding Mumford's warnings that 'such a city the planner improves at his peril', recognizing the role of historic character and cultures in bolstering London's claims to be a world city (Mumford 1945: 3). There was also an implicit understanding of the embeddedness of consumer culture within the existing architecture and urban structure. This represented an important shift in the balance between planning and conservation in the treatment of the West End's shopping areas, and signalled a more 'permeable' and 'flexible' reading of the city, which can perhaps be seen as a very belated, but at least partially successful, response to the vibrant metropolitan consumer cultures that had long been located there and were now flourishing in Soho and Chelsea.

This was not just about architectural conservation, but was also specifically about the sites of many small-scale businesses of the kind that were flourishing in 'Swinging' London. This was a kind of shopping landscape that simply could not be planned in the way of Holford, as Gardiner recognized in his eulogy to the little shop: 'a row of shops with shop atmosphere cannot be system made, mass-produced or manufactured (in the way that a block of flats can), if they are to succeed both visually and, on a larger plane, as a method of integrating new stuff with old stuff'

(Gardiner 1970: 26). Kenneth Browne, another architectural commentator had high hopes for Covent Garden, recast with fashionable boutiques, cafes and artists' studios as a 'Latin Quarter for London', 'the place where all paths cross … a natural melting pot for people and ideas … a place where anything can happen.… . This give-and-take has to be reflected in the architecture; free thought cannot blossom in a gridiron' (Browne 1964: 196–7).

Fashionable consumption was clearly back on the agenda: Covent Garden was intended to emerge as a different kind of market place, where fluid, ephemeral and historic elements were allowed to mingle with the Modern vision. It is significant that such concerns now informed the professional and popular reception of planning schemes: despite earlier opposition, the new Covent Garden of the late 1970s and early 1980s was judged a success because of its treatment of retail and urban space, rather than as a saved urban community. Fashionable consumption was at last being acknowledged as a pivotal and desirable element within the West End's identity.

Conclusion

This has been the story of the renegotiation of the role of fashionable consumption in the city through the imagination as much as the processes of planning. It is clear that in the years after the Second World War, the 'metropolitan', and especially 'fashionable metropolitan consumption', emerged as a problematic issue for urban planning, which existing histories have overlooked. Quite simply, planners, architects, developers and retailers had conflicting visions of the West End shopping street. A history of the West End's retailing geography shows how routes and built structures had developed piecemeal and constantly evolved in *response* to fluid fashionable consumer cultures. This was something that was troublesome for successive generations of planners, difficult to address with directed urban planning and a totalizing vision of modern city. Yet, from a starting point of Abercrombie's denial and curtailment of the metropolitan consumer in the early 1940s, this chapter has described a growing, if under-acknowledged, presence of fashionable consumer culture within urban redevelopment plans. It is precisely through tracking this development that a more nuanced view of the supposedly homogeneous mass of post-war modernist master planning can be constructed.

Fashionable West End shopping has remained an important element within London's identity as a 'fashion city', and these consumer cultures – the consumers, practices and geographies that comprised them – have historically eluded planning because of their very ephemerality and need for constant change. With the onset of the 1970s, as understandings of urban planning shifted, in terms of scope and also in terms of the premium placed on 'special character', it became apparent that a lighter touch was needed if planners, architects and developers were to have a measure of success building consumption cultures into the architectural fabric and traffic systems of a place like the West End.

Part IV
Fashion Cities and Transnational Networks

–11–

La Mode Dakaroise
Elegance, Transnationalism and an African Fashion Capital
Hudita Nura Mustafa

Prologue: From Colonial to Global

The first scenes of Ousmane Sembene's filmic satire of neocolonial elites, *Xala* (1974), present the transfer of power from French officials to the male elite of newly independent Senegal in 1960. Dressed in *petits boubous*, a short version of the 'mbuub' (Wolof), 'traditional' African robes, a group of politicians defiantly expels French advisors along with their busts of French queens and kings from the presidential palace onto the monumental steps and boulevards of Dakar's Plateau district. The fallacy of this defiance is exposed as we see that these same men have exchanged their African *boubous* for exaggeratedly starched *costumes* (French: suits) and even tuxedos. Now acting as the economic elite of the chamber of commerce they eagerly crack open briefcases of money, bribes brought by the same French advisors. Still, they walk through Dakar's elegant, breezy Plateau district, the national administrative centre, with the arrogance of leaders of a newly independent country and men of distinction. These are the descendants of the *evolués*, (F: evolved) civilized assimilated Black Frenchmen of the Four Communes, the urban centres of colonial French West Africa. This political-economic crippling, indeed betrayal, of the new nation is metaphorically explored in the story when the protagonist is cursed with sexual impotence when he refuses to perform a traditional ritual as he arrogantly seeks a third wife. In the final scene, El Hajj, the protagonist is stripped to bareback and spat upon by a street crowd thus facing the worst indignity in Senegal, where nakedness signifies insanity.

Nearly thirty years later, the everyday heroine of Sembene's *Faat Kine* (2001) is a businesswoman always dressed fashionably in the *n'dockette*, a full, flouncy decorative dress, a Eurafrican hybrid dress form of the colonial encounter on the Senegambian coast. Kine's mother's back, scarred by hot water thrown by her father in rage, bears witness to social denunciation at her fateful pregnancy as a young woman. Outcast, a single mother with her hopes for a legal career dashed, she forges a bold path as a gas station owner among the new cohort of women entrepreneurs in 1980s' Dakar. Kine's Dakar, as she drives from upscale residential Point E to downtown Plateau, is laden with memories of both struggle and success. Encounters with betraying men from her past who now come to her in tattered robes, pathetic and financially desperate, depict the reversal of gender positions in the urban middle class as women have replaced unemployed men as income earners. Kine's *sañse* (Wolof: fancy dress, from F: *changer*, transform) represents not just the urban modernity of individual mastery but also a negotiation of contested terrains of wealth, work and beauty. Sembene's representation of the semiotics of dress shows that *sañse* is not a narcissistic changing of one's 'look' as asserted by popular critiques of women entrepreneurs. Set in contrast with the scorched back of the mother under relatively stable patriarchal power relations, Kine's embodied dress practice is the sign of her independent wealth rather than, as has been the case with women's beauty, the dignity of the patriarchal family. *Sañse* here signifies the instability and ambiguity of gendered relations of power under post-colonial conditions of socio-economic and cultural crises and reconfigurations.

Following the course of post-colonial Senegal, Sembene's trajectory of filmic images – the dress, gestures, family forms, work life and urban routes of the two protagonists – portray a political economy and cultural politics of modernity in which the conditions, meanings and institutions of becoming *civilisé* (F: civilized) have changed. These scenarios from one of Senegal and Africa's keenest cultural critics alert us to the complex status of Dakar as an African cultural capital, once the 'Paris of Africa' as Dakarois artists and cultural elites like to say. The personal elegance of the Dakarois and the cultural sophistication of its urban life undergird Dakar's status as a paragon of civilized modernity in Africa. Sembene's two films expose the actuality and contradictions of Senegal's modernity. In *Xala*, official and elite Dakar are a perverse combination of neocolonialism and independence, modernity and tradition, arrogant and impotent colonized masculinity. In *Faat Kine*, the cityscape of crisis and gendered struggle, forty years after independence, is part of a late modern polycentric world, which provides opportunities for middle-class women like Kine. While the tailored suit was the symbol of male power in colonial and early nationalist epochs, as in *Xala*, in the current neo-liberal era the dismantling of elite patriarchy and the ascendance of a religious, commercial elite requires another, indeed multiple, image(s) of wealth, power and modernity. *Cutur* (Wolof from the F: *couture*) emerged from and objectifies this context of change and crisis.

In this chapter, I engage with the aphorism that Dakar is the Paris of Africa by exploring the transformation of couture, the French craft of tailoring, into *cutur*, an interconnected field of garment production, consumption and display.[1] *Cutur* is the social, economic and institutional base for contemporary forms of *la mode Dakaroise*, a constellation of stylish dress objects, images, practices and discourses. *Cutur*, I suggest, makes Dakar both like and unlike 'Paris' and 'Africa', themselves iconic, charged categories. The meanings, agendas and potency of such a characterization situate Dakar variously in a colonial dialectic, in a global hierarchy of cities, as a unique cultural generator and centre of African worlds. Importantly, the economic and cultural conditions of *la mode Dakaroise* both precede and exceed colonial civilizing projects and post-colonial mimicry. There is no question that in both Paris and Dakar, distinction in dress has long been a key form of elite symbolic power and modern fashion processes invigorate contestations thereof. In both cases a feminine beauty culture has long thrived across class and status, indeed, tasteful production and sartorial elegance inspire national pride. Beyond this generality the processes and effects of fashion differ significantly. By examining the gendered transformations and interrelations of production, consumption and display, we can discern the nature of crisis, creativity and flexibility in a post-colonial fashion context.

If in certain 'regards' (F: looks) colonial and newly independent Dakar was a mirror city to Paris, both reflecting and distorting Parisian civilization, *cutur* invites another look.[2] For Kine's crisis-ridden Dakar is not merely a broken mirror. The conceit of the mirror enables us to think about the colonial dialectic, its legacies and the transformation of colonial into global cities. Artists, intellectuals and ordinary persons from Tokyo to New York and Dakar have looked to Paris, long-time capital of the modern Western cultural world, for the 'best' and 'newest' of cosmopolitan urban modernity. Parisian politics, ideas, lifestyle and art are the epitome of sophisticated cultural life. Indeed, Paris as French imperial capital was a model for the rule, planning and image of Dakar, capital of French West Africa. In the mirror cities of Paris/Dakar we may perceive Parisian mappings, technologies, public spaces, images, styles, gestures, scents and words in Dakarois *cutur*. We also see traces of Dakar in the markets, shoppers, greetings and mosques of Paris. But the frames and looks of such a colonial mirror do not contain the actuality of the many streams of culture that compose *cutur*.

Fashion and Gendered Transformations

In the last twenty-five years, processes of decolonization, neo-liberal reform, globalization and French disengagement dismantled the tightly controlled French colonial sphere. Paris 'burned' for two weeks in November 2005, a concrete expression of the post-colonial alienation of French youth of Arab and African origin and the demise of Paris as an imperial centre and ideal. At the same time, New York and other global cities have been revived by the entrepreneurial activity of Senegalese and Malian traders, hair-braiders, tailors, taxi drivers, restaurateurs and students. As a fashion capital, Dakar was forged as a nexus of cross-cultural encounter and conquest. This status precedes and survives its status as a satellite of Paris. To reflect upon these complexities we will ask: Is *la mode Dakaroise* a voracious, even desperately competitive, creativity in a disarticulated market in which nothing is too sacred to be consumed and female beauty is glorified, strategically used and condemned as narcissistic? What has been and is the place of French colonial civilizing urbanism in cultivating a civilized self? What are the global influences on Dakar creativity?

In this changing context sartorial elegance bears heavy burdens, for the gendered body remains a pre-eminent site of civilizing projects. In order to understand how the meanings of *civilisé* and *sañse* have changed we must recall broader historical processes. Under current adverse conditions, Senegambia, always a land of metissage, has re-emerged as a zone of encounter among Africa, Islam, the West and now East Asia. In West Africa, neo-liberal economic reform led to austerity and poverty but also forced local agents to expand transnational connections in a more open, if unequal, global trade arena. The displacement of French by American imperial hegemony is evidenced in economic development infrastructure, popular culture and migration patterns. Ascendant Middle Eastern and East Asian economic spheres supply new transnational commercial networks. As French imperial civilizing cultural projects have been largely abandoned, it is these broader influences of the *longue durée* and new global orders that now generate *la mode Dakaroise*. In turn, *la mode*, reborn of cosmopolitanism and crisis, transforms Dakar from a colonial into a global city.

On the local level, gendered transformations in *cutur* have made fashion an even more crucial arbiter of Senegalese transnationalism, social distinction and female elegance. I have suggested that 'ordinary cosmopolitans' craft not just fashion but Dakarois cosmopolitanism through garments, selves and discourse (Mustafa 1998; Diouf 2000). The new commercial elite is of provincial origin, educated in Koranic schools and based in Islamic brotherhoods. Their success in Dakar, European cities and especially New York finances their investments, marriages and status in Dakar. They challenge the social power of now pauperized long-standing coastal, Francophile, educated middle and elite classes. These various middle and elite classes fragment and reconstitute through entrepreneurship and cloth and tailoring, which were their primary strategic terrains. Their fashion and ceremonial display symbolically expresses new civilities, status and wealth. In the 1980s diversified global networks diversified the prices and qualities of fashion goods and enabled broader sectors of producers and consumers to engage in fashion's pace. Youth fashion expanded with North American trade circuits and influence. *Fuug jaay* (Wolof: dust off and sell), second-hand Western clothes imported from the USA and Europe, are disdained but meet basic clothing needs of youth and children of an increasingly impoverished society. Still, within age/gender patriarchal hierarchies, women's elegance, being *jekk* (Wolof: elegant) symbolizes family dignity, the core of Senegambian values (Diop 1981). Families sacrifice to finance women's dress. Since the 1980s women made production, consumption and display more interdependent by combining work in ateliers, design and trade with sociality and ceremonial life. They created space for themselves in male fields and reinvented femininity as practical elegance. In sum, structural crises, new transnational connections and gendered strategies shape Dakar's fashion processes.

We can specify Dakarois fashion by comparing it to the prominent example of Western fashion processes, Parisian fashion, in four ways. Briefly, we should recall that Parisian fashion, once thriving with a range of artisanal and industrial producers, polarized in the post-Second World War era into very exclusive haute couture houses and mass production, with couture-inspired prêt-à-porter as a small middle level. By contrast, artisanship and small-scale entrepreneurship proliferated in Senegal's economic austerity especially after independence. Among the differences, first, *la mode* and *cutur* are part of a broader discourse and historical consciousness of long-standing Senegambian excellence and exceptionalism in matters of personal conduct and beauty. This could be said of Parisian self-images as well, but the importance here is that such reflection contests colonial constructions of Africa as a culturally regressive space that was awakened by colonial modernity. Second, *la mode Dakaroise* is part of an uneven commodification of urban economy and culture in which the moral economy of cloth, dress and display has in fact intensified rather than subsided. Third, unlike Western fashion's continual negotiation of art and industry, standardization and flexibility, *cutur* is a hybrid, artisanal field, which combines an indigenized Western craft, deeply rooted artistic sensibilities and dependence upon global industries.

Fourth, in contrast to North Atlantic fashion capitals such as London, Paris, Milan and New York, contemporary Dakar fashion is shaped by economic decline rather than growth. Its flexibility is shaped by economic volatility and marginalization to global processes rather than industrial growth strategies in competitive markets. *Cutur* may actually be much more important to the urban economy and middle-class survival than couture has been in Paris. Yet its flexibility allows expansion but little hope for accumulation, equity or sustained economic development. In this crisis context, elegance, the pride of Dakarois who have felt themselves in a respectful dialogue with Parisian distinction, is an even more critical terrain of material and symbolic power in periods of social contestation and change. Dress has a long history as symbol of power and self-reflexive discourse on modernity. The mimicry or similitude implied by comparing Dakar to Paris legitimizes Dakar as a modern cultural centre but obscures the multiple processes that shape *la mode Dakaroise* independently of Paris.

Like many globally oriented urban cultural centres, Dakar fashion is shaped by dense networks of skilled producers, effective distribution circuits, proclivity towards learning and experimentation, and vertical disintegration in cultural products sectors (Scott 2000a). Like Paris, Dakar fashion is imprinted with a unique 'feel' which imbues world cities with charisma as if they were a person. Importantly for the embodied practices of fashion, a loyal, discerning home market advertises, monitors and creates fashion. Hollywood film can only be made in Hollywood, a French film in France. Blue jeans would not be the global icon of American masculinity they are without Hollywood Westerns and Parisiennes would not be known globally without Catherine Deneuve's seductive allure in French films. Similarly, a Dakar-made *taille bas* (F: 'stocking' waist) skirt suit or embroidered *boubou* is marked by the detailed skill and taste of even market tailors.

As it would be impossible to think about Paris without imagining the Parisienne, her easy elegance gracing charming shops and magnificent avenues, it is impossible to think of Dakar without its *dirriankhes*. Corpulent, wrapped in metres of cloth falling underfoot, they saunter in high heels in the wind-blown, sandy alleys leaving behind the sound of waist-beads and scent of incense. This ambiguous yet ubiquitous figure of feminine elegance animates and eroticizes commercialized public spaces of modernity. Once linked to coastal trade and leisured elites, today's *dirriankhes* are middle-class women who aggressively confront crisis to innovate institutions from tailoring to the family in order to manage familial needs and financial instability. Since the 1980s their entrepreneurship in cloth trade and tailoring ateliers has been the core of many families' survival. The most successful travel to buy fashion goods or sell clothing in Europe, Hong Kong, Nigeria, Las Palmas, Jeddah and New York. For these women elegance expresses status and dignity but also asserts a work identity as tastemakers. Amidst Dakar's polarities, the *dirriankhe* condenses the social processes of cosmopolitanism and crisis that beget cultural creativity. We will return to this figure after tracing the processes resituating Dakar from a French colonial to a global city.

A remapping of the terrains and hierarchies of global cities to include not just command networks of contemporary global capitalism but those of colonialism would better enable us to attend to the interdigitation of global hegemonies, creativity and power (King 1990 supplements the paradigm of Sassen 1991). Since the 1980s there has been a new strategic role for global cities as command centres of late capitalism and a new convergence of culture and economy evident in the growth and agglomerations within the cultural products sector. In this process the symbolic value of individual city cultures is a significant part of urban renewal planning and even a brand linking place, heritage and quality (Scott 2000a). However, the programmatic, normative ambition of this facet of the global cities paradigm de-emphasizes polarities, inequalities and disarticulations both within global cities and between cities of the North and South (Massey 1994; Soja 2000).

By contrast, from the critical perspectives of labour, post-colonialism or neo-liberalism, modern fashion processes appear of the same cloth, so to speak, with imperial domination (Mustafa 2002a, b). Global cities then are not only the Northern command centres (i.e. London, New York, and the exceptional Tokyo) but shaped through webs of unequal exchange, dependence and shared imperial history with cities of the South (i.e. Mumbai, Dakar, Lagos, Mexico City) in a polycentric world. Despite its violent processes such as expansion of mass cultural products, undermining of local artisanal production and extreme exploitation of female producers and consumers, fashion provides a global traffic in culture which enables the colonized to negotiate the dialectic of tradition and modernity with skill, pleasure and pride. Such contradictory economic and cultural processes are intrinsic to post-colonial urban conditions of creativity amidst crisis (Appadurai 1996; Hannerz 1996; Hansen 2000).

Before examining the history of *cutur* a reflection upon what I call the 'words of *cutur*' – the vocabulary of tools, skills, positions, identities and styles – broaches critical issues in the cultural politics of urbanism and fashion. The creole words of Dakar Wolof, *cutur*, *créateur* (from F: creator, artist) and *sañse* (from F *changer*; to transform) highlight the hybridity of French and African practices that produce and are produced by the field of fashion. *Créateur* and *sañse* highlight the agency and self-cultivation required for production and consumption. *Cutur*, which refers to production, consumption and the object itself, captures the sense of a semi-autonomous world, a social field. *Civilisé*, with its direct reference to colonialism, no longer refers to Francophile language, manners or even hygiene as taught in schools but retains its reference to a propriety of bodily cleanliness, elegance and fashionability, that is to social knowledge and know-how. Fashion categories such as *tubaab* (Wolof: foreign, white), *modern* (F: modern) and *Africain, traditionel* (F: African, traditional) are organized around the polarity of European/African. Yet instead of representing static tradition, as fashion studies would have it, African style is valued for an authenticity that absorbs new, cosmopolitan Islamic, African and European influences (Mustafa 1998; Rabine 1998, 2002). Notwithstanding the hegemony of coastal Wolof culture, the fluidity of Senegambian ethnicities is fertile terrain for innovation (Diouf 1998; Fall 1989; Mclaughlin 2001; Swigart 1992).[3] Fashion, language and music are part of the making of an urban identity, which is increasingly detached from broader national identification and expressed through creolized cultural forms. Even though New Yorkers, Londoners or Parisians would see Dakar as an outpost, Dakarois feel themselves to be a distinct part of global cosmopolitan society.

'The Paris of Africa': Civility and Colonial Urbanism

As capital of French West Africa (1890–1960), Dakar was made and known as the 'Paris of Africa'. The Plateau district contains within a two-mile radius both the official city of boulevards, grand buildings, roundabouts and monuments as well as the downtown of boutiques, cinema, museums, theatres, cafes and hotels. The coastal road bordering this area leads out to more leisure sites, the airport and French military bases. These spaces of political power and order, leisure, sociality, culture and display are familiar to French expatriates, enjoyed by the Senegalese elite and dreamt of by aspirants. The university, newspapers, theatre and intellectual life have attracted bright minds from across the francophone and African diasporic world. The first world festival of Negro Arts was held here in 1965 and the Dakar visual arts biennial is the most enduring one in Africa. Blaise Diagne was the first to articulate African anti-colonialism here in the 1920s. Leopold Senghor, Negritude philosopher, poet and first President developed a national culture promoting arts and Africanity. Colonial civility became part of Dakar's historical role as a site of metissage and then of global African culture.

A capital in all ways – administrative, diplomatic, commercial, cultural, military – Dakar is centre of not just a nation but of African worlds. This centrality harbours a violent birth as a segregated colonial city, for Plateau was created for French officials through the forced removal of Lebou villages from seaside cliffs to create an African district, the Medina. The harmonizing of colonial modernist norms and forms was always disrupted by African social life and needs. Streets made for rational circulation of goods and persons were always used for ceremonies and trading. Concrete box houses built for nuclear families house extended families, tailoring shops and suitcase trade (Seck 1970; Rabinow 1989; King 1990; Wright 1991; Mustafa 2002b). Through practices such as *cutur* the colonial city has now been fully recuperated by popular needs and desires.

Before examining *cutur* we must recall that the history of sartorial elegance in Senegal reflects and shapes larger processes of colonization, decolonization and modernity. Modern fashion is part of a long regional history of cloth as currency, gift, weaving traditions of hereditary castes, symbol of political and social status and aesthetic object. In the terrain of distinction, the body is a key site for producing ideologies and practices of propriety, civility and elegance. Women's beauty always registered metissage and Western dress was never imposed upon them. 'We learned it from our grandmothers ... have you heard about the St Louisiennes ... they were beautiful, always well-dressed and elegant' I was told. St Louis was a seventeenth-century trading enclave and became the first colonial capital in the nineteenth century. Icons of female beauty and cultivated elegance, St Louisiennes' art of living guarded tradition but absorbed cosmopolitan European and Arab influences (Niang 1990). In my interviews older women St Louisiennes recall memories of post-harvest shopping at French trading houses, ceremonial gift exchanges of heavy woven cloth, thrilling studio portraits and intricate hairstyles with wool wigs and gold decorations. Theirs is the exemplar instance of Senegambian negotiations of colonial influence, imposition and metissage. In their *sañse* the distinct restraint and bodily adornment valued by regional societies, norms of modesty considered to be Islamic, and French elegant fashionability together compose a sartorial performance that weds elegance with foundational values of dignity (Sylla 1978).

As a project of colonial modernity, Dakar evolved through economic and cultural projects, which relied upon the bifurcation of the colonial population into urban citizens and rural subjects and the uneven development of the urban coast and rural interior (Seck 1970; Cruise O'Brien 1975; Conklin 1997).[4] After the Second World War, the 'pacte colonial' closely knit metropolitan and colonial economies favouring French merchant capital. Local handicraft cloth production was undermined by multiple European trading interests in the nineteenth century, then by French control of the colonial market (Pitts 1978; Barry 1992, 1998). African markets provided outlets for declining French industry, including textiles, after the World Wars and the depression, at times providing the only growth market (Boone 1992). By the late 1970s, rural droughts, the global energy crisis and national debt led the country into World Bank structural adjustment reforms. These 1980s reforms undermined education, state services, bureaucratic employment and hence the institutional bases of the middle classes and their patriarchal relations.

The dominating force of colonial urbanism and civilizing projects has to be placed in the longer history of metissage in the trading enclaves of Gorée, St Louis, Rufisque and Dakar, all at or near the Petit Cote of Atlantic Africa. Designated as the Four Communes in the early colonial period they were centres of modernization projects (Biondi 1987; Diouf 1998). For five centuries they were part of coastal Eurafrican societies of Portuguese, French, Wolof and Arab influence, and then sites of European competition for markets, goods and territories. Trans-Saharan trade has been traced back to the tenth century and the scholarly cliché that this coast is a gateway between Islam, Africa and the West holds some truth. In the early 1900s, Dakar became a focal point of modernization with a solid infrastructure of schools, clinics, commerce and military bases to ensure the 'assimilation' of Africans to civilized modernity as Black Frenchmen, *evolués* and citizens (Crowder 1967; Gellar 1982).

The Senegalese incorporated colonial technologies from photography to the sewing machine into their sartorial ecumenes of objects, images, events and meanings. In studio portraits from the height of colonial rule in the 1940s and 1950s we see the hybrid elegance of the women of St Louis and Dakar with heavy gold jewellery, braided hair, woollen wigs, elaborate headscarves and henna-ed hands emphasizing the beauty of head, neck and corpulence. They wear hybrid dress styles such as the *Robe bloc*, perhaps a version of Dior's New Look (Rabine 1998) in European cloth, but these colonized bodies assert the long metissage of the coast. As pioneer Malian studio photographer, Seydou Keita said, 'Above all the attire had to come out in the photo. Hands, long slender fingers, jewels … were very important. It was a sign of wealth, elegance, beauty.' In today's world, such performances of dignity, which may not be grounded in reliable income or social status, become more important to the negotiation of social power.

Men were more engaged with colonial institutions and the costume expressed an ambiguous colonized masculinity. On one hand, punitive civilizing strategies included suspending schoolboys for not wearing suits in public in order to '*faire la rupture*' (F: create a rupture) between the male *evolué* and his community (Rabine 1998: 99). Stifled in the heat, boys rushed home to change. For popular sectors, however, as it continues to be, the suit was the sign of leisured urban modernity. In the 1990s, on otherwise bare shop walls, Keba Fall, tailor to Dakar's elite since the 1940s, displayed photos of youthful memories of Sunday suits and promenades in 1950s' Plateau. In the 1960s while artists held pan-African festivals, youth across the continent adopted flashy Western styles in a rebellious leisure culture allied with African-American rhythm and blues, dances, cinema and new, unsupervised courtship. People threw stones and called the police on girls who wore pants or miniskirts but youth '*ont tenu la coup*', persisted, to impose the European style explains tailor Abdou Niang (Rabine 1998: 99). In the 1960s Senghor prescribed the suit for and banned the boubou for official contexts. The boubou was reinstated in the 1980s by Abdou Diouf as official dress and is now accepted as dress for every Friday, the holy day. As colonial institutions collapse so do their prescriptions for male dress and the boubou is legitimate throughout social contexts.[5] Jewels of the cosmopolitan coast, St Louis and Dakar, never quite conceded to mirror Paris. In becoming *civilisé* their inhabitants used multiple, sometime hybrid, forms of dress, language and conduct as they negotiated colonial institutions and new urban spaces.

Couture to *Cutur*

Dakar's real and imagined city of *cutur* was produced by popular economic strategies and culture in the 1980s. This city of spectacles of both lavish display and inequality reconfigured socio-spatial boundaries, social hierarchies and identities. Local strategies and then neo-liberal reform expanded the informal economy and liberalized trade, which reopened the restricted neocolonial trade regime, though on unfavourable terms of global engagements (Mustafa 1998; Dieng 2000; M. Diop 2002; Simone 2004). Dakar's artisanship in clothing, hair and style relies on rapid, diverse global circulations of industrial productions in technology, cloth, fashion accessories and visual images (see Figure 11.1). Dakar's marketplaces register a new commercial terrain in an urban economy of expanded global trade networks organized through Islamic brotherhoods, unprecedented female entrepreneurship and drastic periodic ebbs and flows of cash flows and consumption. With the demise of the educational system, commerce and small business have become the ground of the reshaped middle classes. The crisis strategies of the 1980s led to gendered transformations in tailoring, as in other domains, as women and youth faced more vulnerability but also opportunity.

While post-Fordist flexibility advances standardization and massification of fashion through highly mobile capital and labour, *cutur's* flexibility of artisanal production enables individual producers and consumers to realize their dreams and participate in fashion's paces. Despite a volatile, seasonal consumer market with unstable cash flows, several factors intensified and expanded competition, creativity, tailoring skills and social knowledge of fashion. These were expanded trade regimes and diversity of raw materials, extreme (self-) exploitation of labour, price cutting, social pressures to reduce prices and expansion of apprenticeship to include middle-class youth who faced collapsed schools, especially girls. It is precisely this volatility throughout production and consumption, which makes fashion important for securing multiple forms of wealth such as income, reputation

Figure 11.1 Cyberfemme (Cyberwoman). Costume by Senegalese costume designer, Oumou Sy. Sy often parades and photographs her costumes in the urban decay of Dakar's streets. Credit: Metissacana 1997.

and social networks. After the 50 per cent devaluation of 1994 the local market polarized even further. Many turned to ever-cheaper materials and revived local techniques such as dyeing, while relatives of Senegalese migrant traders express and claim new status through ostentatious consumption in fashion and ceremonies.

Tailoring entered Senegalese society as a French colonial technology and knowledge in Catholic schools and colonial institutions. During the 1930s male tailors were trained and employed in the French artisanal tradition in urban colonial institutions. In hospitals and military camps they produced *confection*, uniforms. In trading firms they sewed for clients who bought cloth at the shops. By the late 1940s, these *tailleurs militaires* were training their own apprentices and had shops in city avenues catering to Senegalese clients.[6] In the 1970s rural droughts led to the migration of young men to Dakar and into the artisanal trades (see Figure 11.2). In the early 1980s middle-class women entered the field as entrepreneurs and then as apprentices. They have relied upon the reserve male labour in tailoring and built their clientele base from social networks. In this last phase, overlapping categories of *cutur femme* and *cutur africaine*, have been the principal focus of expansion, consumption and creativity. *Cuture africaine* includes embroidered *boubous* for both genders and the hybrid *n'dockettes* and *taille bas* for women. The *n'dockette*, '*mbuub a la francaise*', French robe, resembles the dress of coastal metisse women in St Louis (Biondi 1987: 52). The *taille bas* is a skirt suit with tight bodice and decorative neckline, sleeves and hip areas. *Cutur femme* includes both Western and Eurafrican hybrids for women – *taille bas, n'dockettes* and dresses, skirts, jackets and trousers for young, usually unmarried, women.

The expansion of *cutur femme* exemplifies the way networks at multiple levels and scales enable local agents to negotiate instability in this post-colonial, globalized context. As structural adjustment programmes designed by the IMF led to

Figure 11.2 A tailor in the HLM5 market, the major cloth market of Dakar. Small, artisanal workshops with simple machines predominate in Dakar's garment production sector. Credit: Hudita Nura Mustafa, 1993.

austerity, the state disengaged from services, parastatals and employment. Male unemployment skyrocketed through white-collar sectors and small business. By the early 1990s, middle-class women in Dakar had intervened decisively to transform a male, artisanal craft of tailoring into an occupation based upon wage labour, female social networks, competitive design and marketing.[7] Given the low status of tailoring for urban, middle-class women, they reinvented themselves as couturieres, women of taste with natural gifts for design. Not just in ceremonies but in everyday life they are tastemakers, as one told me sarcastically, 'when I wear something to take out the garbage my neighbours think it is a new style and order it.' In particular, women reinvigorated ceremonial life and its social and financial networks, which served to generate capital and clientele hence intensifying both rivalry and solidarity among women. Families and women strategize to dress by borrowing clothes, gift-giving and organizing savings groups. In weddings and naming ceremonies, individual dress display and gift-giving of cloth are equally important.

Cutur, perhaps more than Western fashion processes, is a field in which production, consumption, exchange and display are deeply interdependent. In the 1980s, by opening shops in markets and at home and 'walking around the city' to 'look for money', women occupied public space and challenged norms of modesty and propriety. As they began in the 1990s to travel to Jeddah, Las Palmas, Gambia and Nigeria to buy cloth, gold, cosmetics or shoes they further destabilized such norms (Grandmaison 1972; Kane 1977; Sarr 1998 on this trajectory). While all ateliers are new public spaces of conviviality, women's ateliers become salons of friends in the afternoons, supporting social networks in times of crisis. Transnational religious diasporas and women's social networks have knitted together a citywide network, linked to other commercial urban centres, which circulates labour, style, materials, cash and connections. Women strategically linked entrepreneurial, ceremonial and personal agendas and in so doing rearticulated institutions, practices, discourses and hence, social domains and the city space.

Several master tailors trained as *tailleurs militaires* adapted to the new terrain of competition by changing their focus in the 1980s to the niche market of *cutur femme*. For instance, Babacar N'diaye was trained as a *tailleur militaire* but strategically turned his eye and hand to this market. By the late 1980s his prize-winning designs, Eurafrican hybrids in evening dresses, *taille bas* (Wolof/F: skirt suits) in cotton prints, were shown on televised fashion shows. His signature is recognized, his clients say, by an elegantly sharp silhouette, itself derivative of his cut, which is based upon his training in men's blazers. In a tragic case, one of the most senior tailors in Dakar closed his shop to work for a businesswoman. When her shop closed he was forced to sit on a bench in a road waiting for his old clients in the same Plateau district where he had been a master artisan for the previous forty years.

The rapid expansion of *cutur* was enabled by multiple forms of global and local flexibility with diverse but mutually reinforcing dynamics. The flexibility and range of new transnational connections are managed by wholesalers connected to a pyramid of smaller traders. For example, Senegalese traders design and order motifs at factories of Dutch 'wax' prints and German damask.[8] Wholesalers then order cheaper copies from Hong Kong and Chinese factories, or purchase the cheapest from Nigeria, which has one of the few viable textile industries on the African continent. *Basin bu riche,* high quality, German damask is CFA (Communauté Financiere Africaine) Fr. 6,000 (US$10) per metre in contrast to the Hong Kong cheaper quality of CFA Fr. 3,000. The major markets in Dakar are situated in the middle-class districts of Sandaga and Habitations Loyers Modérés section 5 (HLM5). These markets are regional centres of trade and contain shops of all these levels of traders. The accessibility of cloth is crucial to the democratizing, if emulative, dynamic of fashion.[9] Flexible forms of artisanal production respond to the short cash flow periods at the beginnings of months and at the peak seasons of the two Muslim Eid holidays.[10] Despite the high rates of consumption at peak season and in ceremonial life, Sotiba, the national textile company has captured neither the luxury nor the low-end local market. Its factories are plagued by mismanagement and are often closed. This exemplifies the disarticulated nature of the fashion process, which serves to support foreign over national industry.

Création and Global Culture

While 'before it [the *boubou*] was for princes and marabouts, now it is for everyone' old hand-embroiders say. Indeed, the embroidered *boubou* is now the main canvas for *création* and its gravitas is disregarded in a wild play with cloth, colour and decoration.[11] The transformation of the *boubou* shows that despite an oppositional semantics of European/modern versus African/traditional, in Dakar's fashion schema new and traditional are not opposed. Notwithstanding an invocation of a colonial dialectic, African style is more valued than European style. Its valorization is based upon an authenticity created from the hybridity of forms and a complex assembly of values rather than the pursuit, always illusory, of fixity or purity (see Figure 11.3). More than nationalism or a revival of tradition, African styles produce an African modernity developed through cosmopolitanism and crisis.

The innovative assembly of forms and values occurs in ateliers through *création*, the collaborative design process between tailor and client, which – at once intimate and public – combines personal fantasy, artisanal skill and social knowledge of fashion. In contrast to the sober artisan–client relations of the past, focused on reproducing styles, in this active consumption clients work with producers to valorize cloth, garments and their bodies through cut and decoration. A valuable garment produces a person of *maana* (Wolof: value, presence). A central practice of *cutur*, *création* is embedded in multiple scales from the local scale of the atelier with its convivial joking, confidences and creativity to the regional scale of materials, skill and style distribution, to the global scale of transnational trade. Its interdependent

Figure 11.3 A 'couturier's' shop window in the Medina district of Dakar, a popular centre for shopping and promenading. Seye's designs show the recent use of 'modern' marketing and publicity techniques. His designs are part of the popularization of the *boubou* robe and use festive, multicoloured cloth, embroidery and motifs to transform the formerly sober, masculine style. Credit: Hudita Nura Mustafa, 1993.

production and consumption produces new social relations and spaces. As such, it is diagnostic for the transformation of the colonial modernity of couture into the globalized modernity of *cutur*.

The versatility of the *boubou* as a form has led to a popularization that some consider banalization or even degradation. The traditional *boubou* has always been requisite for ritual contexts and an unquestioned pinnacle of sartorial prestige. A simple form of robe made from a six-metre length of cloth, its neck is cut out at the fold and ends are sewn at the base of the length to create arm openings. It is worn with pants and kaftans by men, and wrappers and headscarves by women. As a regal male dress the *boubou* was made in white damask, sometimes hand-dyed to the pious sky blue, three pieces being cut from a ten-metre length of cloth to make pants, kaftan and covering robe. Imposing, costly hand-embroidered Islamic motifs in silver or gold thread took months to complete. Second-hand machines, diverse materials from the highest value threads in French silk to Nigerian polyester make embroidery available for increasingly bold, diverse types of garment and clienteles.

While women wore *boubous* in cotton prints, in the 1960s the embroidered *boubou* entered women's fashion. As such it became subject to rapid variations of cloth, materials, colours and motifs and simulations of motifs such as appliqués and hand-painting. Traditional Islamic motifs were replaced by inspirations from the cloth's motifs or even pop art-like geometrics. Damask cloth is supplemented by luxurious feminine materials such as Swiss voiles, Japanese jacquards or, for a more imposing look, heavy German brocades. While the sober blues and browns of prized *tuub* hand-dyed *boubous* are worn by older women or at times by Toucouleur women, most women follow the seasonal fashion in colour, which is determined in large part by what the traders order. Scandalously, *boubous* and *n'dockettes* are even made in percale, the cheap white cotton used to wrap the deceased, and decorated with appliqués or even painting that imitate embroidery. Conservative older tailors who refuse fashion insist on the sober colours and Islamic motifs. The banalization they say results from women copying celebrities on television in 'extravagant and folkloric dress ... and they follow not knowing that dress has its proper context.' For elite embroiderers, like the Guinean couturiere celebrity Douma Diakhate, the *boubou* has generated great wealth and an international African clientele of elites and even presidents.

Unlike ready-to-wear, which conceals labour processes, *création* enables both clients and tailors to exercise imagination and choice. Furthermore, evaluation of a garment is based in part upon the skill of sewing and its final value is based upon personal elegance in wearing. As for any migrating friend, at my departure my tailor and key interlocutor, Babacar N'diaye of Weekend Elegance insisted on making a collection for me. We chose models by scouring magazines, a photo album of his designs and my own notebook of fantasy styles. We shopped for cloth in markets, went through my own collection of cloth and, as he cut, he reinvented our designs. At the end, I had several dressy skirt-and-pant suits in black chiffon, white damask, cotton prints and hand-dyed damask. Western cuts were combined with 'African' cloth of prints, *tuub* or damask. Decorative highlights such as the full sleeves like the *taille bas*, embroidery on necklines, lace cuffs, rows of tiny buttons were based on both Parisian haute couture models and the Senegalese emphases of head and shoulders. Many were variations of the Eurafrican *taille bas* that modify recent neck or sleeve styles from Paris seen in the prêt-à-porter magazine from Paris, *Rendezvous*, in *Amina*, a women's magazine published in Dakar, on television or film (see Figure 11.4). In the early 1990s *Rendezvous*' photographs of Victorian balloon sleeves in Parisian shows inspired virtual flower bouquets of sleeves. Among my skirts were flared models and the popular Alexis long split skirt named after the *Dynasty* soap opera character. For Babacar, this collection was an opportunity for his designs to be seen in elite, foreign contexts such as hotels, conferences or receptions.

Figure 11.4 A bride from an affluent Dakar family with her entourage of friends. This white Eurafrican *taille bas* style is one of three outfits for the day and is made in European luxury cloth. Credit: Hudita Nura Mustafa, 1993.

Dakar's allure for West African consumers rests upon its creative producers, diverse materials and quality. Malian and Guinean women traders purchase stocks of *n'dockettes* made in the HLM market by women entrepreneurs and their employed tailors. There cheap cloth such as percale, sheer cotton Khartoum or Chinese damask is valorized with 'eccentric' trims of eyelet lace, ribbons or embroidery that often cost more than the dress itself. These women claim to be *créateurs*, but as one told me, 'we are all cheats [of others' designs].' For educated elites, such garments demonstrate poor taste, for the value and quality of cloth is more important than decoration. The trajectory of the most popular *n'dockette* style in the 1990s, the jaxass style of patchwork, shows how the fashion process circulates and masticates images. Jaxass originated with the founder of the Baye Fall sect of the Mouride brotherhood, Cheikh Ibra Fall, whose tattered clothes signified world renunciation and hard work. Today's disciples beg but also drink alcohol and perform ecstatic ceremonies of drumming, singing and self-flagellation. They make baggy pants and tunics made of patchwork panels. In the free for all of contemporary fashion this inspired the national textile producer to make a cotton print for cheap pants, tops and bags for tourists and exported it to the United States. By the 1990s, jaxass inspired an enduring style of *n'dockettes*. The irony was that patchwork was a costly design because it needed multiple symmetric panels in new, even luxury, cloth whose many seams were decorated with costly trimmings. As fashion, patchwork catered to consumer desire in commodified transnational markets for Dakarois authenticity, the opposite of its origin in worldly renunciation in pursuit of a sacred Senegalese community.

Youth style has most leeway to engage directly with images of not only European but with parallel modernities in Asia or the Islamic world. Young women (under the age of thirty-five) enjoy the most diverse array of styles. For example, in the 1990s, a stitched-skirt Indian sari was worn with so-called 'Naomi Campbell' wigs of straight hair and bindis on the forehead. Veiling, usually done by women for only a few years in their twenties, is more controversial as it is generally seen as a repressive, 'un-African' practice; and, though covered from head to toe, these women are usually colour coordinated in fashionable cloth. As in most major cities, blue jeans are part and symbol of a larger youth culture of associated accessories (T-shirts, baseball caps, sneakers, lycra leggings, miniskirts), music (rap or local *mbalaax* music) and leisure activities (cinema, dances, hanging out). For everyday wear, male youth, teenage girls and children rely on second-hand clothes. For important dances at Christmas or New Year, youth order tailor-made outfits. In the poorest sectors, tailors creatively use *fuug jaay* or even curtains to make stylish outfits. Many apprentices use their first salary as a tailor to buy, overnight, an image of urban sharpness in a pair of jeans, a shirt and leather shoes.

So, to return to our basic questions, is *la mode Dakaroise* voracious creativity a result of colonial legacy or a disarticulated globalized economy? What is the place of colonial civilizing urbanism in the making of Dakarois modernity today? It is telling that unlike East and Southern Africa in which Western style has long replaced local dress, *fuug jaay* is disdained. This contrasts with other East and Southern African states where Western styles are the standard, and second-hand clothes are central to fashion processes (Hendrickson 1996; Hansen 2000). It is the limit against which we can discern the current meaning of *civilisé*. While African dress is now acceptable across all social contexts, Western clothes have become limited to offices, youth social contexts and casual everyday dress mostly for male wearers. Since education and bureaucracy have been displaced by commerce as routes to socio-economic position and mobility, the men's suit has been displaced by the *boubou* and the *n'dockette*. Through *création,* the *boubou* and *n'dockette* bear the agendas and burdens of contemporary crisis and cosmopolitanism. For the new class of entrepreneurs these styles create a new image of Dakarois civility and elegance based not on francophone education as it has been for a century, but on successful negotiation of transnational trade, renewed cosmopolitan influences and very specific valorization strategies in *cutur*. With the decline of French influence and collapse of neocolonial institutions, being *civilisé* through comportment is rerooted in popular Senegalese practices as part of broader struggles around distinction, class restructurings and global hegemonies.

A Cityscape of *Dirriankhes*

Fashion needs a stage, we know, and cities need spectacles. The specificity of Dakar's stage is the heterogeneity of the spaces for fashion competition and recognition.

From ateliers and markets to ceremonies and streets and television and music videos, the *dirriankhe* is the ideal of feminine elegance. The *dirriankhe* is above all a corporeal, multi-sensorial and eminently visual spectacle of mature femininity – overflowing robes that fall underfoot, a voluptuous body cared for by lotions and incense, clinking waist-beads, slow, seductive gait – all performed for the audiences of urban streets, ceremonies and markets. This *sañse* of various sensory effects plays at revealing and concealing the body, and an air of nonchalance belies the great effort that enables such dress. Urban lore contends that this sight was said to 'drive the Yankees crazy' in post-Second World War naval postings in Dakar and hence the word, '*dirriankhe*'. An etymology, however, suggests that her name comes from her gait, the Wolof '*dirri*', to drag. In the heterogeneity and polarization of urban spaces, her presence is pervasive.

Urban legends, visual images and music reiterate the *dirriankhe*. A drawing by an early documentarian of Senegal, the metisse priest, David Boilat presents historical images of the pre-colonial coastal culture of beauty. In his *Esquisses Senegalaises* (1984 [1853]) Wolof queens and mixed-race Signares, female traders in eighteenth- and nineteenth-century St Louis, wore multiple layers of woven cloth and towering headscarves. In 1950s studio portraits, St Louisienne women assert hybrid aesthetics amidst the colonial assimilation policy and these portraits grace many domestic interiors. They also serve as models for wall murals in Dakar and for the unique genre of miniature glass paintings. Griot singers or women politicians are celebrated in music videos and television newscasts. Televised fashion shows and beauty contests both promote and satirize this model of corpulence and nonchalance. Gossip about neighbourhood fashion queens or wealthy women traders circulate stories of ceremonies, wealth, marriages and dress. Such enactments reinvent the *dirriankhe* for the contemporary purposes of celebrity. They also take the *dirriankhe* from circumscribed contexts of conjugal domesticity, familial ceremony or collective leisure into ambiguous commercialized, mediatized contexts and even to foreign travel.

Like the American New Woman or Parisian *grisette,* the *dirriankhe* represents experiments in and cultural anxieties about modernity. In Senegambian traditions of elegance women's beauty represents familial dignity as well as individual mastery. Any single performance of dress is enabled by a host of collective financial and social investments from advice on fashion, borrowed gold jewellery to gifts of cloth or cash loans. Furthermore, the sites of sartorial display were limited to familial ceremonial life, collective leisure activities or conjugal seduction. As an ideal of masterful elegance, the *dirriankhe* was linked to leisured elites but today she is linked to mobile, public businesswomen. For these women an elegant dignity secures not only respect and familial reputation but also credit, clients and business connections. Their expenditures on ceremonies, dress and financial (and possibly sexual) autonomy incite a critical popular discourse on the immorality of women's consumption, public work and narcissism. One legend of a cloth trader, Anta Gueye, known for her beauty, recalls that she wore a *boubou* costing CFA Fr. 800,000.00 (nearly US\$ 3,000.00 or about a year's salary for a bureaucrat) and spent 10 million on ritual gifts of cloth for her daughter's baby's naming ceremony. Whether or not this is true, such legends inspire the self-destructive excesses of ordinary women, which then lend fuel to ambivalent gendered discourses on modernity. While self-transformation, *sañse*, is valued, businesswomen's fashion is seen as false display of ambiguous wealth.

Most importantly, the *dirriankhe* is a crafted identity of middle-class business-women whose sartorial performances reinvent work identities as tastemakers rather than accept disdain as common manual workers or traders. They strategically weave together work, sociability and self-fashioning. As patriarchal norms are challenged and displaced by the reality of male disempowerment and female economic activity, the ideal of femininity as nonchalant elegance has a new edge as the woman who comes face to face with crisis: juggling obligations, time and money, some even advancing, and doing so with the pleasure of looking good, 'feeling good in one's skin', my friends say. In sum, the current appeal of the ideal of the *dirriankhe* is not that she represents static tradition but rather that she represents contemporary disintegrations, reinventions and recuperations of power, culture and values in a transnational world. It is for this reason – her disruptive as well as recuperative capacity – that the *dirriankhe* is the focus of cultural anxiety around gender and work, consumption and morality. A figure of elegance, transnationalism and Senegambian modernity, the *dirriankhe*, as image and lived reality, is embedded in the *longue durée* of Senegambian cosmopolitanism as well as more recent colonial and global encounters. As such, she condenses the multiple streams of history, culture and power through which Dakarois agents negotiate with the crisis strategies and creativities of cutur. On a broader scale, *la mode Dakaroise* emerges from these negotiations and transforms Dakar from a colonial capital to a global city.

Mirror Cities: Colonial Spheres and Global Cities

The conceit of the mirror for inter-urban influences in fashion aptly raises questions of imitation, narcissism, image-making and ephemeral images. The mirror reminds us of what is at stake in discussing Paris and Dakar, or any post-colonial dynamics of emulation, recognition and hierarchies of cultural capacity. Coastal global history, colonial projects and contemporary global restructuring created conditions of crisis and cosmopolitanism for *La mode Dakaroise* that endow it with a remarkable capacity to hybridize, reinvent and resist global hegemonies. As a nexus for Western European, Islamic and African cultures, Dakar has for centuries been a fashion capital of cultivated elegance of persons and things. The sartorial excellence of Dakarois is a living tradition that far exceeds French projects of colonial civility. Dakar is not a mirror city to Paris or anywhere else. Rather it provokes reflection upon the many spheres and hegemonic struggles that intersect in any city in Europe or Africa. As colonial cities transform into global cities, conceits such as the mirror and fashion city remind us that currencies of cultural brokerage and resistant creativities continually rearticulate local and global hierarchies. In Dakar's ruins of the colonial mirror, spectacles of globalized hybrid creativity forge a contemporary fashion capital.

Notes

1. I wish to thank Leslie Rabine and Didier Gondola for their helpful comments as I was preparing this chapter.
2. I am inspired here by Didier Gondola's invention of the term *villes miroirs* (F: mirror cities) to describe the intertwined histories of Kinshasa and Brazzaville as they looked at each other across the river Congo. See his study (1997) of La Sape, a fashion cult of male migrants between Congo and Paris.

3. The exception to ethnic tolerance is the recent secession struggle of the Diola in Casamance region, who were long neglected by the central government. There the state has been repressive and violent.

4. In the interior, colonial cash-cropping relied upon cooperation of marabouts, leaders of the Mouride, Sufi Islamic brotherhood, who organized hard labour to grow peanuts to be sold to French trading firms, which were managed by Lebanese. In response to ecological crisis in the region they have expanded into urban and, since the 1980s, transnational bases in the informal sector and trade. They now form a powerful and wealthy trade diaspora, and effectively partners of the state. Throughout satellite communities in New York, Turin and other Western cities their web of finance, advice, support and knowledge links urban entrepreneurs, male traders and artisans and young male migrant traders to maraboutic leaders to whom they tithe.

5. By contrast to Senghor, Mobutu Sese Seko's policy of cultural authenticity in culture banned European names, dress and culture generally when he seized power in 1971 in Zaire, formerly Belgian Congo. He banned European suits for men and pants and dress for women. He wore a signature leopard skin hat and promoted the *abacos*, a version of the suit, as official men's dress (MacGaffey and Bazenguissa-Ganga 2000).

6. In pre-colonial Senegambia, crafts had been organized through hereditary, low status castes of weaver, black/goldsmiths, praise singers/musicians, leather and woodworkers. While tailoring is not casted, many persons of caste entered into it. In Dakar, it is considered at once clean and modern but is considered a low status, manual occupation among the middle classes.

7. While there are a few sweatshops in Sandaga market and a few elite shops of around twenty-five tailors, most ateliers are *petit tailleurs*: one man, his machine and apprentice. Some men share rental of a shop space and many are continually looking for day jobs. Women opened ateliers in their homes in garages, corridors, courtyards and spare rooms. Women's shops, usually with one or two tailors, are riddled with tension. Tailors leave jobs suddenly, steal and sabotage. Aspiring to be artists, being exploited as workers, tailors complain of low wages, disrespect and being forced to do quick, shoddy work, which ruins their hand. I found that these complaints describe actual conditions for tailors and businesswomen in my research.

8. Vlisco in Netherlands has long been a main wax producer, but Manchester, England also makes some. Wax is a cotton print that imitates the batik the Dutch saw in their Indonesian colonies and is exemplary of the circuits of colonial culture through one colony and imperial centre to another colonial zone. This of course debunks the authenticity of African cotton prints with stereotypically bright colours and 'loud' designs.

9. Similarly, second-hand sewing machines, such as the lightweight Butterfly made in Taiwan, or the German Bernina for embroidery are brought in crate loads from

Germany by Mouride traders. They are then modified for local styles and labour processes. Trade-in of second-hand goods from car parts, refrigerators, magazines to clothing is a large part of trade.

10. Home-based operations open and close for peak season. There is a range of wage types from piecework to daily and monthly. Prices range from credit, often never fully repaid, to bargained prices. Free labour within social networks aids many to dress especially as the apprenticeship and community centre sewing schools expand. Some clients never pick up their orders because they cannot pay.

11. This was explained to me by one of the few surviving hand-embroiderers of *boubous*, one of a few men who sit outside a mosque in Plateau. In the early 1990s such an elaborate motif cost from CFA Fr. 30,000 up to CFA Fr. 100,000, the same range as for the cloth and embroidery for a custom-made machine-made boubou. European damask cost CFA Fr. 3000, Taiwanese CFA Fr. 1500. These prices doubled after the 1994 devaluation. For holidays, marketplace sweatshops in Sandaga churn out ready-made boubous at CFA Fr. 10,000 in cheap Taiwanese damask and Nigerian thread for adults and children. This enables shoppers to dress for holidays with cash procured at the last minute.

–12–

Far Out and Way In

London as Fashion Cosmopolis 1945–1979

Sonia Ashmore

In February 1970, *Vogue* reported on an aristocratic wedding at the Grosvenor Chapel, in London's Mayfair, one of the most exclusive areas of the city. Among the guests, royalty and politicians mixed with figures from the media and the world of pop music. 'The congregation looked different', noted *Vogue*. In place of the usual uniform outfits, the silk coats and matching hats worn season after season at society weddings, guests at the marriage of Lord Harlech to Pamela Colin were described as, 'Beautiful, young, long-fringed people … dressed like Augustus John gipsies.' Lord Harlech's daughters, Alice and Victoria Ormsby-Gore, famed for 'looking as if they had been rummaging in the Wilton dress-up chest' (Beaton 2003: 98), wore a brocaded velvet kaftan and a silk tribal coat from Asia, with patchwork boots. (The bride's dress by Jean Muir, in cream wool incorporating a Celtic motif is now in the V&A (T.268-1986).) The Harlechs had previously been photographed in similar exotic dress at their ancient family seat in Wales (*Vogue* July 1969). Such English aristocrats in hippy 'ethnic' clothes were in some ways style leaders of their generation, both signifiers and signified. At an earlier society wedding celebration, in 1966, the photographer Cecil Beaton had observed similar transgressive mores: 'Not one person was in evening dress, not a sign of a gala flower. No buffet with little cakes: beats, open necks, blue jeans, sweaters, shoulder-length hair for men and women, Shrimpton, the model, in football boots…' (Beaton 2003: 97–8). In Britain, social dress codes were changing.

The emergence of exotic dress styles in Britain during the 1960s and early 1970s, was neither a designer-led phenomenon, nor quite a 'street style', but a form of counter-cultural expression that arrived through less predictable routes and cultural milieux. This chapter, as part of a larger study of fashion consumption in the West End of London during the post-war period, explores some of these routes and also considers broader aspects of the appropriation of 'ethnic' dress styles by the London fashion market. It examines aspects of the context, representation and discourse around this phenomenon and identifies how the 'ethnic' or indigenous clothing of non-Western cultures was absorbed into the British, and implicitly London-based fashion boom of the period, in the context loosely referred to as 'Swinging London'.

In another chapter, and in earlier discussion, Claire Dwyer has analysed issues of dress and ethnicity in relation to transnationalism, and to 'the spaces of commodity culture' in the context of cultural geography (Dwyer and Crang 2002; Crang, Dwyer and Jackson 2003). An extensive literature has attempted to formalize and model the patterns of diaspora and 'global cultural flows' of an apparently rootless, boundaryless postmodern world and their reflection in material culture. It has been argued that the more ethnographic approach emerging from this has produced more 'grounded' versions of transnationalism as it is actually experienced (Crang, Dwyer and Jackson 2003). Appropriation has not all been one way; Western fashions have also been adopted by Asian women, and British-Asian entrepreneurs 'continuously reformulate their 'ethnic' traditions through the filters of their British class and local cultures', such cultural intermediaries can be said to have opened 'new spaces', generate new landscapes and ethnicities and new consumer styles (Jackson 2002). Some of these issues have been brought into the domain of consumption via the cultural repositioning of immigrant cultures on specific London streets. This has resulted in the 'aestheticisation and promotion of inner-city streets as exotic landscapes of consumption' and an 'inherent imbalance of power, wealth and mobility between the visitors and the visited' (Shaw, Bagwell and Karmowska 2004). While it may be useful to apply some of these perspectives to the wearing of ethnic dress in 1960s' and 1970s' London, the frame of reference of much of this recent discussion is not always historically relevant to the specific context of London during that period, when the term 'diaspora' still referred specifically to the Jewish experience, and 'identity' tended to be used in the context of psychology rather than sociology.

In the post-colonial era, cosmopolitanism, defined as 'the place which encompasses the variety of human cultures' (Chaney 2002), also has different meanings than it did in the 1960s and 1970s, at the 'end of empire'. While the period in principle saw a changing, less patriarchal relationship with the Commonwealth, in reality attitudes changed slowly. Post-war attitudes to immigration were formed by colonial experience and decolonization. In sociopolitical terms, and in terms of legislative policies towards immigrants, 'multiculturalism' is also a relatively recent concept; colour was an obstacle to assimilation, marked by Powell's 'Rivers of Blood' speech in 1968 (Goulbourne 1998). The novelist and writer on black British culture Mike Phillips noted in his autobiography that,

In the span of about ten years, London's role as the capital of the Empire evaporated, and the city began to struggle with its new post-imperial identity... For the bulk of Londoners the period was marked by the continuing arrival of Afro-Caribbeans in the city, followed by waves of Asians from Africa and the subcontinent. Accompanying this movement was the continuous irritation of transport strikes or housing shortages, and the trauma of Powellism, all of them object lessons that prompted the sense that the city was going through a process of fundamental and unstoppable change. (Phillips 2001: 40)

Thus the apparently trivial act of white British elites 'dressing up' in the kind of exotic dress that could be disruptive when worn by the actual immigrant 'owners' of those garments may have rehearsed some of the issues of 'transnationalism' currently under discussion, but it also pre-dates them. In the 1950s and 1960s, turbans may have been chic in *Vogue*, but were not acceptable for Sikh bus conductors; in some ways the *hijab* issue is not new (Wilson 2003; Maynard 2004).

Given the issue of historical differences, alternative interpretative contexts are needed for the wearing of 'ethnic dress' in this period. The idea that 'early twentieth-century consumer culture provided "other" fashions and cultural products which seeped into the popular imagination and helped develop a cosmopolitan consciousness' (Featherstone 2002) might be useful here, but it was equally true for London in the late nineteenth century, where large shops such as Liberty and Co. successfully provided just such exotic and alternative fashions and cultural products for consumers from 1875 onwards in an evocatively orientalist environment.

According to recent definitions (Eicher 1995; Maynard 2004), 'ethnic dress' is linked to ethnicity; it is perceived as the opposite of Western clothing and fashion cultures, relatively stable, beyond fashionable change, and worthy of appropriation. 'Ethnic' is the opposite of 'world fashion' (Eicher and Sumberg 1995: 300), which in its current meaning is about similarity. 'Ethnic dress' is intrinsically about marking differences between social groups by means of clothing and personal adornment. To avoid confusion with the more recent notion of 'style tribes' (Polhemus 1994), we can also take the term to refer to non-Western societies.

Such scholarly definitions of 'ethnic dress' have emerged from a wider, post-colonial examination of conscience initiated by Said's *Orientalism* (1995 [1978]) and from ethnographic discussion of issues of authenticity and appropriation. In the context of the applied arts, orientalism in dress has been connected to the fine art avant-garde; Poiret, Bakst and Matisse 'each ... created a scenography of the Orient that enabled him to redefine the image of the body, especially, but not exclusively, the female body' (Wollen 1993: 13). *Orientalism*'s notion of pervasive imperial ideologies has also been challenged; within the 'cosmopolitanism of commerce', orientalism has been seen as a liberating force. Selfridges department store in the West End of London exploited the Russian Ballet and the tango as 'a kind of generic popular cosmopolitanism – a commercial orientalism – with a distinctive libidinal economy in which women were key players' (Nava 1998). In a different discussion – about French interiors of the 1950s and their symbolic relationship with decolonization – it has been argued that exoticism in interior decorating offered possibilities of 'authenticity' in a world of 'disrupted certainties' (Sherman 2004). Fantasies of the 'primitive' were constructed through assemblies of objects 'styled' by magazines, juxtaposing objects from different cultures, in direct opposition to 'barren' Modernism; style leaders were declaring 'a war on good taste'. This idea of disruption and challenges to accepted taste is also an appropriate concept in the social and cultural environment of Britain in the late 1960s and early 1970s when interior design reflected a similar fascination with the 'exotic' at different economic levels, from the embroidered floor cushions and bedspreads that were affordable to students to the harem-like rooms and interior oriental 'tents' created by professional designers for wealthy clients and featured in glossy magazines.

It is evident that the 'West' imbues 'ethnic' dress and decoration with its own meanings and values, constructing it as sensual, handmade, decorative, different and allowing symbolic participation in the global arena. In the context of the Western fashion industry, 'ethnic' is a vague term, which has varied from 'Indian', both from the subcontinent and the Americas, to 'peasant', located anywhere from Eastern Europe to a Japanese rice field. These inconsistencies have been reflected in the fashion media. The cavalier and consumer-oriented approach of the fashion media to the notion of 'ethnic dress' is exemplified by a fashion feature in the women's magazine *Nova* as part of a special issue on Japan in 1972.

> The Indian thing has gone and in its place the oriental thing ... is influencing us Westerners. We are adapting their style to suit our way of life: taking bits of it and using them much less formally with our own things ... wide kimono sleeve and its variations – the dolman or batwing sleeve ... big clumpy shoes or sandals ... very much the dress of Japanese labourers. The layered look is also oriental: blouse upon blouse ... the kimono – copied too of course, but Westernised, softened up ... sometimes worn loose like a smock ... A tranquil alternative to western fashion. (*Nova,* March 1972)

While the notion of an alternative to Western fashion is significant, and despite *Nova*'s deserved reputation as a publication for thinking, independent-minded women, the language still carried the cultural baggage of colonialism, the ephemeral enthusiasms of the fashion media and the industry's impatience with the concept of 'authenticity', in itself a problematic term. As Leslie Rabine (2002) has noted in relation to West African fashion, ethnic authenticity is a term used by Westerners 'to add value to an object as commodity when it has left their original daily or ritual use.' Hazel Clark (1999) has also noted that 'authentic' dress has sometimes been reclaimed by its originators, after becoming 'ethnic chic' to tourists and expatriates, as in the case of the Chinese *Cheung Sam*. Yet stereotyped interpretations are actually the substance of this chapter; literal transcription is not fashion's business. As Colin McDowell has remarked, fashion designers' selective and romanticized view of exotic cultures has often been mediated through the visions of orientalist painters and other secondary imagery. 'Reality has never been part of the equation' (McDowell 2000: 328).

Interest in non-Western dress was one aspect of a spectrum of changes in the production and consumption of fashion during the 1960s, particularly evident in the boutique boom. It was a period when the fashion press and retail trade began to embrace a greater eclecticism than in the immediate post-war years when national reconstruction had precedence. Opposition to established conventions of fashion developed in parallel with other forms of social and political resistance: the 'counter-culture' and political protest. As Elizabeth Wilson has noted, fashion, being 'at the heart of history' has consistently embodied the most shocking and subversive ideas, sometimes in the form of 'oppositional dress' (Wilson 2003: 277). Valerie Steele (1997a) has suggested that the hippy effect was 'to destroy every rule' ... it was dressing to suit oneself. The transformative aspects of fashion have been discussed more generally by Caroline Evans, who argues that it 'can act out instability and loss but it can also, and equally, stake out the terrain of "becoming" – new social and sexual identities, masquerade and performativity' (Evans 1997; 2003: 6). This concept fits both Phillips's notion of the mood of 1960s' London trying on post-imperial identities and the late 1960s' concept of experimenting with cultural and political 'alternatives.'

Other 'fashion cities' besides London also had their flirtation with 'exotic' clothing. Italian and Parisian designers incorporated details of 'ethnic' dress into high fashion, notably Yves Saint Laurent who produced major collections with 'African', 'Russian' and 'Chinese' themes between 1967 and 1976, with a variety of other cultural excursions en route. It was 'Swinging' London, however, that was attracting the Western world's attention as a source of fashion and cultural innovation and was also engaging with a wider world through travel, fashion, art and pop music, sometimes all at once, as with the Beatles' flirtation with Indian mysticism. As Jonathon Green (1999) has noted, there were different locations of fantasy and 'otherness': America was admired for its popular culture, India for spiritual values. At the same time, different images of 'Englishness' continued to be successfully promoted and retailed in London's West End and in the fashion media. Examples of this were the traditional, formal tailoring rooted in an upper-class English lifestyle, with wardrobes designed to 'suit the social calendar' by designers such as Hardy Amies, although continuing to use French as well and British materials (Ehrman 2002); the new 'Pop' Englishness of Carnaby Street, with its debased, Union Jack decorated forms, and the 'English' styles designed by Laura Ashley that shifted from an early nineteenth-century 'peasant' look to country house gentility.

Historically, the wearing of oriental dress by Europeans began with the physical exploration of the world beyond Europe, but it was not until the late nineteenth and early twentieth centuries that non-Western approaches to garment making began to be incorporated into the cut of dress in the West, referred to as the 'flat terrain of cloth, the looping and wrapping of the garment, and the integrity of the untailored textile' (Martin and Koda 1994: 13). By the early eighteenth century there had been precedents for hybrid oriental garments in Britain; 'Indian Gowns' or 'banyans', loose garments for men of oriental inspiration and worn about the house, were often 'made up, and remade when worn, in London' even though they might have been made from Asian textiles (Swain 1972). Experiments with 'fancy dress' were made on designated occasions by both the middle and upper classes throughout the nineteenth century, but the idea of diverting from the Paris-dominated dictates of fashionable Western dress was promoted at market level by businesses like Liberty and Co. For Lasenby Liberty, the store's founder, Japan set a new aesthetic standard for dress; he admired the 'soft and clinging ... daintily coloured ... classic draperies of old Japan' (Liberty 1893). From the 1880s both historical and non-European garments were of direct inspiration to Liberty and Co. in their quest for 'permanent fashions' that liberated the female body simultaneously from the prison of the corset and the tyranny of Paris; even in the nineteenth century, progressive thinking about dress in the British capital was set against the perceived fashion leadership of the French one. Liberty's widely imitated 'artistic' garments also provided an outlet for the qualities of craftsmanship promoted by the store in the form of embroidery and decoration. The Liberty clothes were generally interpretations and not copies of garments such as kimono; they were translated into less structured and more fluid designs than were the common currency of late nineteenth-century dress, in harmony with the soft Liberty silks. Mixed sartorial metaphors were common then as now and can be seen on a series of cloaks inspired by the North African *burnous*, now in the Museum of London collections, which promiscuously combine African, Celtic and Aesthetic movement motifs. In Europe, designers such as Fortuny, Poiret and Vionnet also explored the possibilities of non-Western clothing beyond the borrowing of surface decoration, and it is not surprising that Poiret, whose reputation was by then in decline, should have been invited to produce collections for Liberty in the 1930s.

The adoption of elements of oriental dress in the West was selective, differentiating texture, motif and cut. Meaning was also complex and often conflicting, but in relation to clothing as an expression of the status and independent tastes of the wearer rather than an overt expression of imperial attitudes. In nineteenth-century America for example, the kimono suggested an interior, domestic life for women while also allowing the introduction of more relaxed forms of dress (Corwin 1996). In the later twentieth century, Japanese clothing design still offered the opportunity for radical change and reinvention in Western fashion, both in its styling and its symbolic order (Martin 1995b).

In Britain, during the 1940s and 1950s, war, shortages, rationing and reconstruction dominated the economy, clothing and notions of 'abroad'. The dress of immigrants had little to do with 'ethnic' dress; in terms of Caribbean immigrants, an identifiable 'Black Style' developed much later (Tulloch 2004). In *Small Island* (Levy 2004), the hat, white gloves and Sunday handkerchief worn by Hortense, a young teacher from Jamaica, put into symbolic relief her own palpable disappointment with the dirt and decay of post-war London.

By the 1960s and 1970s, the use of 'ethnic' dress as a symbolic gesture of a renewed, more empathetic, or familiar relationship with the world beyond Europe coincided with increased leisure, travel and also with movements of resistance to Western 'rules' and global events such as the Vietnam War. One might also refer to Appadurai's notion of 'armchair nostalgia' increasingly exploited in marketing

– 'nostalgia without lived experience or collective historical memory' (Appadurai 1996: 79) – to account for the apparently meaningless eclecticism of the way in which 'exotic' dress has been appropriated in the West. In terms of the fashion industry, its distribution was facilitated by the small, independent boutique and the rise of the street market as a source of alternative fashion (McRobbie 1989; Wilson 2003).

The use and meaning of the term 'ethnic' has frequently mutated in the fashion press and in popular jargon, and fashion journalism and photography have transmitted uneven messages regarding the notion of 'ethnic' clothing and its place on the fashion agenda. These related to their broader scope, perceived readership and, of course, advertisers. While *Vogue* remained committed to high fashion and the fashion cycle, it was forced to take account of the tastes of a new generation of consumers. Its ambivalence to the 'ethnic' was shown in its juxtapositions of alternative style options, constantly redefining the 'ethnic' on its own terms in its perpetual quest for novelty and being in front of the game. Signalling 'New interpretations of ethnic, all out glamour, new simplicity… The New Look of Ethnic Fashion', in 1976, it advised readers to, 'Mix yourself a potent Eastern evening.' It was a sort of luxury 'Pick and Mix' of world wardrobes where the emphasis on the word 'new' was antithetical to the 'tradition' it romanticized in aesthetic terms. Evening dress was now a 'Gold lame turban' and 'Asian pantaloons in shocking pink satin feathers … exotic follies for formal evenings' (*Vogue* 1 October 1976).

The then separate society magazines *Harpers* and *Queen*, which on the whole suggested dress for a structured social life, were sometimes unexpectedly iconoclastic during this period, particularly in the promotion of unorthodox styles for men. The use of a fashionable young male actor, Michael York, as a model associated with the exotic location of his current movie, increased the acceptability of garments such as embroidered kaftans. The *Times* correspondent Prudence Glynn, Lady Windlesham, a keen promoter of new talent and a democratized fashion industry, also reported on exotic fashion trends. Perhaps reflecting her own lifestyle, but with tongue in cheek, she recommended kaftans for country house parties. 'Christmas dinner sees you giving the county a glimpse of swinging London in your kaftan which should be warm enough to withstand the months of cold stored up in the seldom used dining room' (Glynn 1966). *Nova*, overtly rejecting the high fashion that was *Vogue*'s central mission, encouraged a more streetwise approach. Its fashion features mixed locally sourced garments with European ones, although it did not entirely dispense with stereotypes. In 1969, Brigid Keenan, reporting from Paris on Dior's new 'gypsy' look, stated that, 'The smartest woman in Paris last January was the gypsy outside the Plaza Hotel.' The model chosen for the feature was described as a 'half gypsy actress' who chose the clothes she modelled herself (*Nova,* August 1969).

Examples from *Vogue* illustrate how the magazine maintained a difference between the indigenous 'ethnic' garments that it sometimes celebrated and their commodification and consumption by the West. This was particularly evident on location in remote corners of the globe, where a peculiar 'ethnography' evolved. In April 1945, *Vogue* recommended transforming 'treasure' sent home from the East by one's menfolk in the services and turning saris into evening gowns; this conveniently sidestepped the problem of textile rationing. In May 1954, Wenda Parkinson was photographed looking elegant and patrician, but not at all 'ethnic', in Tangier; she wore an immaculate white cotton coat, three-quarter length white nylon gloves and court shoes, with an anonymous Moroccan woman sitting veiled, in matching white, at her feet. This was a typical use of aestheticized exotic settings as a background for Western fashions. Norman Parkinson, a master of the imaginative use of outdoor locations, made no attempt at empathy; the colonial imagery is striking, even though the picture was put together with his customary skill. In January 1969 David Bailey photographed Penelope Tree in Kashmir; the approach was more 'naturalistic', attempting to match clothes to setting and even using some locally sourced garments, yet the feature now appears no more culturally sensitive. In the same issue, *Vogue* also published Parkinson's fashion shoot in Ethiopia, to post-colonial sensibilities, perhaps the nadir of *Vogue*'s 'ethnography'. In one photograph a model, waited on by native 'attendants', wore a 'borrowed' local wedding dress; on the facing page, she wears a black *ciré* catsuit, from Harrods 'Way In' boutique, posed among semi-naked local women, the shiny black material intentionally echoing their skin colour. While this attempted a kind of physical rapprochement between 'them and us', the appropriation by the Western wearer of ritual indigenous dress and the overt distinction made between the raw, naked 'them', and the smooth, modern 'us', remain uncomfortably apparent. There were also many advertising promotions, which overtly commodified the 'exotic other.' In August 1979, *Vogue* promoted the 'Chinoiserie' of Saint Laurent's Rive Gauche as a main fashion trend; the magazine also carried double page spreads of Saint Laurent's notoriously *risqué* advertisements for its new 'Opium' perfume. In October of that year, *Vogue* was on location in China; the magazine carried advertisements for Revlon's 'China Reds' lipsticks and nail polish.

Ethnic dress did not initially arrive in London's shops and drawings rooms via conventional routes of fashion distribution. As social codes changed in the post-war period, prescriptive dress codes for the British social 'Season' became less relevant. As already noted, the changes were closely observed by the photographer Cecil Beaton (2003), familiar with the old English aristocratic style and a younger 'bohemian' upper class, a wealthy 'international set' and new 'classless' style setters such as rock musicians, photographers and fashion designers and stylists. Socialite 'stylists' such as Christopher Gibbs also had their influence. An old Etonian antique dealer, frequently in Morocco, at ease with both the old aristocracy and new London plutocracy and its drug scene, Gibbs wrote for *Vogue*, designed the 'exotic' sets for Nicholas Roeg's film, *Performance*, and lent his flat in Cheyne Walk to Beaton, style setter for a previous generation, as an exotic set for *Vogue*. Other wealthy socialites and 'jet setters', such as the younger Gettys with their house in Marrakech, were featured in the fashion and other press wearing de luxe exotic garments, often emphasizing their authenticity, antiquity and implied costliness. Less visible in the fashion media were lower budget 'hippy' types and students who assembled their clothes inventively both from necessity and principle (McRobbie 1989; Wilson 2003). Finding clothes that were inexpensive, yet romantic, they were saluted by *Nova* as practitioners of an independent, grassroots style; 'Do you think they will let anyone tell them what to wear?' it asked (*Nova* September 1968).

Beside the imagery and the social production of this new style of dress is the question of its diffusion. Ethnic dress arrived partly through non-commercial routes, via travellers from both the jet set and low budget hippy trail. Some of these set up market stalls and shops according to their means in London, importing directly from Asia, North Africa and Central America, through local wholesalers or having clothes made up in quasi-ethnic styles. Recognizing the demand, importers soon set up wholesale businesses in the East End of London and the rag trade area of the West End and advertised in the trade press.

Many of London's more exclusive 'ethnic' shops started in Belgravia, like Savita, which sold expensive, tailored clothes from India in luxurious fabrics, and Malabar on Brompton Road. Chelsea, on the map of 'Swinging London' since the arrival of Mary Quant's Bazaar in 1955, was the favoured location for small 'bohemian' and usually short-lived boutiques often started by relatively wealthy aristocrats. Michael Rainey's Hung on You, which initially catered to the bohemian dandy, moved into a more 'hippy' phase in its Kings Road premises, stocked with carpets and embroidered cushions, Afghan robes and oriental kaftans like those worn by his wife, Jane Ormsby-Gore, at her father's wedding (Figure 12.1). Nearby, London Docks and Oxus had similar merchandise. Countdown on the Kings Road was a more typical contemporary boutique that also sold exotic clothing, such as embroidered Romanian blouses. The Third Eye opened behind Oxford Street in 1969, in the then exclusive and hidden niche of St Christopher's Place; it sold exotic clothes and accessories. The cheaper Forbidden Fruit was in the then more socially more questionable and eclectic zone of Portobello Road and also in shabby Kensington Market. All these shops imported clothes directly, or through intermediaries, from sources in Asia. There was no doubt of the excitement caused by the appearance of these sumptuous textiles and gorgeous hand-decorated garments in a boutique scene that was gradually becoming increasingly mass-market driven with clothes of degraded quality. Designers from haute couture to the mass market also took on the 'ethnic' look: from Dior and Saint Laurent to young London designers such as Bellville Sassoon who catered for the debutante class, Thea Porter, herself of Lebanese/Syrian origin, Foale and Tuffin, John Bates and later Zandra Rhodes and Bill Gibb. Clearly such designers had no interest in offering reproductions of ethnic styles, but interpretations of them (Figure 12.2). In the mid 1960s Porter also had a decorating shop in Berwick Street selling eclectic objects and textiles from Syria and other parts of the Middle East and Europe.

Figure 12.1 Modelling in Chelsea, September 1967. The male models, from the English Boy agency, wear a 'peasant' outfit of embroidered blouse, jeans and sheepskin boots, probably from a Chelsea boutique, and an imported silk kaftan and embroidered slippers from Michael Rainey's shop Hung on You. The girls, with 'natural' bare feet and heavy make-up, wear dresses by Alice Pollock and Ossie Clark. © Celia Birtwell. Permission given gratis.

With their high profile and long-lived exposure in fashionable circles and the fashion press, the West End rag trade and mass-market retailers inevitably appropriated ethnic styles. Carnaby Street filled up with cheap cheesecloth clothes from India. The fashion trade inevitably diluted the original 'ethnic look', in one sense reaffirming the power of the white, Western fashion system over more 'primitive' sources, although it must be added that indigenous producers were also willing to increase production of these 'hand-crafted' clothes to supply Western consumer demand. East End wholesalers advertised limitless supplies of 'Afghan' coats and dresses. At all levels of the fashion industry, 'authentic' ethnic styles were reproduced and distorted through the use of synthetic or otherwise inauthentic materials, colours, fastenings, decoration and accessories. The *Drapers' Record* was particularly keen on promoting 'ethnic' clothing in patent synthetic fabrics, such as 'Banlon', 'Tricel' and Tootal's 'Sahara' range; these directly contradicted the

Figure 12.2 'Kaftan' by John Bates for Jean Varon, London, 1971. Art deco inspired patterns are applied to a garment based loosely on a traditional North African striped *djellabah* and Berber style desert head dress. The shoes were not typical desert wear. Photograph: Evening Standard © Getty Images. Getty Editorial 3267953.

'natural' fabrics and handmade qualities for which ethnic garments were appreciated (Figure 12.3).

Companies like Monsoon and East were later 'involved in the active construction of difference through the process of commodification' in a more formalized way, but during this intermediate and less formalized period, other discourses were also being rehearsed around the wearing, representation and reproduction of 'ethnic' clothing in London's fashion 'renaissance' (Dwyer and Jackson 2003). With hindsight, it is now possible to identify a dialectic between radical and conservative attitudes to dress and to ethnicity, to tradition and innovation, to stereotypes of race and gender, to nationalism and cosmopolitanism, to fashion elitism and the mass market.

The use of clothing unconnected with the Western fashion system was in many ways a radical gesture of resistance. It broke with the designer-led fashion cycle, with class-based dress codes, with the seasonal dress cycle and, temporarily, with mass-market capitalism. Where 'ethnic' dress represented resistance to consumption,

Figure 12.3 A fashion promotion for Tootal Fabrics' new 'Atlas' and 'Strata' Terylene Georgette, determinedly associating new synthetic fabrics with the ancient Mediterranean world and fashionable North Africa. These were made up into styles such as an 'exotic 4 piece harem set' and 'dainty kaftan' and were available in shops around the country from Abergavenny to Kilmarnock. Tootal Sahara advertising promotion in *Vogue*, February 1972.

Figure 12.4 Street style: a boy in 'ethnic' shirt and 'gypsy' neck scarf dances at a pop concert in Trafalgar Square, London, late 1960s. Photographer, Bill Coward. © Mary Evans Picture Library.

market stalls were as much staple sources of supply as Chelsea boutiques were. 'Hippies' favoured flea markets and old clothes shops (McRobbie 1989), and preferred natural fibres such as cotton, lace, silk, wool, rejecting synthetics. They preferred craft values to factory production and industrialized clothing; they developed independent entrepreneurial networks serving the counter-culture. 'Ethnic dress' also broke with gendered dress codes, representing men in frock-like kaftans, jewellery, sensual fabrics and flowered patterns (Figure 12.4). It was sanctioned by rock musicians like Mick Jagger and Jimi Hendrix, whose sexual preferences were not in question. 'Ethnic' dress' was also associated with social and political resistance, exemplified in the United States by empathy with Native Americans, the rural commune movement and the 'alternative' fashions of frontier style dress and nakedness. (For a discussion of counter-cultural dress see Wilson 2003 and Maynard 2004: 117–33.)

The ways in which 'ethnic' dress and exotic locations were commodified and represented, however, were also fundamentally reactionary. Images in the fashion press preserved a separation between the ethnic 'other' and the Western viewer or consumer. Marie Helvin, a successful fashion model of Hawaiian-Japanese origins, said she was at first considered 'too exotic' to work for Western fashion magazines (Helvin 1985), although her representation by photographer David Bailey put her onto the covers of *Vogue*. Ethnicity was portrayed aesthetically; there was no dirt and no poverty. Drugs were often an important factor in the appreciation of 'exotic' fabrics, colours and decorative detail, yet these were not referred to in the fashion press. 'Ethnic' dress was often an elitist form of consumption and display, based on the wearing of clothing appropriated from the poorest people in developing countries with which Britain had a legacy of colonial associations. While it could appear as a 'counter-cultural' stance, choosing to wear 'ethnic' dress in mid twentieth-century

London had a different ideological loading from the choice between Indian and European dress confronting Indian women in the colonial period (Bhatia 2003).

Despite such moralizing conclusions, the fashion plate remains the fashion plate. Most people dressed eclectically – an Indian *kurta* with jeans, an Afghan coat with Kings Road boots – and according to their budget, as they do today. As Margaret Maynard has suggested, 'Bi-cultural dressing' does not mean straightforward choice of one or other; 'fashionably ethnic' usually means indiscriminate sourcing. With mass-produced clothing, 'it is consumers who bring meaning to bear in their choice of clothing.' Cultural and personal identity is 'subject to constant repositioning' (Maynard 2004: 4–5). Remote from their ethnographic sources, 'ethnic' clothes were, and are, rarely worn in indigenous style. The defence of such 'cultural surfing' is that it inspires and regenerates longitudinally as well as historically (Johnson 2004). In terms of the inbuilt perversity of the fashion cycle, it was also perhaps not surprising that sensual, layered, complicated, 'handmade' clothes should follow the quintessentially 'sixties' look pioneered by designers like Quant, with a modern, clean-cut school uniform or 'space age' look using contemporary fabrics, represented with dynamic, minimalist imagery and worn with geometric haircuts. 'Ethnic' clothes were pretty, sensual, romantic and worn with long, preferably 'pre-Raphaelite' hair and languorous body language.

There are different ways of reading statements such as the one from *Nova* quoted earlier in this chapter: as ephemeral fashion journalism, with all the attendant ironies of wearing Japanese labourers' clothes in Bond Street, or as a statement of cultural appropriation that reflects the Western attitude that 'the world is ours' and paves the way for aggressive neocolonialist globalization strategies (Price 1981: 5). In terms of the production and diffusion of fashion, however, globalization is a more recent and specific concept, part of an 'interwoven macro-culture' (Maynard 2004), which does not fit Britain in the period of the 1960s and 1970s. On the other hand, linear notions of cultures dying out have also been rejected in favour of more optimistic botanical metaphors of the pollination and regeneration of cultures (Appadurai 1996; Clifford 1998; Rabine 2002). It has also been recognized that 'ethnic' style is not unchanging; traditional clothing can develop its own inner logic as a modern fashion system. In another chapter of this book, Rabine reminds us of the conditions of production and unfair trade practices relating to ethnicity in the 'rag trade' in West Coast cities, which are also universal, yet in one sense this has always been a continuous dark side of the fashion industry.

London, at the 'heart of Empire' in the nineteenth and early twentieth centuries, was the nexus of an imperial trade in which the global politics of cloth, both cut and uncut, played a significant and symbolic part. The textile trade with Asia formed a significant part of Britain's imperial trade, and historically influenced both dress and the decoration of the home. This legacy was manifested in the 'ethnic' revivals of the mid twentieth century, which referenced Asia over other non-Western countries. The appropriation and commodification of other people's clothing styles has historically been recurrent and, arguably, culturally stimulating. Martin and Koda have indeed argued in broader terms that, 'We cannot conceive of dress today without the East' (Martin and Koda 1994: 2). Other commentators have also noted that reinterpretation of ethnic dress can also have a regenerative effect in relation to issues of negotiating cultural identities today. Yet the reduction of a 'cultural tradition' to a fashion moment suggests a continuing attitude of condescension that derives from that earlier colonial era, generating problematic forms of representation, with uncomfortable visual juxtapositions of smooth Western models alongside rough 'natives', appropriating indigenous dress, yet still representing a duality of the primitive 'them' and the 'civilized 'us'. It was surely fun, but not entirely innocent.

–13–

Fabrications of India
Transnational Fashion Networks
Claire Dwyer

In October 2000 the British model Jodie Kidd was on the front cover of the Indian fashion magazine, *Gladrags*, to mark the launch of India's first fashion week held in Delhi (Figure 13.1). The knowing staging of this image resonates with critiques about re-Orientalization in its deliberate tropes of whiteness, sexuality and 'the exotic' (Jones and Leshkowich 2003; Nagrath 2003). At the same time there is something about the grins on the faces of the young men behind Jodie Kidd, carefully positioned as signifiers of the Indian traditions of the Jaipur palace in which the photographs were taken, to suggest, perhaps, ways in which some of the fixities of 'East' and 'West' implicit in this staging, might be disrupted opening the way for thinking about more *transnational* fashion cultures.

In this chapter I want to explore the transnational fashion cultures linking Britain and India as a way of thinking about fashion cities. I will draw on some empirical work, conducted between 1999 and 2002 with a range of fashion companies all based in Britain but selling clothes that are linked to the subcontinent in various ways. This research was part of a broader project on commodity culture and South Asian transnationality[1] through which we sought to understand the transnational networks, flows and imaginaries associated with commodity cultures of food and fashion (Crang, Dwyer and Jackson 2003). We were interested both in the transnational practices and spaces within which the fashion companies we interviewed operated, but also in how discourses or ideas about transnationality were mobilized in the stylization and marketing of clothing. We also wanted to understand how consumers understood transnationality (Dwyer 2004). Here I want to extend some of the arguments we have made elsewhere about transnational fashion cultures to think about fashion cities (Crang et al. 2003; Jackson, Crang and Dwyer 2003). By tracing the transnational networks and linkages through which British-South Asian fashion cultures are made, I focus on the ways in which these networks can be traced in and through specific urban spaces. This understanding of fashion cities as produced through a geography of transnational fashion networks and cultures is linked to recent geographical writing on fashion cities that emphasizes the importance of linkages, networks and flows (Gilbert 2000; Scott 2002; Rantisi 2004a).

Figure 13.1 Jodie Kidd modelling in Jaipur to promote the first Indian Fashion Week (*Gladrags Magazine*, October–November 2000). © *Gladrags Magazine*.

I begin by outlining our theorization of transnational commodity cultures and drawing on examples from a number of different British-South Asian fashion trajectories. I then focus on two different case studies from our research: the specialist Asian clothes retailer, Daminis, based in London and Leicester, and EAST, a high street retailer with outlets across the UK. In my analysis I trace the transnational relations evident in these companies, which operate in a range of different ways including material, aesthetic and imaginative connections. These transnational fashion cultures are also produced in and through specific urban spaces. Here I focus on such spaces in London, Delhi and Mumbai.

Transnational Fashion Cultures

This chapter is drawn from our wider study of transnationality and the commodity cultures of South Asian food and fashion. In this research we sought to expand existing definitions of the transnational, which we argued often focused narrowly on the flows of 'transnational' peoples and their associated goods from one place to another. Instead we adopted a more expansive conception of transnational space that understood social spaces themselves as constitutive of transnationality (Crang et al. 2003). We argued that transnational spaces were produced not only by the material geographies of transnational flows of labour or goods but also by the symbolic and imaginative geographies through which we understand transnationality. Transnational space was then both multidimensional but also multiply inhabited – by those with varying investments in transnationalism (Crang et al. 2003). Our focus upon the transnational spaces of commodity culture draws inspiration from Leontis's discussion of a topography produced through the notion of *emporium* – or commerce – which creates 'not a world of boundaries that separate but of routes that connect' (Leontis 1997: 189). It is also inspired by Appadurai's injunction 'to follow things themselves, for their meanings are inscribed in their forms, their uses, their trajectories.' (1986: 5) Tracing 'traffic in things' (Jackson 1999) involves the exploration of both the physical movement of people and goods across different geographical spaces, and also the processes of commodification that accompany this circuitry (see also Cook and Crang 1996; Cook 2004).

The case studies we selected for our investigation of British-South Asian transnational fashion cultures are embedded in different ways in the broader transnational trajectories linking Britain and the subcontinent. These trajectories include a long history of Western designers seeking inspiration in 'the East' – from William Morris, through Zandra Rhodes to Matthew Williamson – as well as a newly emerging British-Asian fashion industry (Bhachu 2003). Post-colonial transnational fashion cultures retain the resonances of histories of empire within which cultural and economic imperatives and imaginaries were entwined (Thomas 1991). Thus, as Emma Tarlo (1996) illustrates, Gandhian politics of the *khadi* placed dress at the heart of colonial contestation. The question of 'what to wear' in India remains, as Tarlo argues, bound up with contested imaginations of 'modernity' and 'tradition', 'indigenous' or 'Western'. At the same time the complexity and instability of these imaginaries is inherent if we consider the linkages between the British Arts and Crafts movement and the 'revival' of craft production in India in the nineteenth century (Metcalf 1989). This legacy, articulated through key sites such as the West End orientalist emporium, Liberty of London (Calloway 1992), is re-echoed in the emergence of twentieth-century transnational fashion cultures of 'ethnic' fashion such as those discussed by Ashmore in this volume. More recent enthusiasms for Indian-inspired (although not always Indian-produced) fashion in the high street have been paralleled with an enthusiasm for the aesthetic style of Bollywood and Asian music (Sharma and Sharma 2003). Analysis of these transnational fashion cultures highlights themes – such as issues of fair trade and ethical consumption (Hale 2000); accusations of neocolonialism, re-Orientalism or cultural appropriation (Hutnyk 2000; Puwar 2002) – which again find resonance within imperial histories (see Thomas, forthcoming).

A second way into the analysis of British-Asian transnational fashion cultures is to examine the history of Asian fashion in Britain. Histories of Asian fashion in Britain emphasize the different ways in which transnational connections have produced what Bhachu defines as 'diaspora economies' (Bhachu 2003; see also Khan 1992). While much of the earlier Asian fashion retailing of loose fabrics was male dominated, Bhachu celebrates the emergence of a women-led fashion culture, which includes both the long-standing tradition of skilled home-based seamstresses, early pioneers who sold 'suitcase collections' from home, and younger fashion designers, usually British-born and trained, who have created a vibrant and distinctively British-Asian fashion culture. Asian fashion histories are also made through particular geographies. These can be traced through the significance of key centres for Asian fashion such as the upmarket retailing spaces of Ealing Road in Wembley, where some of the first fabric shops run by Gujarati migrants in London were established. Bhachu argues that Asian diaspora economies produce distinctive hybrid fashion cultures, which are made both transnationally and locally. Asian fashion cultures reflect both the diversity of the Asian population in Britain, differentiated by religion, language and class, and the rooting of British-Asians in particular British regional fashion cultures (Bhachu 1988).

Linking both these trajectories is a consideration of the ways in which distinctive fashion cultures have emerged in India itself. Banerjee and Miller (2003) capture the complexities and diversity of women's fashion in India through an analysis of the significance of the sari. They chart both the contexts within which new traditions of Asian dress have emerged – the transition for many women from the sari to the shalwar kameez or Punjabi suit, for example – while also undercutting any assumptions about the meanings of different forms of dress. In contrast, Emma Tarlo (1996) traces the emergence of 'ethnic chic' or ethnic revivalist fashion in India embodied in the work of Ritu Kumar, the doyenne of Indian fashion, whose highly expensive clothes feature the most intricate hand-beaded embroidery. Kumar has sought to catalogue and revive embroidery and craft traditions of India both through her own incorporation of them in her modern designer clothing and in her work as a writer on the Indian textiles. The transnational trajectories work in different ways here. Kumar describes visiting the Victoria and Albert museum in London to trace designs no longer made in India that she seeks to revive (Bhachu 2003: 76). Ritu has been active in the institutionalization of design and textile education in India through the establishment of the Delhi Crafts Council and the National Institute of Fashion Technology also based in Delhi. The significance of Delhi as a site for the revival of Indian craft traditions through their re-working as ethnic chic is described in Tarlo's case study of the designer Bina Ramani and her establishment of the urban fashion village Hauz Khas (now somewhat eclipsed by more corporate shopping malls).

This is a significant established Indian fashion culture with continuities with the textile-based politics of earlier elite Indian nationalist figures (for example, the 'All India Handicraft Board' founded in 1952, which campaigned that urban Indians had a moral duty to support Indian handicrafts). However, alongside this are new fashion cultures whose exponents are young Indians capitalizing on a newly globalized economy. Key figures here include Ritu Beri, Rohit Bal and Rina Dhaka. Many of these designers were educated at the premier fashion institutions in Delhi but have chosen to relocate in Mumbai. It is here that new fashion cultures are being created by the vibrancy of the Bollywood film industry and sustained by Mumbai's rapid growth as a global financial and culture centre. This tension between the different fashion cultures of Delhi and Mumbai is played out within debates about where key events such as the India Fashion Week should be held (Nagrath 2003).

While offering a context for the various case studies selected for our research on British-Asian fashion cultures, this discussion of the different transnational fashion cultures linking Britain and the Indian subcontinent also highlights the significance of key urban centres. Jaipur, Delhi and Mumbai all function as fashion cities in India but in different ways: Jaipur remains a centre of 'traditional' skills and crafts; Delhi is a highly linked centre of production and design expertise; while Mumbai is an aspirant fashion city through its role as a centre of consumption. At the same time the transnational fashion cultures linking Britain and the subcontinent are articulated through specific urban sites and spaces within the UK.

Transnational Fashion Cultures: Two Case Studies

Our two case studies offer contrasting insights into the transnational fashion cultures linking Britain and India. EAST is a major high street retailer with more than fifty outlets across the UK. Daminis is a retailer within the specialist Asian fashion market, and one of the few companies that operates as a branded chain in this sector. Our case studies were based on in-depth research with the companies between 1999 and 2001, which included interviews with key personnel, attendance at meetings, visits to suppliers and buyers, and shadowing of some employees. Our research coincided with a significant period in the development of both companies when expansion, rethinking and rebranding were taking place.

Daminis

The specialist Asian retailer Daminis has been at the forefront of changes in Britain both in garment design and its retailing strategies. Daminis has its origins in a fabric shop opened on Green Street, East London, in 1970 by Damini Mohindra a refugee from Iraq. Using finance from the family's transnational business interests in Switzerland and building up a network of suppliers in India, the shop was part of the 'first-wave' of Asian fabric retailers described by Parminder Bhachu (2003: 103). Damini Mohindra's son, Deepak, joined the business in the early 1980s after training as an accountant and sought to change the direction of the company from wholesale fabric towards ready-made clothes with their greater profit margins. The expansion of the business into ready-made shalwar kameez and *lenghae* reflected both developments in the fashion industry in India but also increasing demand from British-born consumers of Asian fashion. This trend has been followed by a whole range of new Asian retailers in Britain. Daminis have also been pioneers in selling men's tailored suits (which they see as a growing market) and a wide range of children's clothing. The expansion into ready-made clothes was accompanied by new retailing practices, including the provision of multiple sizes, rather than 'one-off' pieces altered to fit on site, and by new forms of standardized merchandising, which were part of broader ambitions to transform Asian retail spaces in Britain.

The Daminis store located in the heart of the Asian shopping district of Southall, in West London, is a dramatic contrast to many of the other, older or more established specialist retailers of Asian clothes with its bright lit, airy interior and colour-coded garment displays. This shop opened in 1999 during a period of expansion of the Daminis chain following the remodelling of its existing shops in Green Street (opened in 1995) and Belgrave Road in Leicester (opened in 1989). To design the new 'flagship' store in Southall, Daminis employed for the first time a design consultant, Redjacket, chosen for their previous work with high street names such as Oasis and Kookai. For Deepak Mohindra, managing director of Daminis, this choice marked a recognition that the predominantly British-Asian customers buying his Asian clothes needed a shopping experience that reflected the other 'mainstream' stores they might also visit. At the same time, the new retail spaces were intended to welcome non-Asian customers as Daminis, like many other Asian retailers, sought to capitalize on the enthusiasm for Indian-inspired fashion. In 2001 the company realized its ambitions for a 'West End' store, opening a new shop on the Edgware Road, their first shop outside a recognized Asian retail centre and intended to attract non-Asian shoppers including a significant local Arab population. However this shop has now closed.

The locations of the Daminis shops in London reflect the geographies of Asian fashion in the capital and a recognition of the fashion cultures associated with particular sites as differentiated spaces for the consumption and display of clothes (cf. Gilbert 2000). The Green Street shop, the successor to the original shop, caters for a diverse immigrant population as well being an emerging Asian retail centre. However, it is also seen by the company as a less prestigious and less affluent location. The expansion to the Southall site was carefully considered. Deepak had originally intended to locate in Ealing Road in Wembley and he described this predominantly Gujarati area as being the most 'upmarket Asian shopping area in London – like Knightsbridge'. In contrast, Southall, which was eventually chosen, was described as 'more Oxford Street, you get a real frenetic feel there'. Eventually the choice was for an area with more passing trade rather than the more exclusive shopping area of Ealing Road, reflecting Daminis positioning of themselves as 'more in the middle' of the market than some of the more exclusive Asian designer stores located in Wembley. Southall is also a tourist site attracting both visitors from the subcontinent but also non-Asians seeking 'ethnic' goods – and Daminis were particularly keen to attract more customers from this group. The opening of the shop in Edgware Road was accompanied by advertising that announced Daminis arrival in the 'West End', drawing on all the resonances of this globally significant retail district. Although Daminis had long aspired to open a shop in the 'West End' of London, they recognized the pitfalls for retailers of 'Asian' fashion of moving beyond what the co-director Dax describes as their 'bread and butter' local 'Asian' market. Its subsequent closure suggests that the caution was correct and that the anticipated markets did not materialize, and that the high costs of maintaining a presence in this area were not justified.

Daminis describe their clothes as 'East-meets-West' or 'a fusion of East and West' and this is a theme that recurs in the stylization, advertising and marketing of the clothes and in the imagining of the retail spaces. In 1999 they produced a glossy catalogue that sought to expand their customer base beyond Asian consumers. Entitled 'Fashion from the East' (Figure 13.2) and marketed through *OK!* magazine (which had recently published an article about actress Melanie Sykes featuring Daminis clothes). The models used in these advertisements were all Indian and the photographs were taken in India (where costs were much cheaper). Deepak explained, however, that they were careful to produce 'neutral' backgrounds avoiding any ethnic referents, thus locating their clothes in a space that did not appear too 'Asian' (in contrast, for example, with how their clothes are often marketed in Asian wedding magazines).

In the making of the new Daminis stores the aim was to produce shops that mirrored mainstream high street shops such as Oasis with their open and airy interiors, but also to combine 'Western influences … [with] … elements and shapes from Indian architecture' (www.redjacket.co.uk). The resulting designs are described in typically overblown style as 'paying homage to elements of Le Corbusier's Chandigarh' by the designers themselves (www.redjacket.co.uk). The reference here is clear – the shops are supposed to evoke modernity, both through their links to the design of other mainstream high street stores and through reference to a particular version of India's modernity in the shape of Le Corbusier's Chandigarh. Within the

Figure 13.2 Daminis Advertising Catalogue. © Daminis, used with permission

shops themselves there is a careful juxtaposition of objects intended to evoke India but with no particular concern about 'authenticity'. Thus, in the Leicester store, furniture from India is placed alongside earthenware pots that were actually bought from a garden centre in Swindon.

The clothes sold by Daminis include more ordinary or everyday clothes, but the retail space and advertising is dominated by clothes produced for extended Asian weddings and other festivals and parties. When asked to define how their 'East/West' or 'East meets West' stylization works, Deepak Mohindra emphasizes that their clothes are driven by trends in 'Western markets' rather than from 'India'. He insisted that the ideas for the styles of the clothes are inspired by both Asian and non-Asian clothes in 'the West' while manufacturing takes place in India. Thus the design input is seen to come from London, via the provision of sketches or copies of magazines and samples that are either brought over to India on frequent visits or faxed back and forth.

Tracing the trajectory of the clothes manufactured for Daminis suggests a more complex interweaving of transnational design geographies. Clothes produced for sale in Daminis come from a range of sources. Some garments are bought direct from designers/manufacturers in India with whom the company have built up good ongoing relationships. One example is a small factory on the outskirts of the Indian city of Jaipur owned and run by a local businesswoman and designer Manisha, whose husband ran a large export business. On a visit to her business in November 2000 Manisha explained that her brief from Daminis was very broad-brush – emphasizing styles and colours. She would develop a set of samples drawing on her own designs, including pieces that she also sells in boutiques in India, as well as to buyers for shops in Los Angeles and Malaysia. Pictures of designs or samples are sent or faxed back to Daminis in London before multiples are ordered. Her small-scale operation can nonetheless produce rapid turnaround when particular samples are ordered.

A key supplier of Daminis clothes is the company Vanshik based in the suburb of Bandre in Mumbai, which also produces clothes for designer shops in the most prestigious shopping districts of the city such as Crawford Market and Crossroads Mall. If specialist Asian retailers have previously been more closely linked to production sites in Delhi, Daminis has self-consciously developed production sites in Mumbai identifying it as the 'new' fashion city within India, particularly because of the influence of the film industry in shaping contemporary trends in Indian fashion (Nagrath 2003). Viki, Vanshik's director and Deepak at Daminis work closely together, coordinating designs and manufacture on a daily basis via fax and phone. While some garments, particularly the men's range are manufactured in Vanshik's own workshop, located in the labyrinthine backstreets of Bandre, others are outsourced to more than thirty workshops in the local area. The intricate hand-beaded embroidery that adorns most of these garments is executed by young men, most of whom are poor migrant workers from Bihar. Talking to supervisors in the factory I learnt that the embroiderers would make their own decisions about how the complex beaded patterns were to be arranged, while other alterations were often made, for example, in the tapering of sleeves or trouser legs. Again then, much scope remains at the site of manufacture for clothes to be subtly altered and changed, often reflecting what is currently in vogue within local markets. The interlinking between the Daminis London stores and Mumbai's fashion retail spaces is manifest by the same advertising posters produced by Daminis/Vanshik, which hang both in Sheetals, an upmarket fashion store in Mumbai, and in the Daminis store in Southall.

The case study of Daminis reveals some of the ways in which we might trace transnational fashion cultures both operating through and shaping urban spaces. Our ethnography of the commodity cultures of Daminis revealed some of the instabilities or complexities in the narrative of 'East' and 'West' produced both through Daminis advertising and in their own telling of the design and production process. Although this narrative places the design process in 'the West' (an evocation of 'the modern') following the object itself (cf. Appadurai 1996) reveals the role of many different actors, in different places, who have some influence on the garment that is eventually produced. This would not be surprising to the consumers of the clothes themselves. Consumers we interviewed in both India and in Britain were likely to locate the source of innovation and 'modernity' in Indian clothing in the subcontinent (see Jackson, Thomas and Dwyer, forthcoming). For Daminis, the signifiers of 'East' and 'West' operate in a number of different ways. Defining themselves as innovators in the field of Asian clothing, the trope of 'modernity' is important in the shaping of Asian retailing spaces and practices as they seek to attract a new generation of thoroughly Westernized young Asian consumers. At the same time, the idea of 'East' and 'West' is deployed to attract consumers who are not Asians and for whom buying clothes from Daminis is about consuming ethnic difference (see Dwyer and Crang 2002). For this differentiated group of consumers the shops must be 'Western' enough to attract them, but the clothing must offer the mark of ethnicized difference, 'even authenticity', marked as coming from 'the East'.

This case study of the material, aesthetic and imaginative networks and practices of a specialist Asian retailer such as Daminis illustrates how we might think about transnational fashion cultures. As I have argued, Daminis is embedded within practices of transnational commodity culture through which clothes are designed, manufactured, advertised, retailed and consumed. For Daminis, as I have illustrated, this transnational fashion culture is narrated through an opposition of 'East' and 'West'. This transnational fashion culture also operates through the making of fashion city spaces, which are understood as produced through these complex material and imaginative linkages. Thus Mumbai is produced as a site for the innovation of contemporary Indian design for consumers both within India and in the diaspora (see Harris 2005). In the UK, differentiated urban spaces of Asian consumption are also produced by Asian retailers who self-consciously produce for different markets.

EAST

EAST is a high street fashion retailer with sixty stores in the UK selling women's clothes, which they describe as an 'international collection' which 'celebrates colour and decorative hand crafted details, using luxurious, natural fabrics'. EAST was chosen as a case study for our research on transnational commodity culture because we were fascinated by the history of this company, which began in 1986 and emerged from a very particular set of transnational relations with the subcontinent. The origins of EAST are linked to the histories of two other companies involved in British-Indian transnational fashion cultures, the Indian-based company Anokhi and the high street name Monsoon.

Anokhi, based in Jaipur, was established in 1967 by Faith, a British woman with a missionary childhood in India, and John Singh, a member of the elite Rajput princely family. The company was established to 'preserve and revive traditional textile skills' focusing in particular on developing Western markets for clothes made using the hand-blocked textiles that are characteristic of the Jaipur area but were in decline in the late 1960s. The 'revival' of craft production in India has a long and fascinating transnational history (see Metcalf 1989: 159). Members of the Arts and Crafts movement in nineteenth-century Britain, such as John Ruskin and William Morris, championed the quality of Indian craftwork as an alternative to the mass-produced world of industrial manufacture, celebrating India as a locus of timelessness and tradition, beyond the destructive reach of the West. This was particularly true of the princely states whose preservation was seen as both a political and an aesthetic priority. Most active in the craft 'revival' were the successive maharajas of Jaipur. Anokhi clothes were first sold in Liberty of London, the 'emporium' whose origins lie in the import of Oriental textiles and in the nineteenth-century English Arts and Crafts movement in the late 1860s (Calloway 1992).

Liberty was also a significant fashion retailing site for the emergence of a new ethnic chic in swinging sixties London (see Ashmore in this volume). In the early 1970s the Singhs met Peter Simon, who was to become the founder of the well-known high street chain Monsoon, and Anokhi became the founding brand of the Monsoon chain, whose first shop opened in Beauchamp Place in Knightsbridge in 1973. However Anokhi and Monsoon were to part company in the late 1970s – Anokhi could not reconcile their own ideals as a company with a strong sense of commitment to a local workforce with the more expansive commercial ambitions of Monsoon. They feared becoming marginalized as 'simply a supplier'. In 1986, three former employees from Monsoon (Clive Pettigrew, Penny Oliver and Jonathan Keating) approached Anokhi to sell their products. They founded a new company (Anokhi Wholesale Limited), which opened its first shop on the Kings Road, London in 1986 selling Anokhi's distinctive hand-block printed clothes and other textiles.

This new company soon began to diversify its range and in 1994 the first EAST collection was launched. The new brand sought to expand the business beyond its existing customer base to attract a younger market – in the words of several interviewees within the company to move beyond an association with a 'hippy' image. A new designer, Francine Seward, was brought into the company to produce a new collection and to establish the EAST brand. According to their corporate publicity, the intention was to 'extend the range of fabrics and design ... whilst still retaining some of the ethnic roots, colour and fashion quirkiness that originally drew the Anokhi fans'. In seeking to position the EAST brand in a crowded retail marketplace, emphasis was placed on the use of natural fabrics and techniques such as hand-embroidery. Thus corporate publicity from 1999 described their clothes as 'designed to be individual' for 'women who want something a little exotic but also wearable'.

By the late 1990s the company had rebranded all its stores as EAST and had begun to grow rapidly, opening new stores and expanding others. In January 2005 they appointed a new chief executive, Yasmin Yusuf, formerly a creative director at Marks and Spencer to spearhead the next phase of expansion for the chain. The establishment of the EAST brand as a high street name has marked some tension in their relationship with Anokhi as their distinctive block-printed clothes have become a less significant part of the company's identity and are sold only in a select number of stores where they are branded as 'Anokhi for EAST'. Instead Anokhi has sought new markets of its own in Britain continued to develop its retailing in India (Dwyer and Jackson 2003).

This brief history of EAST illustrates the transnational connections out of which the company has emerged. Research within the company between 1999 and 2001 allowed us to trace EAST's changing relationship with India in terms of production networks and imaginative connections. EAST retains an Indian-inspired influence within some elements of its design 'handwriting' but operates through a more diffuse notion of 'the exotic'. In common with many other comparable fashion retailers, China and the Far East are now more significant production sites than India for EAST (particularly for winter fabrics and silks) since they are perceived to offer better value in both quality and cost. For EAST, the development of a distinctive brand requires careful management of an association with India and the notion of an 'ethnic' look. While their chief designer explained that 'the ethnic look is part of EAST's distinctive handwriting' – this is a generalized 'ethnic look' rather than a specific connection to India. As their retail manager explained 'we are selling a brand, not clothes which are made in India' while their PR manager points to the pitfalls: 'we don't want to be just *ethnic*'. Instead the EAST brand is articulated through the slogan 'Designed to be individual' and sustained through a range of discourses about fabric, design and handwork and by an engagement with a generalized 'exotic' aesthetic.

This aesthetic works both through the design and marketing of the clothes and through EAST's retail spaces. Interviewed in 2000, designer Francine Seward explained that India remained important to her as a 'source of inspiration' citing the colourful clothing worn by women road workers which inspired her Spring/Summer 2000 collection. These ideas were encapsulated in the following press release:

> The EAST look for Spring/Summer 2000 is a juxtaposition of colour, layering, texture and ornamentation. Strong influences are the eclectic mixing of old and new, encom-passing flower power, the nomadic hippy trail with the romantic feminine nostalgia of grandmother's wardrobe. EAST ornamentation and embroideries this season take to the road looking at the intricate stone works, inlays and carvings seen in the temples and palaces in India and Morocco. A group of easy layering colourful separates are taken from the nomadic Indian Banjaras gypsies highly decorated and colourful work wear.

The Autumn/Winter Collection for the same year also drew heavily on Indian referents. Publicity materials emphasized that designs were 'inspired by Tibetan art and the colourful "Thieves market" in Delhi', while the 'lost dynasties' collection featured embroidery 'reminiscent of ornate Kashmiri tapestries' and 'vintage decorated sari designs'. Yet collections in subsequent years reflected a range of different influences – from the Santorini Party (Spring/Summer 2002) to a more North African theme in Spring/Summer 2003.

Even when clothes are inspired by or draw reference to India they may not necessarily be produced there. A shirt based on an Indian-style fabric print was manufactured in China with silk-printed fabric designed by an Italian-based fabric designer. Often fabrics sourced from India, such as antique saris bought in Benares, will be rewoven to EAST's specifications. What the EAST brand seeks to evoke is a generalized aesthetic of the 'exotic', which is captured through the locations used for photo shoots and their selection of models and in the arrangement of retail spaces – for example, the use of tropical flowers in window displays or the Mughal window feature in their Regent Street store. Another way in which an imaginative geography of 'the East' circulates is through the names of the clothes themselves, which often evoke places such as – Shekhavati, Rajput, Zanzibar, Saltimbocca, Mumbai or Tunis (see Figure 13.3). This is an imaginative geography, which seems to resonate with customers – although perhaps more with EAST's older customers (characterized in their focus group research as 'older explorers') rather than the more recent target group of younger women or 'life managers' (see Dwyer and Jackson 2003, Jackson et al., forthcoming). In contrast with the valorization of indigenous textile traditions such as hand-block printing associated with Anokhi garments, EAST clothes are not usually merchandised through association with their distinctive embodied processes of manufacture – although labels such as 'handmade' or 'hand crafted' are used.

While the Far East is most significant for EAST's production, India remains important for clothing production both in terms of manufacturing and for the provision of particular specialist embroideries. Our research involved accompanying EAST buyers on a visit to India, which gave us some insight into how transnational operations took place. Like most British companies EAST operates primarily in Delhi and works with an agent based there, although they also have long-standing relationships with several different factories specializing in export production. Visits to showrooms in Delhi adhere to the timetable of the fashion cycle, allowing EAST buyers to view samples and check quality. The production process is monitored closely to ensure consistency, particularly with regard to fit and cut, and samples produced by suppliers in India will be returned to EAST in the UK for checking before patterns are made for the final run. However, there is scope for active dialogue between EAST buyers and their Indian export suppliers. One such company, located in an affluent Delhi suburb, produces clothes for export to a range of other Western companies including high street rivals and named designers, and their meetings with EAST buyers which we observed are also a time for mutual exchange of new

Figure 13.3 'Mumbai', EAST advertising catalogue, Spring/Summer 2000. © EAST, used with permission.

ideas or fabrics. EAST will send mood boards to companies for them to supply ideas (for both clothes and accessories) and all the showrooms will have ideas made up (sometime through the inspiration of other overseas buyers) to show visiting buyers. Like most Western buyers EAST has little direct contact with those who make their clothes, the owners of export companies in Delhi negotiate contracts with a host of subcontractors working in small textile workshops around Delhi to produce the garments.

Visits to India may concentrate on quality control and mass production. However EAST's buyers also use these visits to enliven their aesthetic imaginations and connections with the subcontinent. Although EAST was keen to continue buying from India, this was often through smaller scale purchases, such as accessories, shawls or fabric samples. It was also hoped that these might inspire new designs retaining the Indian-inspired aesthetic of the company. This enthusiasm or perhaps romanticism for 'the authentic' was encapsulated in a meeting I observed between EAST buyers and an elderly shawl manufacturer from rural Gujarat whose initial encounter with EAST buyers occurred within the more touristic spaces of the Craft Museum in Delhi. Although he continues to supply EAST with shawls, it was significant that when these shawls appeared in central London EAST stores some months later they were displayed alongside handmade dolls, which were produced by a charity for street children in Delhi with whom EAST was associated, and thus merchandised separately away from the fashion spaces of the store.

In fact it is through charity work that EAST retains perhaps its most explicit relationship with India. Since 2000, EAST has sponsored Disha, a school for handicapped children in Jaipur with which Anokhi is also involved. Previously funding was raised through special shopping days where customers received a discount and a percentage of company profits went to support Disha. While individual employees at EAST have developed strong attachments to Disha through site visits, they also recognize the ways in which such events can have commercial advantages as well. Such events allow EAST to continue to build up a customer database and encourage customer loyalty while also contributing to charity. On these occasions photographs are displayed showing the work of Disha, carefully chosen, as their retail manager explains, to be 'tasteful' and 'not too shocking' so that the relationship between shopping for pleasure and giving to charity can be successfully balanced. To mark its support for a new school in Disha, the company plans to move in 2006 to a new scheme of more sustained support with information about Disha appearing on till receipts, labelling and packaging.

If we return to the question of transnational fashion cultures our research at EAST was marked by a period of rapid expansion which included a reworking of the company's associations and networks in India, most obviously in terms of their changing relationship with Anokhi. For EAST, India remains a contradictory site. It functions as a source of inspiration and aesthetic ideals but often fails to deliver, in comparison with the Far East, in terms of production. Even India as a source of inspiration has to be carefully managed because of the danger of being seen as '*too* ethnic' producing associations not in tune with EAST's aspirations as a designer-led chain. Instead the transnational connection that is evoked by EAST is India as a site that is a point of tradition – where handcrafted skills are valorized and retained. This has parallels with the imaginaries of earlier British transnationals such as those involved in the Arts and Crafts movement and is tinged with both nostalgia and imperial imaginaries. However it is clear that the relationship with India is also pragmatic, and the company is quite self-conscious about how tropes of 'the EAST' and 'the exotic' are mobilized. Our fieldwork with consumers also revealed that they too shared an investment in these imaginaries but were also aware of how these narratives worked in the retailing process (see Jackson et al., forthcoming).

Our case study of EAST is more complex and wide-ranging than that of Daminis because of the company's rapid expansion. While I have highlighted the renegotiation of its transnational fashion cultures, we might also consider the metropolitan – and suburban – fashion cultures within which EAST stores are located. Anokhi's early success in Britain in the early 1960s was integral to the enthusiasm for 'ethnic' fashion that characterized the emergence of 'Swinging London' as a fashion 'cosmopolis' (see Ashmore in this volume). Anokhi's early collections were sold through Liberty and featured in British *Vogue* while the first Anokhi/EAST shop was on the Kings Road, placing it at the heart of a distinctive urban fashion space. Many of the earliest EAST stores, when they were more closely associated with Anokhi, mapped a more suburban fashion geography with strong associations with particular university or market towns in the South such as Cambridge or Cheltenham. EAST directors told anecdotes of loyal Anokhi customers who were typified as schoolteachers, ex-missionaries and the wives of Oxbridge dons! Such local associations, producing particular events like charity fashion shows, are less important as the company has expanded and a more corporate ethos is evident. If EAST has a distinctive retail geography it is marked by the same commercial aspirations that drive other high street names such as Hobbs or Karen Millen. The company seeks sites in upmarket shopping developments that are distinctive by their shared commitment to a particular kind of imagined locality.

Conclusion

In this chapter I have drawn on two case studies from a wider study of the trans-nationalities associated with British-South Asian commodity cultures to illustrate the making of transnational fashion cultures. Through these detailed examples I have sought to illustrate how transnational fashion cultures might be understood as the complex geographies within which clothes are designed, manufactured, retailed and consumed. I have argued that transnational fashion cultures must be understood not only through the material geographies of transnational flows of labour or goods but also through the symbolic and imaginative geographies that accompany these circuits of production. These transnational geographies are also shaped through, and by, specific urban spaces. Thus London emerges as a key fashion city in transnational British-Asian fashion cultures both in the narrative of 'ethnic' fashion in Britain from which EAST emerged and in the history of specialist Asian fashion in the UK for which the history of Daminis is an example. The case studies also illustrate how London is a differentiated urban fashion market (Gilbert 2000) with highly distinctive local histories and identities as the marketing strategies operated by both EAST and Daminis suggest. At the same time on the Indian subcontinent the fashion cities of Jaipur, Delhi and Mumbai are differentiated from each other as sites of craft specialization, export-orientated manufacture or consumption orientated design. Thinking about the making of transnational fashion cultures produces an understanding of fashion cities that resonates with geographer Doreen Massey's arguments about places as dynamic and interconnected (Massey 1994).

These case studies also suggest that the essential relationship between producers and consumers that has long characterized the fashion city remains important, but is reconfigured in an era of globalization (Green 1997). Thinking about fashion cities in the context of transnational fashion cultures illustrates the need to go beyond thinking about cities either as bounded spaces or as spaces with fixed identities. This analysis of the transnational geographies of EAST and Daminis has illustrated how the imaginative geographies of 'East' and 'West', 'India' and 'Britain' are mobilized and deployed in ways that evoke a fixing in place. At the same time, this analysis also emphasizes how these fixities are challenged, complicated and ruptured in the making of transnational fashion cultures.

Note

1. The project 'Commodity Culture and South Asian Transnationality' was undertaken in collaboration with Philip Crang, Royal Holloway, University of London and Peter Jackson, University of Sheffield, and was funded by the Economic and Social Research Council. Award Number: LT214252031. The research was made possible through the support of the directors of the case study companies who were generous in their assistance to us and we gratefully acknowledge their support and enthusiasm for the research project.

–14–

Sewing Machines and Dream Machines in Los Angeles and San Francisco

The Case of the Blue Jean

Leslie W. Rabine and *Susan Kaiser*

Neither Los Angeles nor San Francisco comes to mind as a contender for 'the list of so-called fashion capitals … routinely incorporated into the advertising of high fashion' (Gilbert 2006, this volume). And yet, the status of fashion capital in the mould of Paris and New York has now become 'a goal for city boosters and planners' in these outposts of the Far West. In many ways, the new fashion city boosterism misses the boat. Its striving after unimaginative imitations of New York's Fashion Weeks bespeaks a baffling blindness to the wild, wacky, ethnically diverse and immensely influential contributions to global style that do not fit the mould of runway couture collections or other conventions of what David Gilbert calls 'the city booster toolkit'. In their rivalry and sisterhood, Los Angeles and San Francisco provide a case study for a comparative, relational analysis of fashion cities in the age of global restructuring that suggests alternatives to the homogeneous city booster model.

San Francisco's influence on transnational fashion has emerged from its historical character as haven for gender, sexual and political radicals. For Los Angeles, such influence has come from a population among the most ethnically, culturally and linguistically diverse in the world (with over 100 languages spoken). Both cities' major fashion contributions have therefore come from ethnic and counter-cultural street styles – and, of course, from Hollywood film. Although an inimitable and universally recognizable sartorial ambience emanates from LA and San Francisco as material places, the Hollywood dream machine has been the deterritorializing force that mythologizes homespun street figures from both these cities (not to mention every major city in the world) as globally disseminated glamour. But as centres of garment production, first and third in importance among US cities, they are also noted for the endemic labour abuses that form the invisible underside of fashion glamour. Visibility and invisibility; production of images and production of material garments; Hollywood's cinematic fashion fantasies flowing outward over the globe while Latino and Asian immigrants flow into California to work in garment factories. These are the axes around which revolves the solidly constructed (dis)connect between the in-fact deeply interdependent transnational networks we will symbolize by Hollywood's 'dream machine' and the garment industry's 'sewing machine'.

If one garment sums up the knot of issues tangled between dream machine and sewing machine, it is the blue jean. As material product and mythic fetish, it brings together in a symbolic matrix the contrasting personalities of these rival sister cities, the distinct idiosyncratic influence of each on world fashion, and the hidden immigrant labour haunting images of consumer desire. Acknowledged even by such quintessential world-fashion-city moguls as Bill Blass and Yves Saint Laurent to have originated in San Francisco, the blue jean became a universal icon of global fashionability and sexual magnetism through its dissemination by Hollywood film (Hall 2002: 22; Harris 2002: 95). This garment further warrants a case study because it not only owes its status as fashion star to Hollywood, but also symbolizes the film genre – the Western – to which Hollywood owes its status as world centre of the image industry. Although we will briefly review many of the fashions invented in Los Angeles and San Francisco, the blue jean – ubiquitous, semiotically protean, endlessly adapted to the creation of new genders and sexualities – will serve here as our figure of concentration. As it symbolically concentrates the contrasting hallmarks peculiar to fashion in Los Angeles and San Francisco, the blue jean exemplifies the inseparability between material and symbolic, work and leisure, local and global, the hypervisibility of the image and the invisibility of garment labour. It will serve as prism concentrating and refracting the facets of LA's and San Francisco's ex-centric position with respect to the charmed circle of world fashion cities.

Los Angeles and San Francisco as Distinct Urban Spaces

If Los Angeles lacks a major fashion magazine and tastemakers like Anna Wintour, it has its own representational system based on Hollywood's mass dissemination of visual fantasy. This system challenges and even displaces fashion print culture, as designer Max Azria of BCBG, perhaps indulging in a bit of LA defensiveness, contends: 'Fashion is disseminated via film, television and music videos as opposed to couture crawling catwalks' (Chensvold 2005). By the late 1920s, Hollywood's studio system was gobbling up diverse appearance styles and mythologizing them into glamorous must-haves for spectators around the world. This process paralleled a larger construction of place – of LA as paradise for white, middle-class people to start over in a space of perpetual sunshine, pleasure and promise.

Of decisive consequence for LA fashion is the construction of this space as privatized. It is a truism that in LA there are no 'in between' clothes. White, wealthy Angelinos wear either fabulous evening gowns or jeans and beachwear – and for good reason. In this city where the post-Second World War auto industry destroyed public transportation and built a network of freeways, there is a dearth of middle-class street life. Local-born fashion innovations for which the frenetic megalopolis is famous are outrageously glamorous evening gowns, bathing suits, sportswear separates and surfing gear – not to mention the surgically induced perfect bodies to fit these styles. They appear as if by magic in film and TV images. If the Los Angeles film industry created a medium for disseminating seductive fashion images around the globe, Los Angeles city planning created a model of deracinated urban life perfectly suited to that medium. Angelinos pick up fashions not by observing other people in public spaces, but by receiving them as if beamed from outer space in mass-mediated images.

LA's apparel industry emerged in the 1920s in tandem with Hollywood's film industry. Savvy owners of two knitting mills, based in Los Angeles to produce mundane underwear, recognized the film industry's demand for glamorous, photogenic bathing suits. Changing their companies' names to Cole and Catalina, they 'created the business that would ... become California's claim to fame, the fashion swim suit' (Hall 2002: 43). But as city boosters were rushing to attract tourists and to expand LA's industrial base, the emerging film industry helped to create a space of both escape and erasure. The escape to a Veblenesque 'conspicuous leisure' relied on erasing the histories of the indigenous and immigrant populations to whom the new space was so indebted for inspiration and labour. The labour, in particular, had to remain invisible to sustain the new myth. Nowhere is this more evident than in the labour-intensive sportswear and swimsuit industries.

The largest group of immigrant workers has, from the founding of Los Angeles, come across the stubbornly porous border from Mexico, making Los Angeles the second largest city of Mexican inhabitants after Mexico City itself. Though either ignored or used as serape- and sombrero-laden background by Hollywood until the 1980s, Mexican immigrants created a rich gallery of street figures. Zoot-suited *el Pachuco* of the 1940s and Pendleton-shirted *el Cholo* of the 1960s were perhaps reacting to the exclusionary white images of Hollywood's dream machine. Such looks expressed the will to create 'a public persona that asserted their presence in public spaces in their own ways and on their own terms' (Obrégon Pagán 2003: 218). Despite the Latinos' creativity in fashioning their own leisure styles outside the mainstream, an authoritative history like Hall's *California Fashion* omits these, and calls the mix-and-match aesthetic, assumed Anglo and also developed in the 1940s, the 'single most important innovation in the history of American sportswear' (Hall 2002: 69). In fact, this aesthetic draws heavily on the diverse ethnic influences in California's cultural histories. All too often, however, these influences were uncritically appropriated as precisely the stereotypes they were meant to challenge into a casual, mix-and-match style labelled 'Californian': 'From the cult of California, there came about a design *oeuvre* as mixed as an omelet. Take a bit of Hollywood starlet, a pinch of farmer's daughter, a dash of surfer girl, and stir. For spice, add the charm of old Mexico and the exotic allure of traditional Hawaii' (Reilly 2000: 164). On the production side, garment workers, 70 per cent Latina and 20 per cent Asian, finally became visible in the twenty-first century for their epic struggles for human dignity (Garment Worker Center 2004: 6).

The story of these transnational networks would not be complete without Los Angeles's quaint little sister city San Francisco, even more 'relatively marginal' (Scott 2002: 1300) as a candidate for the title of world fashion city. Yet the largest apparel companies in the world – Levi Strauss and Gap – are located there. Indeed, San Francisco, founded in 1849 as the centre for urban growth during the gold rush, has a longer history of apparel production than Los Angeles, a history not about conspicuous leisure but about a very proud and visible working-class culture. The city has built a culture perfectly fitted to give birth to the blue jean. In 1872, Jewish immigrant merchant Levi Strauss patented Levi's®, an innovative trouser for the most menial, unglamorous labour of cowboys, miners and railroad workers (Figure 14.1). Through the dialectical process that turned them into the universally recognized embodiment of glamour and leisure, 'levis' became the generic term for denim jeans. Speaking with typical US fashion hyperbole, New York's Bill Blass claimed: 'Nothing any fashion designer has ever done has come close to having the influence of blue jeans. That Levi Strauss invention – one of the sexiest items a man or a woman can wear – is the most significant contribution America has made to fashion' (quoted in Hall 2002: 22).

In contrast to LA, San Francisco is a city whose people have a deep concern for community and public space, and where street life of every class and ethnicity thrives. Where LA's counter-cultural styles emerge from the struggles of ethnic minorities,

Figure 14.1 A diverse group of California cowboys or *caballeros* in Levi Strauss denim work trousers with their patented copper rivets. Late nineteenth century. Credit: Courtesy Levi Strauss & Co.

Figure 14.2 Artist Doug Miles in the photograph he submitted to the 1974 Levi Strauss & Co. denim art competition. His hand-painted white jeans won fourth prize. Credit: Courtesy Doug Miles artist.

San Francisco's influential street styles, many of which invented their own versions of jeans, emerged through social, sexual and political movements (Figure 14.2). An exuberant mix of such creative styles includes: the black-clad Beatniks of the 1950s, the hippies and flower children of the 1960s, the Black Panthers across the San Francisco Bay in Oakland, the drag queens and buffed clones of the Castro, and the motorcycling Dykes on Bikes. In both Los Angeles and San Francisco, subcultural and ethnic appearance styles have been the visual force of larger struggles with established authority over the right to control urban public space.

Jeans and Hollywood Film

Admittedly, Hollywood cinema has mined styles from every world fashion city to feed its insatiable dream machine. But Levi's jeans entered the world of cinematic fantasy when the overwhelming popularity of the Western in the early years of commercial film led producers to set up studios in Los Angeles County. The first films were made in Eastern cities, and also in France by Pathé and Gaumont. The actors in Westerns wore their own Eastern clothing, or in the case of Pathé, European riding britches (Everson 1969: 17). In the winter of 1908, producers F. M. Anderson and Fred J. Balshofer set up temporary studios in warehouses near Los Angeles in order to get away from the cold weather and the Edison patent enforcement agents (Bowser 1990: 150–2; Balshofer and Miller 1998: 3–4). William Hart soon followed, and like Anderson, he recruited local, working, Levi's-clad cowboys into his films.

Anderson and Hart discovered the scenic advantages of California, and by the 1910s other producers joined them in setting up permanent studios in Los Angeles County, so that they could film on location at local ranches and in the San Francisco Bay Area, as well as in other western states and Mexico. Los Angeles could thus lay claim to both 'geographic authenticity' (Everson 1969: 17–18) and costume authenticity as capital of the Western film. In Westerns of the 1910s and 1920s, jeans appeared routinely, but almost unnoticeably. Their very inconspicuousness had two features that hinted at their future of fashionable sexuality. In many early Westerns, leather chaps cover the trousers except for a triangle or circle around the crotch. In a fetish-like displacement, denim fills in this gap, foreshadowing (or influencing?) the effects of bleaching or filing that gay men applied to the crotch of their Levi's 501s in the 1970s (Cole 2000: 96). The second feature results from the photographic methods particular to Westerns filmed out of Los Angeles studios. Once producers discovered the visual advantages of majestic scenery, they favoured the high angle long shot in black and white. This made the details of costume disappear. The idealized silhouette – noble, athletic and unconsciously sexual – of the rugged individual stands out. And in twenty-first-century fashion, it is the perfect silhouette, mirage shimmering just beyond the consumer horizon, that countless fashion articles and jeans ads promise.

Hollywood Westerns of the period from 1908 to 1920 also gave birth to the future role of jeans in constructing gender and sexual identities. In US history, the period was marked by 'anxiety ... around the preservation of white Anglo-Saxon-identified, Protestant, middle-class-identified masculinity' (Studlar 1998: 63). In spite of, or because of, California's isolation from the major hubs and institutions of US cultural and political power in East Coast cities, the early Hollywood cowboy films wielded major influence in constructing a distinctive American identity. When urbanization in the Eastern USA created fears of a feminization of America, rugged cinematic cowboy heroes like Douglas Fairbanks offered a 'mythically charged solution to imperiled masculinity' (Studlar 1998: 73). By 1909 critics and the public had claimed the Western as 'distinctively American' (Abel 1998: 78). And so, in a city far from the centres of US legal, political and financial power, an infant creative industry could exert a new kind of power to define an identity for the whole nation – an identity endowed with the physical prowess, moral fortitude and natural innocence to realize the expansion of American rule. Both film genre and blue jean thus became enmeshed in the paradoxical quest for authenticity, an ever-receding ideal haunted by ever-changing images.

Ironically though, the garment so basic to Western film costume, and destined to become just as basic to California's influence on global fashion, represented an ideology that left women far in the background. The Western film, as epic of this ideology, also racialized Native Americans and Mexicans as Others to be conquered or else idealized as the vanishing noble savage or helpless peasant. Asian and African Americans were altogether excluded from their important role in the settling the West (Durham and Jones 1965; Chinese Historical Society 1975; Katz 1987; Chen 2005). Western dress becomes saturated with meanings of a masculinity that is authentic because it comes straight out of nature (the 'wild west') (Gaines and Herzog 1998). The blue jean, as a kind of second skin, aptly signifies this naturalization.

Even in the twenty-first century, Levi Strauss markets its jeans to a multi-gendered, multi-ethnic public by claiming this myth: 'The Levi's® brand has been the most definitive and original jeans brand since 1853. Today, the Levi's® brand is an authentic American icon.... Rooted in the rugged American West, Levi's® jeans embody freedom and individuality' (SF Fashion Week *Official Program*: 2005: 6). The genuine item can now be found 'at the Flagship Levi's store in Downtown San Francisco'. This marketing blurb illustrates sartorial authenticity's paradox as it promises to contain within a commodity precisely what is desirable because it is natural, original, and thus outside of commodification. This Levi's blurb also suggests how jeans work as a figure of concentration reflecting the dialectic between Los Angeles and San Francisco. It was Hollywood cinematic representation that made the scruffy work trouser into a mythic 'authentic American icon'. But a century later, back in San Francisco, Levi Strauss reclaims the myth as if freedom and rugged individuality had always and originally resided in the material jeans themselves.

After the Second World War, Hollywood's role in mythologizing the blue jean took on a second and even more influential life. Like film, commercial television production began in the East, specifically in New York, with live studio production. It ended up centred in Hollywood through the influence of the Western. By the 1950s, the TV networks began producing new B Westerns with William Boyd (as Hopalong Cassidy) and Roy Rogers, because they were much cheaper than the live dramas and variety shows produced in New York City. Although far inferior in quality, they were overwhelmingly popular and profitable. Since the networks relied on the major Hollywood film studios to produce these television Western series, network control switched to Hollywood programming (Boddy 1998). Thus Los Angeles, still bereft of major fashion magazines and collections, extended its influence on global fashion by adding the power of television to its dissemination of fantasy images. One of the first fashions marketed through television – the children's cowboy outfit – provided the model for disseminating all manner of more adult fashions from MTV gangsta' gear to *Dynasty* evening gowns.

As Hollywood stopped producing B Westerns for cinema by 1954, the A Western came into its heyday (Corkin 2004: 1–4), and the mantle of authentic American masculinity fell upon Gary Cooper, Henry Fonda, Ronald Reagan and especially arch-conservative John Wayne. In well-worn boot-leg jeans, but with perfectly shaped Stetsons, they played out the allegory of US imperialism from 1946 to 1960.

Cowboys, Urban Rebels and California in the 1960s

These Hollywood allegorical figures of the cold war influenced California politics, and in a state where mass-mediated elections historically muddle Hollywood fantasy and political reality, Ronald Reagan was not the first (nor the last) actor whose film persona won him an election. When he became governor in 1967, he set out to translate the Hollywood cowboy ideology into a punitive state policy. He targeted the new urban rebels protesting US foreign policy and demanding free speech in the San Francisco Bay Area, especially at UC Berkeley and San Francisco State University. If Reagan glamorized a Southern California or 'Western' version of blue jeans, the young rebels of Northern California chose their own scruffier version of the garment as anchor piece of a new urban, counter-cultural, cross-gender outfit.

In the 1960s, widespread aversion to the Vietnam War, along with movements for women's liberation and against racism, threw into disarray the conservative model of a homogeneous American identity based on white, violent masculinity, and so brought about the decline of the US Western in both film and TV – but definitely not the decline of the blue jean as a staple of California identity construction. On the contrary, in the 1960s and 1970s, this magically mutable garment showed its genius for labyrinthine multiple coding and barely noticeable shifts in looks that relay secret messages to the initiates of subcultural groups. The dialectic shifts back from Hollywood to San Francisco as Haight Ashbury hippies adopted bell-bottom jeans to display a new ambiguous masculinity, and gay clones of the Castro adapted the boot-leg Levi's of the Western in a pastiche of the old 'authentic' masculinity (Cole 2000: 96). But both San Francisco and Los Angeles were trumped by New York designers Gloria Vanderbilt and Calvin Klein who pioneered a new genre of jeans: 'designer' jeans for women.

In the counter-cultural, 'do-it-to-it' creative environment of California's 1960s generation, jeans became more than ever a figure of concentrated meaning. This most basic of garments became not only a second skin but also the canvas upon which thousands of people painted, embroidered, appliquéd, patchworked, trapuntoed and interfaced in brilliant colours the visions, dreams and stories of their era. In 1974, Levi Strauss and Co. sponsored a national denim art contest and sent 100 of the most spectacular jeans, shirts and jackets on a US tour (*American Denim* 1975; Leventon 2005: 32–3).

So agile and rich are the semiotics of blue jeans in this period that they can at the same time signify opposite meanings for two very different California male subcultural groups: 'out' gay men of the Castro and men of the Marxist left (Figure 14.3). While the Levi's 501s expressed for gay men a 'new meaning of overt

Figure 14.3 The Clone look in San Francisco's Castro Street gay community in the early 1970s. The man on the right is wearing the *de rigueur* Levi's 501s. Credit: Photograph Crawford Barton, courtesy Gay, Lesbian, Bisexual Transgender Historical Society.

sexuality' (Cole 2000: 95), California Marxist men, many of whom espoused quite conservative gender and sexual politics, also chose the boot-leg 501s instead of the fashionable unisex bell bottoms, but for opposite reasons. For them the garment became a paradoxical anti-sign, showing that they were above anything so trivially feminine as worrying about show and personal appearance.

Shaun Cole analyses the transatlantic dissemination by which Londoners picked up the clone look: 'the most important item to get right was the jeans' (Cole 2000: 97). And he reports the experience of men importing the prized Levi's 501s from the USA. But to find the impetus behind the transcontinental flow of this look, we must once again look to another flow: that of subcultural clothing styles from San Francisco street figures to the dream machine of Los Angeles. Linda Williams attributes the beginning of cowboy wear as a global gay fashion to the 1969 ground-breaking Hollywood film *Midnight Cowboy* (Williams, personal communication, 2005).

Midnight Cowboy plays upon the conventions of the Western genre to exploit the double and secret coding that had always been inherent to the genre. Naïve young Texan Joe Buck (Jon Voight) hopes his rugged cowboy look will bring him success with wealthy New York women as a male hustler. Like Voight's Levi's 501s, the film expressed one message to its mainstream audience and another to initiates who viewed it through gay codes. In just one example of such double coding, Joe's companion Ratso (Dustin Hoffman) mocks his cowboy gear: 'That's strictly for fags!' But Joe responds: 'John Wayne! You wanna tell me he's a fag?' The film parodies the disavowal inherent in the Western's overt hypermasculine heterosexism. No element of the Western outfit signified and embodied as much as his jeans the often unspoken homoerotic power of the cowboy silhouette.

Gender and Sexuality: Authentic vs Designer Jeans

The traditional ideal of masculinity disavowed the sexiness of jeans, while gay men magnified it but in private codes and subcultural communities. When women finally adopted jeans as a ubiquitous urban fashion, the garment inspired an overt, mass-mediated discourse on the outrageous eroticism of this most materially malleable and symbolically eloquent of garments. This discourse burst into controversy with Calvin Klein's 1980 television ad featuring fifteen-year-old Brooke Shields murmuring 'nothing comes between me and my Calvins.' The slogan takes up the old myth of jeans as Americans' second skin, but sweeps away the old alibi of functionality. Ironically, however, the deliberately shocking Calvin Klein ad uses exactly the same marketing technique as the 1950s ads for wholesome children's cowboy outfits – that of Hollywood celebrity endorsement. Hopalong Cassidy, Roy Rogers and Brooke Shields belong to an already existing genealogy of such endorsers that makes blue jeans, even if designed in New York, inseparable from the myth of Hollywood celebrity.

Although women rarely appeared in the classic Western in anything but the frontier version of Victorian dress, other Hollywood film genres promoted jeans as chic Western resort wear, and so began their celebrity endorsement. As early as 1939, *The Women* features three of Hollywood's most glamorous stars, Norma Shearer, Rosalind Russell and Joan Crawford, wearing sexy versions of the garment at a Nevada resort while waiting for their divorces (Harris 2002: 27). Films like these made jeans popular weekend suburban attire. The most spectacular celebrity endorser was of course Marilyn Monroe. In a 1952 photo she wears nothing but Levi's and a bikini top as workout gear. Thirty years before women engaged in body building, she bench presses free weights from an angle that emphasizes the border between her bare midriff and the fly of her blue jeans, foreshadowing the role jeans would play in signifying and performing women's sexual and gender revolution a generation later.

The Ambivalence of Designer Jeans: Production and Consumption in the Age of Global Restructuring

Like the post-Second World War singing cowboys, designer jeans of the 1970s and 1980s were an ambivalent symbolic force. On the one hand they signified a structural challenge to the dominant white, masculine identity that had underwritten American imperialism from the Indian massacres to the Vietnam War. Their role in expressing a new feminine sexuality was complexly bound up with social and political issues. But on the other hand, designer jeans, even more than the outfits of the 1950s singing cowboys, were central to a historically new and intensified form of consumerism that made possible the global restructuring of the garment industry in the 1980s. It is this restructuring that gave California 'the unfortunate distinction of being the garment sweatshop capital of the nation' (Chung, Marblestone et al. 2005: 6). In the 1990s and 2000s, social movements in LA and San Francisco responded to sweatshop exploitation. These movements have the potential to create alternative models for fashion cities, and in the following we briefly review their achievements as well as some new directions in policy they suggest.

In the 1980s, jeans and T-shirts became the global uniform of youthful hipness at the same time that large US fashion corporations made the decision to radically shift their investment from producing material garments to marketing (Klein 2002). Divesting themselves of their production units, and indeed of responsibility for producers and conditions of production, they outsourced the work to contractors in the USA and around the world. As they wielded their buying power to pay less and less to subcontractors, subcontracted factories became sweatshops, and the gap between workers' decreasing earnings and retailers' increasing profits widened (Bonacich and Appelbaum 2000). Cutting corners on worker salaries and garment quality, the fashion giants lavished investment in brand development and fashion advertising. As jeans brands proliferated, the need to distinguish them created an even greater proliferation of film, magazine and television representations that vied with each other in quantity, lushness, and seductive sophistication. Hence, mainstream US fashion increasingly sold lifestyle and branding, even as the actual garment became more and more indistinguishable from hosts of other garments. The simultaneous exploitations of young, predominantly female, producers and consumers became intimately, reciprocally dependent, and posed a need to find joint solutions.

The centrality of jeans to this process came into indelible focus for one of us (Rabine) when she visited a garment factory owned by a San Francisco Bay Area firm and located in the Export Processing Zone (EPZ) of Nairobi, Kenya, in 1995. The workers, paid twenty-three cents an hour, sat in long rows and columns, their dead eyes bearing a striking contrast to the lively expressions of workers in Nairobi's small tailoring shops. At the front of the cavernous room, a thirty-foot mountain of crumpled blue jeans waited to be finished, pressed and folded. The garments were also waiting to have labels of a well-known designer jeans maker affixed. Several such jeans retailers, each claiming uniqueness, sent their prestigious logo labels along with their orders. The factory manager, who commented that the jeans were all made the same way by the same workers, found these claims highly amusing.

But not all garment production was outsourced to Third World countries. During this period, Los Angeles became the number one centre of garment production in the USA (with San Francisco in third place after New York). Although its production volume peaked in 1997, in 2004 LA had 4,000 to 5,000 factories, and turned out $13 billion in clothing each year (Scott 2002; Garment Worker Center 2004; Chung, Marblestone et al. 2005). About 75 per cent of these factories had serious health and safety violations. Further, in a state where the minimum wage is $6.75, garment workers are paid an average of $5.75 per hour, often not getting paid at all (Garment Worker Center 2004: 3). The California Labor Department estimates $81 million in unpaid wages each year for this highly profitable retail industry (Chung, Marblestone et al. 2005: 5). In one telling case a factory contracted by Disney to make T-shirts and baseball hats owed $200,000 in unpaid wages. To meet Disney's contract, it had been operating on 'a razor thin profit margin and accelerated production schedules' (McDonnell 1998). The private inspector hired by Disney 'failed to notice that the workers were not being paid.' As the Labor Commissioner said, 'They are interested in the quality of the product, not the quality of the workers' lives' (McDonnell 1998).

A Thai immigrant worker in Los Angeles County precipitated public outcry when she managed to escape from a prison-like factory in August 1995, and contact an Asian American human rights lawyer. State inspectors found more than seventy undocumented Thais working in conditions of virtual slavery sixteen hours a day, and forced to sleep as many as ten in a room. The 'disconnect' between dream machine representations for consumers and the grim realities facing immigrant garment workers finally came to light. In response to worker and consumer protest against such abuses, a new breed of vertically integrated apparel firms (e.g., Babette in the San Francisco Bay Area) and human rights organizations (e.g., Global Exchange in San Francisco, the Garment Worker Center in LA) have led the way toward significant strategies for bridging the production–consumption disconnect. In 1999, California passed 'the strongest anti-sweatshop bill in the nation,' making the profitable retail corporations responsible for guaranteeing minimum and overtime wages to workers in contracted and subcontracted factories (Chung, Marblestone et al. 2005: 5). Workers' wage claims have quadrupled, but the California Labor Department has been lax in forcing corporations to comply with the 1999 law. Ingenious new laws, with promising potential for fashion production, do not rely on the Labor Department. Activist organizations have persuaded the LA City Council and the San Francisco Board of Supervisors to pass ordinances requiring city agencies to buy their uniforms from sources that pay workers prevailing wages. The San Francisco law, strongest in the USA, requires that the city purchase all garments from sources that pay at least the minimum wage, and respect all worker and human rights, including freedom of association to form unions. Of great significance is that this ordinance further requires preferences to be given to local clothing manufacturers (Sweatfree Ordinance 2005).

As a result of anti-sweatshop efforts by consumers and workers over two decades, some companies, especially in San Francisco, have taken the lead in setting industry codes of conduct for treatment of production workers. In 2003, Gap began seriously monitoring its subcontractors, and published hard-hitting, self-critical reports (Gap Inc. 2004). Gap owner Donald Fisher challenged other giant retailers to do likewise, and Nike has followed its example. Levi Strauss, during this period of global restructuring, maintained its reputation for ethical treatment of workers, something for which the founder's great-great-grandnephew Robert Haas received much criticism from other businessmen. Levi's profits and sales fell in large measure because it was slow to outsource to Third World sweatshops. As one financier put it, in a world where garment firms divested from manufacturing to focus on marketing, Levi's continued to be a manufacturing firm (Sarker 2005). And so in 1999, a marketing expert from Pepsi replaced Haas as CEO. In 2002, Levi's closed its San Francisco factory and the following year ended all production in the USA. Yet even as Levi's bounces back to profitability as it tries to go high fashion, the company continues to have a reputation for corporate social responsibility.

Ethics, Aesthetics and Economics: The Future of Fashion Design and Production in LA and San Francisco

In the twenty-first century, designer jeans, now called 'premium jeans', are more high fashion than ever, and fashion journalists anoint California's two fashion cities with complementary claims as 'epicenter of the denim industry' (Tschorn 2005a). While Los Angeles is 'the creative capital,' the celebrity endorsed and club scene inspired 'R&D for the whole world of denim' (Tschorn 2005a), Levi's has the most extensive jeans archive in the world: 'In the current crowded jean pool ... its archive collection serves as a reminder that the company invented the most popular piece of apparel in today's global wardrobe. And since Levi's designers can walk into those rooms and draw on the rich history whenever they are so inspired, Levi Strauss & Co. is sitting on a gold mine' (Tschorn 2005b).

This tendency to see LA and San Francisco in binary terms, as opposing poles of glamour and authenticity, may rely more on simplified marketing slogans than complex contrasts. The boundaries between these poles often blur, as when LA's venerable surf wear companies like Quicksilver claim the mantle of 'authenticity' as 'the original true California beach lifestyle brand' (Tran 2005). At the same time Levi Strauss can go for glamour, as in the 2005 San Francisco Fashion Week runway show, where its customization team 'cut up, reconfigured, painted and patched denim jeans, jackets and skirts' (Rubin 2005). Yet the contrast is useful, if replaced within the complexities of these two strikingly different urban spaces, because their production practices provide diverse visions for world fashion cities not in lockstep to the standard model.

For LA, one key lies in the phenomenon of premium jeans, which has shifted the centre of jeans design and production from New York back to this West Coast city, and perhaps more importantly, from foreign sweatshops to local specialty factories. These high-end jeans, selling for at least $US120, require skilled needle workers, small unit runs, specialized washes, quality assurance, and 'a wide variety of contemporary construction details and innovative stitch designs' (Figueroa 2005). They thus cannot be outsourced to factories overseas, and in the wake of global restructuring, Los Angeles remains the only US city with plants to fulfil these requirements. In addition, some of the really high-end jeans, like 7 for all Mankind, can forego conventional advertising to follow Hollywood's venerable marketing tradition of celebrity endorsement (Hall 2002: 71; Lipke 2005). This method of disseminating fashion fits Los Angeles far more than a ridiculed Fashion Week, mocked on the front page of the *Los Angeles Times*: 'Outside the tent at Los Angeles Fashion Week,' the *Times* article began, 'a guy in white angel wings waves C-, D- and E-list celebrities from the valet line to a postage-stamp-size photo backdrop' (Moore 2005). The most prestigious premium jeans producers can avoid this fate-worse-than-death for an Angelino and rely on A-list celebrities to wear their label in all the right places. As a result of all the above factors, 85 per cent of premium jeans, including 110 local brands, are wholly produced in LA (McAllister 2005).

Even these jeans companies, however, are giant enterprises compared with most fashion businesses in San Francisco. Yet the intimate ambience of San Francisco fosters a wealth of small independent designers, who fall under the radar of global fashion and who could not exist in the highly capitalized monster spaces of LA.

They represent the potential for a world fashion city of a distinct type. Many of the more successful designers – like Babette, Erin Mahoney and Freedom Fits – are socially conscious business people as well as creative innovators. Babette Pinsky's high-end, elegant and technically experimental fashions are produced, distributed and sold in a sweat-free, vertically integrated company. This could serve as a model for scores of struggling and talented designers. Although Levi Strauss and Co. showed commendable support to young designers by lending its prestige to the 2005 Fashion Week when San Francisco's other famous fashions brands, Banana Republic and Jessica McClintock, refused to do so, different forms of support could be more sustaining.

The same holds for California state government. Currently it pursues a policy of 'sweeps', surprise inspections of garment factories for labour law violations. These have proven to focus on enforcing arcane bureaucratic obstacle courses of licensing laws and, according to Delia Herrera of LA's Garment Worker Center, do not provide 'any comfort, assurance, or respect to worker rights' (Garment Worker Center 2005). Government and business leaders like Levi Strauss have the resources to encourage independent designers to set up their own sweat-free manufacturing units. Shifting funds from Fashion Weeks, streamlining licensing laws, and mentoring young designers are just three of many practical ways to turn San Francisco's unique social and fashion consciousness into a world fashion reality.

Such policies would allow both California cities to build locally distinct alternatives to the homogeneous model of the world fashion city. In San Francisco, Levi Strauss and Gap, who can claim leadership for inventing jeans and marketing them as global fashion, are beginning to play a leading role in socially responsible manufacture. They could also take leadership in supporting California policies that encourage local sweat-free production. In Los Angeles, the boom in high quality, highly skilled production of premium jeans provides a way to combine world fashion looks with dignity and sustaining pay for garment workers. In both San Francisco's festive spaces of community and LA's massively scaled, privatized spaces, the rich history of mining jeans to find an ex-centric place in the world fashion sun continues into the twenty-first century. In each urban space, the garment remains at the centre of different potential solutions to the multiple (dis)connects between 'sewing machines' and 'dream machines'.

References

Abel, R. (1998) '"Our Country"/Whose Country? The "Americanisation" Project of Early Westerns', in Edward Buscombe and Roberta E. Pearson (eds) *Back in the Saddle Again: New Essays on the Western*, London: BFI Publishing.

Agins, T. (1999) *The End of Fashion: The Mass Marketing of the Clothing Business*, New York: Diane Publishing.

Agnew, J. (1998) *Geopolitics: Re-visioning World Politics*, London: Routledge.

American Denim: A New Folk Art (1975) presented by Richard M. Owens and Tony Lane; text by Peter Beagle; photographs by Baron Wolman and the denim artists, New York: H. N. Abrams, Inc.

Amin, A. and N. Thrift (2003) *Cities: Reimagining the Urban* Oxford: Polity

An Aid to Pedestrian Movement: A Report by a Working Party on The Introduction of a New Mode of Transport in Central London (1971), London: Westminster City Council.

Anderson, F. (2000) 'Museums as fashion media' in S. Bruzzi and P. Church Gibson (eds) *Fashion Cultures: Theories, Explorations and Analysis*, London: Routledge.

Aoki, S. (2001) *FRUiTS*, New York: Phaidon Press.

Appadurai, A. (1990) 'Disjuncture and difference in the global cultural economy', *Theory, Culture and Society*, 7: 295–310.

Appadurai, A. (1996) *Modernity at Large: Cultural Dimensions of Globalisation*, Minneapolis: University of Minnesota Press.

Appadurai, A. (ed.) (1986) *The Social Life of Things: Commodities in Cultural Perspective*, Cambridge: Cambridge University Press.

Balshofer, F. and A. Miller (1998) 'Eluding the Patent Agents' (orig. 1976) in Christopher Silvester (ed.) *The Grove Book of Hollywood*, New York: Grove Press.

Balzac, H. de (1974 [1831]) *La Peau de Chagrin*, Paris: Gallimard.

Balzac, H. de (1984 [1843]) 'La Femme de Province', in *La Muse du Département*, Paris: Gallimard.

Balzac, H. de (2002 [1830]) *Traité de la Vie Elégante*, Paris: Arthème Fayard.

Banerjee, M. and D. Miller, (2003) *The Sari*, Oxford: Berg

Banville, T. de (2002 [1881]) *Le Génie des Parisiennes*, Paris: Mille et Une Nuits.

Barry, B. (1992) 'Commerce et Commercants Senegambiens dans la Longue Duree: Etude d'une formation economique dependante', in *Commerce et Commercants en Afrique de L'ouest: Le Senegal*, Paris: L'Harmattan.

Barry, B. (1998) *Senegambia and the Atlantic Slave Trade*, Cambridge: Cambridge University Press.

Barthes, R. (1990) *The Fashion System*, Berkeley: University of California Press.

Baudelaire, C. (1975 [1857]) *Les Fleurs du Mal*, Harmondsworth: Penguin.

Baudelaire, C. (1986 [1860]) 'A une Passante', in *Tableaux Parisiens*, in *The Complete Verse*, Volume I, London: Anvil Press.

Baudrillard, J. (1993) *Transparency of Evil: Essays on Extreme Phenomena*, London: Verso.

Bazenguissa-Ganga, R. and J. MacGaffey (2000) *Congo-Paris: Transnational Traders on the Margins of the Law*, Bloomington: Indiana University Press.

Beaton, C. (2003) *Beaton in the Sixties: The Cecil Beaton Diaries as they were written*, Hugo Vickers (ed.), London: Weidenfeld and Nicholson.

Beaverstock J., R. Smith and P. Taylor (1999a) 'A roster of world cities', *Cities*, 16: 1133–46.

Beaverstock J., R. Smith and P. Taylor (1999b) 'The long arm of the law: London's law firms in a globalizing world economy', *Environment and Planning A*, 31:187–92.

Beaverstock J., R. Smith and P. Taylor (2000) 'World city network: a new meta-geography?', *Annals of the Association of American Geographers*, 90: 123–34.

Bell, Q. (1947) *Of Human Finery*, London: Hogarth Press.

Benjamin, W. (1997) *Moskovskii dnevnik*, Moscow: Ad Marginem.

Benjamin, W. (1999) *The Arcades Project*, Cambridge, MA: The Belknap Press of Harvard University Press.

Bernstein, R. (1991) *Fragile Glory: A Portrait of France and the French*, New York: Plume.

Bhachu, P. (1997) 'Dangerous designs: Asian women and the new landscapes of fashion', in A. Oakley and J. Mitchell (eds) *Who's afraid of feminism?* London: Hamish Hamilton.

Bhachu, P. (2003) *Dangerous Designs: Asian women fashion the diaspora economies*, London: Routledge.

Bhatia, N. (2003) 'Fashioning Women in Colonial India', *Fashion Theory*, 7: 327–44.

Biondi, J. P. (1987) *Saint-Louis du Senegal: Memoires d'un Metissage*, Paris: Denoel.

Boddy, W. (1998) '"Sixty Million Viewers Can't Be Wrong": The Rise and Fall of the Television Western', in Edward Buscombe and Roberta E. Pearson (eds) *Back in the Saddle Again: New Essays on the Western,* London: BFI Publishing.

Boilat, D. (1984 [1853]) *Esquisses Senegalaises: Physionomie du pays, peuplade, commerce, religion, passé et avenir, recits et legends*, Paris: Karthala.

Bolton, A. (2002) *Supermodern Wardrobe*, London: Victoria and Albert Museum.

Bonacich, E. and R. Appelbaum (2000) *Behind the Label: Inequality in the Los Angeles Apparel Industry*, Berkeley: University of California Press.

Bondanella, P. (1990) *Italian Cinema From Neo-Realism to the Present*, New York: Continuum.

Bonomi, A. (2004) 'Milano, l'importanza di ridiventare leader', *Corriere della Sera*, 22 December.

Boone, C. (1992) *Merchant Power and the Roots of State Power in Senegal, 1930–1985*, New York: Cambridge University Press.

Bourdieu, P. (1993a) *The Field of Cultural Production*, Cambridge: Polity.

Bourdieu, P. (1993b) *La Misère du Monde*, Paris: Editions du Seuil.

Bourdieu, P. (1996) *Distinction: A Social Critique of the Judgement of Taste*, London: Routledge.

Bowlby, R. (2000) *Carried Away*, London: Faber and Faber.

Bowles, H. (2001) *Jackie Kennedy: the White House Year – Selections from the JFK Memorial Library and Museum*, New York: Metropolitan Museum of Art Press.

Bowser, E. (1990) *History of the American Cinema. Vol. 2, The Transformation of Cinema, 1907–1915*, Berkeley: University of California Press.

Bradley, S. and N. Pevsner (2003) *The Buildings of England. London 6: Westminster*, New Haven: Yale University Press.

Braham P. (1997) 'Fashion: Unpacking a Cultural Production', in P. DuGay (ed.) *Production of Culture/Cultures of Production*, Thousand Oaks, CA: Sage.

Braidotti, R. (1997) *Nomadic Patterns*, London: Polity Press.

Brett, L. (1942) 'Doubts on the Mars Plan', *Architect's Journal*, 9 July.

Breward, C. (1995) *The Culture of Fashion*, Manchester: Manchester University Press.

Breward, C. (1999) *The Hidden Consumer; Masculinities, Fashion and City Life 1860–1914*, Manchester: Manchester University Press.

Breward, C. (2003) *Fashion,* Oxford: Oxford University Press.

Breward, C. (2004) *Fashioning London: Clothing and the Modern Metropolis*, Oxford: Berg.

Breward, C. (2006) 'Introduction' in C. Breward, D. Gilbert and J. Lister (eds) *Swinging Sixties: Fashion in London and beyond* London: V&A Publications.

Breward, C. and C. Evans (2005) *Fashion and Modernity,* Oxford: Berg.

Breward, C., E. Ehrman and C. Evans (eds) (2004) *The London Look*, New Haven: Yale.

Browne, K. (1964) 'A Latin Quarter for London', *Architectural Review*, March.

Brunsdon, C. (2004) 'The Poignancy of Place: London and the Cinema', *Visual Culture in Britain*, 1: 59–74.

Buchanan, C. (1963) *Traffic in Towns: a Study of the Long Term Problems of Traffic in Urban Areas*, London: HMSO.

Buckley, R. and S. Gundle (2000) 'Flash trash: Gianni Versace and the theory and practice of glamour', in S. Bruzzi and P. Church Gibson (eds) *Fashion Cultures: Theories, Explorations and Analysis*, London: Routledge.

Bullock, M. (2002) *Building the Post-War World: Modern Architecture and Reconstruction in Britain,* London: Routledge.

Butler, J. (1999) *Gender Trouble*, London: Routledge.

Calloway, S. (1992) *The House of Liberty: Masters of Style and Decoration*, London: Thames & Hudson.

Capote, T. (1958) *Breakfast at Tiffany's*, London: Hamish Hamilton.

Carter, M. (2003) *Fashion Classics: From Carlyle to Barthes*, Oxford: Berg.

Certeau, M. de (1988) *The Practice of Everyday Life.* Berkeley, CA: University of California Press.

Chaney, D. (2002) 'Cosmopolitan Art and Cultural Citizenship', *Theory, Culture and Society*, 19: 157–74.

Chase, E. W. and I. Chase (1954) *Always in Vogue*, London: V. Gollancz.

Chen, Y. (2005) *Chinese San Francisco, 1850–1943: A Trans-Pacific Community*, Stanford, CA: Stanford University Press.

Chenoune, F. (1993) *A History of Men's Fashion*, Paris: Flammarion.

Chensvold, C. (2004) 'That's Entertainment: Apparel Companies Cross into Entertainment—To Varying Degrees of Success', *California Apparel News*, 22–28 October: 18.

Chinese Historical Society (1975) *The Life, Influence and the Role of the Chinese in the United States, 1776–1960* Proceedings/Papers of the National Conference Held at the University of San Francisco, 11–12 July.

Chung, C., Marblestone, J. et al. (2005) *Reinforcing the Seams: Guaranteeing the Promise of California's Landmark Anti-Sweatshop Law: An Evaluation of Assembly Bill 633 Six Years Later*, Los Angeles: Asian Pacific American Legal Center of Southern California, September. Available online at: http://apalc.org/pdffiles/SWReportFinal.pdf

Clark, H. (1999) 'The Cheung Sam: issues of fashion and cultural identity' in V. Steele and J. Major (eds) *China Chic: East meets West*, New Haven: Yale University Press.

Clarke Keogh, P. (1999) *Audrey Style*, London: Harper Collins.

Clarke Keogh, P. (2001) *Jackie Style*, London: Aurum Press.

Clifford, J. (1998) *The Predicament of Culture: Twentieth Century Ethnography, Literature and Art*, Cambridge, MA: Harvard University Press.

Clunn, H. (1937) *The Face of London: The Record of a Century's Changes and Development*, London: Simpkin Marshall.

Cole, S. (2000) *'Don We Now Our Gay Apparel': Gay Men's Dress in the Twentieth Century*, Oxford: Berg.

Colomina, B. (1994) *Privacy and Publicity: Modern Architecture as Mass Media*, Cambridge, MA: MIT.

Comité Colbert. Le (2002/2003) Les Expoirs de la Création.

Conklin, A. (1997) *A Mission to Civilize: The Republican Idea of Empire in France and West Africa, 1895–1930*, Stanford: Stanford University Press.

Cook, I. (2004) 'Follow the thing: papaya', *Antipode*, 36: 642–64.

Cook, I. and P. Crang (1996) 'The world on a plate: culinary culture, displacement and geographical knowledges', *Journal of Material Culture*, 1: 131–53.

Corkin, S. (2004) *Cowboys as Cold War Warriors: The Western and U.S. History*, Philadelphia: Temple University Press.

Corwin, N. (1996) 'The Kimono in American Art and Fashion, 1853–1996' in Stevens, R. and Y. Wada (eds) *The Kimono Inspiration: Art and Art-To-Wear in America*, Washington: The Textile Museum.

Craik, J. (1994) *The Face of Fashion*, London: Routledge.

Crane, D. (1993) 'Fashion Design as an Occupation', *Current Research on Occupations and Professions*, 8: 55–73.

Crane, D. (1997) 'Postmodernism and the Avant-Garde: Stylistic Change in Fashion Design', *MODERNISM/modernity*, 4: 123–40.

Crane, D. (2000) *Fashion and Its Social Agendas: Class, Gender, and Identity in Clothing*, Chicago: The University of Chicago Press.

Crang, P., C. Dwyer and P. Jackson (2003) 'Transnationalism and the spaces of commodity culture', *Progress in Human Geography*, 27: 438–56.

Crowder, M. (1967) *Senegal: A Study in French Assimilation Policy*, London: Methuen.

Cruise O'Brien, D. (1975) *Saints and Politicians: Essays in the Organization of a Senegalese Peasant Society*, Cambridge: Cambridge University Press.

Cullerton, B. (1995) *Geoffrey Beene*, New York: Harry N. Abrams.

De la Haye, A. (1998) 'Foreword', in R. Violette (ed.) *One Woman's Wardrobe*, London: Victoria and Albert.

De Marly, D. (1980) *The History of Haute Couture, 1850–1950*, New York: Holmes and Meier.

Department of Culture, Media and Sport (2005) *Understanding the Future: Museums and 21st Century life*, www.culture.gov.uk/museums_and_galleries.

Dieng, A. (2000) *Senégal à la Veille du Troisième Millénaire*, Paris: l'Harmattan.

Diop, A. B. (1981) *La societe Wolof: Tradition et Changement: Les Systemes d'inegalite et de domination*, Paris: Karthala.

Diop, M. C. (2002) *Le Senegal Contemporain*, Paris: Karthala.

Diouf, M. (1998) 'The French Colonial Policy of Assimilation and the Civility of the Originaires of the Four Communes (Senegal): A Nineteenth-Century Globalization Project', *Development and Change*, 29: 671–96.

Diouf, M. (2000) 'The Senegalese Murid Trade Diaspora and the Making of a Vernacular Cosmopolitanism', *Public Culture*, 12: 679–702.

Dodd, P. (2005) 'China chic, not China cheap', *Observer*, 4 December (www.guardian.co.uk).

Domosh, M (1998) 'Those "Gorgeous Incongruities": Polite politics and public space on the streets of nineteenth-century New York City', *Annals of the Association of American Geographers*, 88: 209–26.

Durham, P. and E. Jones (1965) *Negro Cowboys*, New York: Dodd, Mead.

Dwyer, C. (2004) 'Tracing transnationalities through commodity culture: a case study of British-South Asian fashion', in P. Jackson, P. Crang and C. Dwyer (eds) *Transnational Spaces*, London: Routledge.

Dwyer, C. and P. Crang (2002) 'Fashioning ethnicities: The commercial spaces of multiculture', *Ethnicities*, 2: 410–30.

Dwyer, C. and P. Jackson (2003) 'Commodifiying difference: selling EASTern fashion', *Environment and Planning D: Society and Space*, 21: 269–91.

Edwards, B. (2003) 'A Man's World? Masculinity and Metropolitan Modernity and Simpson, Piccadilly', in D. Gilbert, D. Matless and B. Short, B. (eds) *Geographies of British Modernity*, Oxford: Blackwell.

Edwards, B. (2005) 'West End Shopping with Vogue: 1930s Geographies of Metropolitan Consumption', in J. Benson and L. Ugolini (eds) *Cultures of Selling: Perspectives on Consumption and Society since 1700*, Aldershot: Ashgate.

Edwards, B. (2006) '"We are fatally influenced by goods bought in Bond Street": London, shopping and the fashionable geographies of 1930s *Vogue*', *Fashion Theory*, 10 in press.

Ehrman, E. (2002) 'The Spirit of Style: Hardy Amies, Royal Dressmaker and International Businessman', in C. Breward, B. Conekin and C. Cox (eds) *The Englishness of English Dress*, Oxford: Berg.

Eicher, J. (ed.) (1995) *Dress and Ethnicity: Change Across Space and Time*, Oxford: Berg.

Eicher, J. and B. Sumberg (1995) 'World fashion, ethnic and national dress', in J. Eicher (ed.) *Dress and Ethnicity: Change Across Space and Time*, Oxford: Berg.

Elias, N. (1987) *The Court Society*, Oxford: Blackwell.

Entwistle, J. (2000) *The Fashioned Body: Fashion, Dress and Modern Social Theory*, Cambridge: Polity Press.

Evans, C. (1997) 'Dreams that only money can buy ... or the shy tribe in flight from discourse', *Fashion Theory*, 1: 169–88.

Evans, C. (2003) *Fashion at the Edge: Spectacle, modernity and deathliness*, London: Yale University Press.

Evans, G. (2003) 'Hard-branding the cultural city – From Prado to Prada', *International Journal of Urban and regional Research*, 27: 417–40.

Everson, W. (1969) *A Pictorial History of the Western Film*, New York: The Citadel Press.

Ewen, S. (1976) *Captains of Consciousness: Advertising and The Social Roots of the Consumer Culture*, New York: McGraw-Hill.

Ewing, E. (1992) *A History of Twentieth Century Fashion,* London: Batsford.

Fall, Y. (1989) 'Les Wolof au miroir de leur langue: quelques observations', in J. P. Chretien and G. Prunier (eds) *Les Ethnies ont une Histoire*, Paris: Karthala.

Featherstone, M. (2002) 'Cosmopolis: an Introduction', *Theory, Culture and Society,* 19: 1–16.

Fedosiuk, Iu. A. (1991) *Moskva v kol'tse Sadovykh*, Moscow: Moskovskii rabochii.

Fedosiuk, Iu. A. (2004) *Utro krasit nezhnym svetom... Vospominaniia o Moskve 1920–1930 godov*, Moscow: Flinta; Nauka.

Figueroa, C. (2004) 'Los Angeles Becoming a Mecca for Premium Denim Makers', *California Apparel News*, 17–23 September: 1, 8–9.

Finkelstein, J. (1996) *After a Fashion*, Melbourne: Melbourne University Press.

Flaubert, G. (2000 [1881]) *Dictionnaire des Idées Reçues*, Paris: Mille et Une Nuits.

Foot, J. (2001) *Milano dopo il miracolo*, Milan: Feltrinelli.

Forshaw, J. H. and P. Abercrombie (1943) *County of London Plan*, London: MacMillan.

Fortassier, R. (1988) *Les Ecrivains Français et la Mode*, Paris: Puf.

Foucault, M. (1997) *The Archaeology of Knowledge*, London: Routledge.

Friedberg, A. (1994) *Window Shopping: cinema and the postmodern*, Berkeley: University of California Press.

Friedmann, J. (1986) 'The world city hypothesis', *Development and Change,* 17: 69–83.

Friedmann, J. (1995) 'Where we stand: a decade of world city research', in P. Knox and P. Taylor (eds) *World cities in a World-System*, Cambridge: Cambridge University Press.

Friedmann, J. and K. Wolff (1982) 'World city formation: an agenda for research and action', *International Journal of Urban and regional Research*, 6: 309–44.

Frisby, D. (1985) *Fragments of Modernity: Theories of Modernity in the Work of Simmel, Kracauer and Benjamin*, Cambridge: Polity Press.

Fujita, A. (2005) 'Tokyo Hatsu: Pari Tsuigeki-e [Fashion from Tokyo: Challenging Paris]', *Sankei Shimbun*, 28 July: 20.

Gaines, J. and C. Herzog (1998) 'The Fantasy of Authenticity in Western Costume', in E. Buscombe and R. Pearson (eds) *Back in the Saddle Again: New Essays on the Western*, London: BFI Publishing.

Gandee, C. (1999) '1950s: Designer Bill Blass Remembers the Years of Cocktails, Café Society and Cool American Chic (An Interview with Bill Blass)' *Vogue*, November, 470: 537–8.

Gap, Inc. (2004) *Corporate Responsibility Report*, www.gapinc.com/public/documents/CSR_Report_04.pdf.

Gardiner, S. (1970) 'Little shop – what now? Natural street art and the planners', *The Architect and Building News*, 3 September.

Garment Worker Center (2005) 'Labor Commissioner's Surprise Raids Wreak Havoc in Los Angeles Garment Factories', 10 August, www.garmentworkercenter.org

Garment Worker Center and Sweatshop Watch (2004) 'Crisis or Opportunity: The Future of Los Angeles Garment Workers, the Apparel Industry, and the Local Economy', www.garmentworkercenter.org

Gastel, M. (1995) *50 anni di moda italiana*, Milan: Vallardi.

Gastel, M. (2003) 'L'incontro fra domanda e offerta della moda: l'esperienza di Beppe Modenese' (Interview with Beppe Modenese), *Women & Fashion* website: www.womenandfashion.it/allegati/convegni_domanda_offerta.pdf

Gay-Fragneaud, P. and P. Vallet (2004) 'Une Histoire des Revues de Mode des Origines au XIXe Siècle', in S. Richoux-Berardand F. Bonnet (eds) *Glossy*, Musée de la Mode de Marseille: Images en Manoeuvres Editions.

Geinike, N. A., N. S. Elagin, E. A. Efimova and I. I. Shits (eds) (1991 [1917]) *Po Moskve*, Moscow: Izobrazitel'noe Iskusstvo.

Gellar, S. (1981) *Senegal: An African Nation Between Islam and the West*, Boulder: Westview Press.

George, J. (1998) *Paris Province: de la Révolution à la Mondialisation*, Paris: Fayard.

Giddens, A. (1991) *Modernity and Self Identity*, Cambridge: Polity Press.

Gilbert, D. (1999) '*London in all its Glory – or how to enjoy London:* guidebook representations of Imperial London', *Journal of Historical Geography*, 25: 279–97.

Gilbert, D. (2000) 'Urban outfitting. The city and the spaces of fashion culture', in S. Bruzzi and P. Church Gibson (eds) *Fashion Cultures: Theories, Explorations and Analysis*, London: Routledge.

Gilbert, D. and Hancock, C. (2006) 'New York City and the transatlantic imagination: French and English tourism and the spectacle of the modern metropolis, 1893–1939', *Journal of Urban History* in press.

Ginsberg, M. (ed.) (1971) *Fashion: an anthology by Cecil Beaton*, London: Victoria and Albert Museum.

Glennie, P. and N. Thrift (1992) 'Modernity, urbanism, and modern consumption', *Environment and Planning D: Society and Space*, 10: 423–43.

Glynn, P. (1966) 'Altogether Now', *Times*, 13 December.

Gold, J. (1997) *The Experience of Modernism: Modern Architects and the Future City 1928–1953*, London: Spon.

Goldberg, V. (2001) 'A Certain Look the Camera Sold', *The New York Times*, 18 November.

Goldman, E.S. (1949) *The New York Story: A History of the New York Clothing Industry, 1924–1949*, New York: The New York Clothing Manufacturers' Exchange Inc.

Goldstein Crowe, L. (2005) 'Moscow: New Time, New Fashion', *The Times*, 23 June.

Gondola, D. (1997) *Villes Miroirs: Migrations et Identites urbaines a Kinshasa et Brazzaville (1930–1970)*, Paris: L'Harmattan.

Goulbourne, H. (1998) *Race Relations in Britain since 1945*, London: Macmillan.

Grandmaison, C. (1972) *Femmes Dakaroises: Roles Traditionnels Feminins et Urbanisation,* Abidjan: Annales De L'Universite d'Abidjan.

Greater London Council, City of Westminster and London Borough of Camden, (1968) *Covent Garden Area Draft Plan*, London, November.

Green, J. (1999) *All Dressed Up: The Sixties and the Counterculture*, London: Pimlico.

Green, N. (1997) *Ready-to-Wear and Ready-to-Work: A Century of Industry and Immigrants in Paris and New York*, Durham: Duke University Press.

Green, N. (2002) 'Paris: A historical view', in J. Rath (ed.) *Unravelling the Rag Trade. Immigrant Entrepreneurship in Seven World Cities*, Oxford: Berg.

Griboedov, A. (1993) *Woe from Wit* trans. A. S. Vagapov, http://spintongues. vladivostok.com/griboyedov.htm

Gropius, W. (1937) 'The Store of Tomorrow', *Store*, April: 119–200.

Gubskii, A. (2005) 'TsUM dolzhen stat' dostupnym univermagom' An interview with Vittorio Radice, *Vedomosti*, 4 May.

Guilbaut, S. (1983) *How New York Stole the Idea of Modern Art*, Chicago: University of Chicago Press.

Hale, A. (2000) 'What hope for "ethical" trade in the globalised garment industry?' *Antipode*, 32: 349–56.

Hall, M., with M. Carne and S. Sheppard (2002) *California Fashion from the Old West to the New Hollywood*, New York: H. N. Abrams, Inc.

Hall, P. (1963) *London 2000*, London: Faber and Faber.

Hall, P. (2000) 'Creative cities and economic development', *Urban Studies*, 37: 639–51.

Hammack, D. (1991) 'Developing for commercial culture', in W. Taylor (ed.) *Inventing Times Square: Commerce and Culture at the Crossroads of the World*, Baltimore: John Hopkins University Press.

Hancock, C. (1999) '*Capitale du plaisir*: the remaking of imperial Paris', in F. Driver and D. Gilbert (eds) *Imperial Cities: landscape, Display and Identity*, Manchester: Manchester University Press.

Hannerz, U. (1996) *Transnational Connections: Culture, People, Places*, New York: Routledge.

Hansen, K. (2000) *Salaula: The World of Secondhand Clothing and Zambia*, Chicago: University of Chicago Press.

Harley, J. (1988) 'Maps, Knowledge and Power', in D. Cosgrove and S. Daniels (eds) *The Iconography of Landscape: Essays on the Symbolic Representation, Design and Use of the Past Landscape*, Cambridge: Cambridge University Press.

Harris, Alice (2002) *The Blue Jean*, New York: Powerhouse Books.

Harris, Andrew (2005) 'Branding urban space: the creation of art districts in contemporary London and Mumbai', Unpublished PhD Thesis, University of London.

Harvey, D. (1989) *The condition of postmodernity*, Oxford: Blackwell.

Hebdige, D. (1988) *Hiding in the Light,* London: Routledge.

Heinich, N. (2003) *Les Ambivalences de l'Emancipation Féminine*, Paris: Albin Michel.

Helfgott, R. (1959) 'Women's and Children's Apparel', in M. Hall (ed.) *Made in New York*, Cambridge, MA: Harvard University Press.

Helvin, M. (1985) *Catwalk*, London: Pavilion.

Hendrickson, H. (1996) *Clothing and Difference: Embodied Identities in Colonial and Post-Colonial Africa*, Durham: Duke University Press.

Hill, A, (2005) 'People Dress So Badly Nowadays: Fashion and Late Modernity' in C. Breward and C. Evans (eds) *Fashion and Modernity,* Oxford: Berg.

Hirschberg, L. (2001) 'Tom Ford, Ensuring a Place for Gucci in Hard Times', *The New York Times Magazine*, 2 December.

Hobhouse, H. (1975) *A History of Regent Street*, London: MacDonald and Jane's.

Hughes, A. (1994) 'The City and the Female Autograph', in M. Sheringham (ed.) *Parisian Fields*, London: Reaktion.

Hunt, L. (1993) 'Introduction: Obscenity and the Origins of Modernity, 1500–1800', in L. Hunt (ed.) *The Invention of Pornography: Obscenity and the Origins of Modernity, 1500–1800*, New York: Zone Books.

Hutnyk, J. (2000) *Critique of Exotica: Music, Politics and the Culture Industry*, London: Pluto Press.

Ilyin, P. (2004) 'Geografia kyltyri v Moskve v kontse XIX – nachale XX veka' in P. Ilyin and B. Ruble (eds) *Moskva rubezha XIX i XX stoletii*, Moscow: Rosspen.

Ivanov, E. (1986) *Metkoe moskovskoe slovo. Byt i rech' staroi Moskvy*, Moscow: Moskovskii rabochii.

Jackson, K. (1995) 'Garment district', in *The Encyclopedia of New York City*, New Haven, CT: Yale University Press.

Jackson, P. (1999) 'Commodity cultures: the traffic in things', *Transactions, Institute of British Geographers*, 24: 95–108.

Jackson, P. (2002) 'Commercial culture: transcending the cultural and the economic', *Progress in Human Geography*, 26: 3–18.

Jackson, P., M. Lowe, D. Miller and F. Mort (2000) *Commercial Cultures: Economies, Practices, Spaces*, Oxford: Berg.

Jackson, P., P. Crang and C. Dwyer (2003) *Transnational Spaces*, London: Routledge.

Jackson, P., N. Thomas and C. Dwyer (forthcoming) 'Consumer culture in London and Mumbai: exploring the transnational geographies of food and fashion' *Geoforum.*

Jenkins, R. (2004) *Social Identity*, London: Routledge.

Johnson, A. (2004) 'Cultural Surfing', *Vogue Australia*, 2 February: 104–9.

Jones, C. and A. Leshkowich (2003) *Re-orienting Fashion: The Globalization of Asian Dress*, Oxford: Berg.

Jones, J. (2004) *Sexing La Mode*, Oxford: Berg.

Kagan, M. (2004) 'Moskva pri novom rezhime: dinamika funktsii mesta' in P. Ilyin and B. Ruble (eds) *Moskva rubezha XIX i XX stoletii*, Moscow: Rosspen.

Kane, F. (1977) 'Femmes proletaires du Senegal, a la ville et aux champs', *Cahiers d'Etudes Africaines*, 17: 77–94.

Kanunikova, I. A. (2003) 'Kontsept 'Moskva' v rasskaze I. A. Bunina 'Chistyi ponedel'nik', in *Moskva i moskovskii tekst v russkoj literature XVIII-XIX vekov i folklore*, Moscow: MGPU.

Katz, W. (1987) *The Black West: A Documentary and Pictorial History of the African American Role in the Westward Expansion of the United States*, New York: Touchstone.

Kawamura, Y. (2004a) *The Japanese Revolution in Paris Fashion*, Oxford: Berg.

Kawamura, Y. (2004b) *Fashion-ology: An Introduction to Fashion Studies*, Oxford: Berg.

Kerr, J. and A. Gibson (eds) (2003) *London: From Punk to Blair*, London: Reaktion Books.

Khan, N. (1992) 'Asian women's dress: from burqah to Bloggs', in J. Ash and E. Wilson (eds) *Chic thrills: a fashion reader* Berkeley: University of California Press.

King A. (1990) *Global Cities: Post-Imperialism and the Internationalism of London*, London: Routledge.

King, A. (1990) *Urbanism, Colonialism, and the World Economy*, London: Routledge.

King, A. (1995) 'Re-presenting world cities: cultural theory/social practice' in P. Knox and P. Taylor (eds) *World cities in a World-System*, Cambridge: Cambridge University Press.

Klein, N. (2002) *No Logo: No Space, No Choice, No Jobs*, New York: Picador.

Koenig, R. (1973) *The Restless Image*, London: George Allen and Unwin.

Koenig, R. (1974) *A la Mode: On the Social Psychology of Fashion*, New York: Seabury Press.

Korn, A. and F. Samuely, (1941) 'A Master Plan for London', *Architectural Review*, June: 143–50.

Koroleva, Iu. and I. Zakharova (2001) 'PR v Fashion-biznese', http://pr-club.com/PR_Lib/fashion.shtml.

Kuczynski, A. (1999) 'Conde's Latest Acquisition Has Fashion Industry Fidgeting', *The New York Times*, 23 August 1999, Section A: 1.

Lash, S. and J. Urry (1994) *Economies of Signs and Space*, London: Sage.

Le Corbusier (1998) *Essential Le Corbusier: L'Esprit Nouveau Articles*, Oxford: Architectural Press.

Lecercle, J-P. (1989) *Mallarmé et la Mode*, Librairie Séguier.

Lee, S. (ed.) (1975) *American Fashion The Life and Lines of Adrian, Mainbocher, McCardell, Norell, Trigere*, New York: Quadrangle/New York Times Book Co.

Leontis, A. (1997) 'Mediterranean topographies before Balkanization: on Greek diaspora, emporium and revolution', *Diaspora*, 6: 179–94.

Leventon, M. (2005) *Artwear: Fashion and Anti-fashion*, San Francisco: Thames & Hudson, Fine Arts Museums of San Francisco.

Levin, B. (1959) 'The Monster of Piccadilly Circus', *The Spectator*, 11 December.

Levy, A. (2004) *Small Island*, London: Review.

Lewis, P. (1978) *The Fifties*, London: Heinemann.

Liberty, A. (1893) 'On the Progress of Taste in Dress, III: In Relation to Manufacture', *Aglaia, Journal of the Healthy and Artistic Dress Union*, 3: 27–31.

Lipke, D. (2005) 'The Cool Factor: How the Right Buzz Can Help Brands Break through the Clutter of Today's Crowded Denim Scene', *Daily News Record*, 13 June: 40–2.

Lipovetsky, G. (1994) *The Empire of Fashion. Dressing Modern Democracy*, Princeton: Princeton University Press.

Lockwood, L. (1995) 'ICB: High Expectations in Japan', *Women's Wear Daily*, August, 16: 8–9.

London County Council (1951) *Administrative County of London Development Plan 1951: Analysis*, London: LCC.

London County Council (1960) *Administrative County of London Development Plan First Review 1960: County Planning Report*, London: LCC.

London: A Combined Guidebook and Atlas (1937) London: Thomas Cook and Son.

Loos, A. (1998) *Ornament and Crime: Selected Essays*, A. Opel (ed.) and M. Mitchell (trans.), Riverside: Ariadne Press.

Luckett, M. (2000) 'Travel and Mobility, Femininity and National Identity in Sixties British Cinema', in J. Ashby and A. Higson (eds) *British Cinema: Past and Present*, London: Routledge.

Lurçat, H. and I. Lurçat (2002) *Comment devenir une Vraie Parisienne*, Paris: Parigramme.

Lury, C. (1999) *Consumer Culture*, Cambridge: Polity.

Lykova, A. (2004) TsUM, *Afisha,* 30 June.

MacAdams, L. (2001) *Birth of the Cool: Beat, Bebop and the American Avantgarde*, New York: Free Press.

MacInnes, C. (1959) *Absolute Beginners*, London: Allison and Busby.

Mandelstam, O. (2003) *Ocherki*, Augsburg: In Werden.

Marcus, M. (1986) *Italian Film in the Light of Neorealism*, Princeton, NJ: Princeton University Press.

Martin, R. (1995a) 'Fashion in the Age of Advertising', *Journal of Popular Culture*, 29: 235–55.

Martin, R. (1995b) 'Our Kimono mind: reflections on Japanese design: A survey since 1950', *Journal of the Design History Society*, 8: 215–23.

Martin, R. (1997) *Fashion Memoir: Charles James*, London: Thames and Hudson.

Martin, R. (1998) *American Ingenuity: Sportswear 1960s–1970s*, New York: The Metropolitan Museum of Art.

Martin, R. and H. Koda (1994) *Orientalism: Visions of the East in Western Dress.* New York: Metropolitan Museum of Art.

Maspero, F. (1994) *Roissy Express*, London: Verso.

Massey, D. (1994) *Space, Place, and Gender*, Minneapolis: University of Minnesota Press.

Matless, D. (1998) *Landscape and Englishness*, London: Reaktion.

Maynard, M. (2004) *Dress and Globalisation*, Manchester: Manchester University Press.

McAllister, R. (2005) 'Denim Boom Brings Bounty for L.A. Wash Houses', *California Apparel News*, 29 April–5 May: 1, 14.

McColl, P. (2001) 'The American Coup of Versailles', *The New York Times' Fashion of the Times Magazine*, 19 August: 138.

McDonnell, P. (1998) 'Industry woes help bury respected garment maker', *Los Angeles Times*, 1 December: A1, 33.

McDowell, C (2000) 'Ethnic Influences and the Art of Selection', in *Fashion Today*, London: Phaidon.

McDowell, C. (2002) *Ralph Lauren: The Man, The Vision, The Style*, New York: Rizzoli.

McKendrick, N. (1983) 'The consumer revolution of eighteenth-century England', in N. McKendrick, J. Brewer and J. Plumb (eds) *The Birth of a Consumer Society: The Commercialisation of Eighteenth-Century England*, London: Hutchinson.

McLaughlin, F. (2001) 'Dakar Wolof and the Configuration of Urban Identity', *Journal of African Cultural Studies*, 14: 153–72.

McRobbie, A. (1998) *British Fashion Design: Rag Trade or Image Industry?* London: Routledge.

McRobbie, A. (2002) 'Fashion Culture: Creative Work, Female Individualization', *Feminist Review*, 71: 52–62.

McRobbie, A. (ed.) (1989) *Zoot Suits and Second Hand Dresses: An Anthology of Fashion and Music*, Boston: Unwin Hyman.

Mellor, H. (1997) *Towns, Plans and Society in Modern Britain,* Cambridge: Cambridge University Press.

Menkes, S. (2003) 'Liberty, Equality, Sobriety', in G. Celant, H. Koda and G. Armani (eds) *Giorgio Armani*, New York: Guggenheim Museum.

Menkes, S. (2005) 'Spotlight: Retailing Czar Becomes a Caesar', *International Herald Tribune*, 7 May.

Merkel, J. (2000) 'Fashion Art in New York', *Architectural Design*, 70(6): 62–7.

Messana, P. (2004) 'Tret'iakovskii prospect', *Novyi ochevidets,* 20 (27 December).

Metcalf, T. (1989) *An Imperial Vision: Indian Architecture and Britain's Raj*, London: Faber.

Meyer, L. (1976) 'The city that dresses the nation', *New York Sunday News*, 15 February: 67–9.

Michault, J. (2004) 'The road to China? A soft approach' *International Herald Tribune* on-line version, 7 December, www.iht.com/articles/2004/12/06/style/fhong.php

Milbank, C. (1989) *New York fashion: The Evolution of American Styl*e, New York: Harry N. Abrams.

Miles S. and M. Miles (2004) *Consuming Cities*, Basingstoke: Palgrave Macmillan.

Moeran, B. (2005) 'More Than Just a Fashion Magazine', paper presented at *the Encounters in the Global Fashion Business conference*, Copenhagen Business School, Denmark, 20–21 April.

Molotch, H (1996) 'L.A. as design product: how art works in a regional economy' in A. Scott and E. Soja (eds) *The City: Los Angeles and urban theory at the end of the twentieth century*, Berkeley: University of California Press.

Moore, B. (2005) 'In L.A. Fashion, Celebrity Trumps Couture,' *Los Angeles Times*, 22 October: A1, 19.

Moore, C. (2000) 'Streets of Style: Fashion Designer Retailing within London and New York', in P. Jackson, M. Lowe, D. Miller and F. Mort (eds) *Commercial Cultures: Economies, Practices and Spaces*, Oxford: Berg.

Mort, F (1996) *Cultures of Consumption; Masculinities and Social Space in Late Twentieth-century Britain*, London: Routledge.

Mort, F. (2004) 'Fantasies of Metropolitan Life: Planning London in the 1940s', *Journal of British Studies*, 43: 120–51.

Moseley, R. (2003) *Growing Up with Audrey Hepburn: Text, Audience, Resonance*, Manchester: Manchester University Press.

Moseley, R. (2005) 'Dress, Class and Audrey Hepburn' in R. Moseley (ed.) *Fashioning Film Stars: Dress Culture Identity*, London: BFI.

Mulvagh, J. (1999) *Vivienne Westwood: An Unfashionable Life*, London: Harper Collins.

Mumford, L. (1940) *The Culture of Cities*, London: Secker and Warburg.

Mumford, L. (1945) 'On the Future of London', *Architectural Review*, 97: 3–10.

Mustafa, H. (1998) 'Practicing Beauty: Crisis, Value and the Challenge of Self-mastery in Dakar, 1980–1998', Doctoral Dissertation, Harvard University.

Mustafa, H. (2002a) 'Portraits of Modernity: Fashioning Selves with Dakarois Popular Photography', in P. Landau and D. Kaspin (eds) *Images and Empires: Visuality in Colonial and Postcolonial Africa*, Berkeley: University of California Press.

Mustafa, H. (2002b) 'Ruins and Spectacles: Fashion and City Life in Contemporary Senegal', *Nka: A Journal of Contemporary African Art*, 15: 47–53.

Nagrath, S. (2003) '(En)countering Orientalism in High Fashion: A Review of India Fashion Week 2002', *Fashion Theory*, 7: 361–76.

Nava, M. (1996) 'Modernity's disavowal. Women, the city and the department store', in M. Nava and A. O'Shea (eds) *Modern Times: Reflections on a Century of English Modernity*, London: Routledge.

Nava, M. (1998) 'Cosmopolitanism of commerce; Selfridges, Russian Ballet and Tango', *International Journal of Cultural Studies*, 1: 163–96.

Nead, L. (2000) *Victorian Babylon: People, Streets and Images in Nineteenth-Century London*, New Haven: Yale University Press.

Niang, F. (1990) *Reflets de Modes et Traditions Saint-Louisiennes*, Dakar: Editions Khoudia.

Noiray, J. (2002) 'Préface' to E. Zola *Paris*, Paris: Gallimard.

Nora, P (1989) 'Between memory and history: Les lieux de memoires', *Representations*, 26: 7–25.

Nurok, A. Ju. (2005) Interview with Olga Vainshtein.

Obregón Pagán, E. (2003) *Murder at the Sleepy Lagoon: Zoot Suits, Race & Riot in Wartime L.A.*, Chapel Hill and London: North Carolina University Press.

Ogborn, M (1998) *Spaces of Modernity: London's Geographies 1680–1780*, New York: Guilford.

Paris, B. (1997) *Audrey Hepburn*, London: Weidenfeld and Nicolson.

Pawley, M (2000) 'Introduction', *Architectural Design*, 70(6): 6–7.

Peers, J. (2004) *The Fashion Doll*, Oxford: Berg.

Phillips, M. (2001) *London Crossings: A Biography of Black Britain*, London: Continuum.

Piganeau, J. (1986) 'Le Japon travaille a devenir un centre mondial de mode', *Journal du Textile*, 24: 3.

Pile, S. (1996) *The Body and the City*, London: Routledge.

Pitcher, H. (1993) *Miur i Meriliz: shotlandtsy v Rossii,* Moscow: Moskovskii rabochii.

Pitts, D. (1978) 'An Economic and Social History of Cloth Production in Senegambia' Unpublished Doctoral Dissertation: University of Chicago.

Polhemus, T. (1994) *Streetstyle: from sidewalk to catwalk*, London: Thames and Hudson.

Polhemus, T. (1996) *Style Surfing*, London: Thames and Hudson.

Porter, R. (1994) *London: a Social History*, London: Hamish Hamilton.

Prasso, S. and D. Brady (2003) 'Can the High End Hold Its Own?', *Business Week*, 30 June.

Price, S. (1981) *Primitive Art in Civilised Places*, Chicago: University of Chicago Press.

Puwar, N. (2002) 'Multicultural fashion ... stirrings of another sense of aesthetics and memory', *Feminist Review*, 71: 63–87.

Rabine, L. (1994) 'A Woman's Two Bodies: Fashion Magazines, Consumerism, and Feminism', in Benstock and Ferriss (eds) *On Fashion*, New Brunswick: Rutgers University Press.

Rabine, L. (1998) 'Dressing in Dakar', *L'Esprit Createur*, 37: 84–107.

Rabine, L. (2002) *The Global Circulation of African Fashion*, Oxford: Berg.

Rabinow, P. (1989) *French Modern: Norms and Forms of the Social Environment*, Cambridge, MA: MIT Press.

Radner, H. (2001) 'On the Move: Fashion Photography and the Single Girl in the 1960s', in S. Bruzzi and P. Church Gibson (eds) *Fashion Cultures: Theories, Explorations, Analysis*, London: Routledge.

Rantisi, N. (2002) 'The Local Innovation System as a Source of Variety: Openness and Adaptability in New York's Garment District', *Regional Studies*, 36: 587–602.

Rantisi, N. (2004a) 'The Ascendance of New York Fashion', *The International Journal of Urban and Regional Affairs*, 28: 86–106.

Rantisi, N. (2004b) 'The Designer in the City and the City in the Designer', in D. Power and A. J. Scott (eds) *Cultural Industries and the Production of Culture*, London: Routledge.

Rappaport, E. (2000) *Shopping for Pleasure: Women and the making of London's West End*, Princeton: Princeton University Press.

Rappaport, E. (2002) 'Art, Commerce, or Empire? The Rebuilding of Regent Street, 1880–1927', *History Workshop Journal*, 53: 94–117.

Rath, J. (ed.) (2002) *Unravelling the Rag Trade. Immigrant Entrepreneurship in Seven World Cities,* Oxford: Berg.

Reed, C. (1996) *Not at Home: The Suppression of Domesticity in Modern Art and Architecture*, London: Thames and Hudson.

Reich, J. (2001) 'Undressing The Latin Lover: Marcello Mastroianni, Fashion and *La Dolce Vita*', in S. Bruzzi and P. Church Gibson (eds) *Fashion Cultures: Theories, Explorations, Analysis*, London: Routledge.

Reilly, M. (2000) *California Couture* Atglen, PA: Schhiffer Publishing.

Reynolds, J. (2003) 'Gown or Butter?' *The New York Times*, 20 April.

Ricci, S. (ed.) (1999) *Audrey Hepburn: Una Donna, Lo Stila*, Milan: Leonardo Arte (for Museo Salvatore Ferragamo).

Richards, C. (1922) *Art in Industry*, New York: Macmillan Co.

Richards, F. (1951) *The Ready-to-Wear Industry, 1900–1950*, New York: Fairchild Publications, Inc.

Rocamora, A. (2001) 'High Fashion and Pop Fashion: The Symbolic Production of fashion in *Le Monde* and *The Guardian*', in *Fashion Theory*, 5: 123–42.

Rocamora, A. (2002) 'Le Monde's *Discours de Mode*: Creating the *Créateurs*', *French Cultural Studies*, 13: 83–98.

Rocamora, A. (2006) 'Over to you: Writing Readers in the French *Vogue*', *Fashion Theory* 10(1) in press.

Roche, D. (1994) *The Culture of Clothing: Dress and fashion in the Ancien Regime*, Cambridge: Cambridge University Press.

Roshco, B. (1963) *The Rag Race: How New York and Paris Run the Breakneck Business of Dressing American Women*, New York: Funk and Wegnalls.

Rubin, S. (2005) 'Local Colors: Emerging Talent, Not Big Names, Was the Draw to Fashion Week 2005', *San Francisco Chronicle*, 4 September.

Sadler, S. (2005) *Archigram: Architecture without Architecture*, Cambridge, MA: MIT.

Said, Edward (1995 [1978]) *Orientalism: Western Concepts of the Orient*, London: Penguin.

Sainderichinn, G. (1998) *Kenzo*, Paris: Editions du May.

San Francisco Fashion Week (2005) *Official Program*, 24–28 August.

Sarker, P. (2005) 'Haas to Keep Hand on Levi's: Last of Family to Run Jeansmaker to Stay Active in S.F. Firm', *San Francisco Chronicle*, 24 July.

Sarr, F. (1998*) L'Entrepreneuriat Feminin au Senegal*, Paris: l'Harmattan.

Sassen, S. (1991) *The Global City: New York, London, Tokyo*, Princeton: Princeton University Press.

Sassen, S. (2001) *The Global City* 2nd ed. Princeton: Princeton University Press.

Sazheneva, E. (2004) 'Pokhodka ot Kremlia', *Moscovskii komsomolets*, 9 December.

Scaasi, A. (1996) *Scassi: A Cut Above*, New York: Rizzoli.

Scott, A. (1996) 'The Craft, Fashion, and Cultural Products Industries of Los Angeles: Competitive Dynamics and Policy Dilemmas in a Multi-Sectoral Image-Producing Complex', *Annals of the Association of American Geographers*, 86: 306–23.

Scott. A. (1997) 'The cultural economy of cities' *International Journal of Urban and Regional Research* 21: 323–39.

Scott, A. (2000a) *The Cultural Economy of Cities: Essays on the Geography of Image-Producing Industries*, London: Sage Press.

Scott, A. (2000b) 'The Cultural Economy of Paris', *International Journal of Urban & Regional Research*, 24: 567–82.

Scott, A. (2002) 'Competitive Dynamics of Southern California's Clothing Industry: The Widening Global Connection and its Local Ramifications', *Urban Studies*, 39: 1287–306.

Scott, W. B. and Rutkoff, P. (2001) *New York Modern: The Arts and the City,* Baltimore, MD: John Hopkins University Press.

Scranton, P. (1998) 'From Chaotic Novelty to Style Promotion: The United States Fashion Industry, 1890s-1970s', in G. Malossi (ed.) *The Style Engine*, New York: Monacelli Press.

Seck, A. (1970) *Dakar Metropole Ouest-Africaine*, Dakar: Institut Fondamental D'Afrique Noire.

Segre Reinach, S. (2005a) 'China and Italy: Fashion Fashion versus *Prêt à Porter*. Towards a new culture of fashion', *Fashion Theory*, 9(1): 43–56.

Segre Reinach, S. (2005b) *La moda. Un'introduzione*, Rome: Laterza.

Sharma, S. and A. Sharma (2003) 'White Paranoia: Orientalism in the age of Empire', *Fashion Theory*, 7: 301–18.

Shaw, S., S. Bagwell and Karmowska, J. (2004) 'Ethnoscapes as Spectacle: Reimaging Multicultural Districts as New Destinations for Leisure and Tourism Consumption', *Urban Studies*, 41: 1983–2000.

Sheringham, M. (1996) 'City Space, Mental Space, Poetic Space: Paris in Breton, Benjamin and Réda', in M. Sheringham, (ed.) *Parisian Fields*, London: Reaktion.

Sherman, D. (2004) 'Post-Colonial Chic: Fantasies of the French interior 1957–1962', *Art History*, 27: 770–805.

Simmel, G. (1957 [1904]) 'Fashion', *The American Journal of Sociology*, 62: 541–58.

Simmel, G. (1996) *Izbrannoe*. In 2 vol. Volume 1. Moscow: Jurist publishers.

Simone, A. (2004) *For the City Yet to Come: Changing African Life in Four Cities*, Durham: Duke University Press.

Sischy, I. (1998) *Fashion Memoir: Donna Karan*, London: Thames and Hudson.

Sischy, I. (2000) *The Journey of A Woman: 20 Years of Donna Karan*, New York: Assouline.

Skov, L. (1996) 'Fashion Trends, Japonisme and Postmodernism', *Theory, Culture and Society*, 13:129–51.

Slonov, I. A. (2003 [1914]) *Iz zhizni torgovoi Moskv,* Moscow: Vendina, O.I.

Soja, E. (2000) *Postmetropolis: Critical Studies of Cities and Regions*, Oxford: Blackwell.

Soupault, P. (1997) *Les Dernières Nuits de Paris*, Paris: Gallimard.

Steele, V. (1988) *Paris Fashion: A Cultural History*, New York: Oxford University Press.

Steele, V. (1997a) *Fifty Years of Fashion: the New Look to Now*, New Haven: Yale University Press.

Steele, V. (1997b) 'Anti-Fashion: The 1970s', *Fashion Theory*, 1: 279–96.

Steele, V. (1998) 'A museum of fashion is more than a clothes bag', *Fashion Theory*, 2: 327–36.

Steele, V. (2004) 'Femme Fatale', *Fashion Theory*, 8: 315–28.

Stierle, K. (2001) *Le Mythe de Paris: La Capitale des Signes et son Discours*, Paris: Ed. de la Maison des Sciences de L'Homme.

Storper, M. (1997) *The Regional World*, New York: Guilford.

Studlar, G. (1998) 'Wider Horizons: Douglas Fairbanks and Nostalgic Primitivism', in Edward Buscombe and Roberta E. Pearson (eds) *Back in the Saddle Again: New Essays on the Western,* London: BFI Publishing.

Styles, J. (1998) 'Dress in History: Reflections on a Contested Terrain', *Fashion Theory*, 2(4).

Swain, M. (1972) 'Nightgown into dressing gown: A study of men's nightgowns in the eighteenth century', *Costume*, 6: 10–21.

Sweatfree Ordinance (2005) Chapter 12U, *San Francisco Administrative Code*, San Francisco Board of Supervisors, 13 September http://www.globalexchange.org/campaigns/sweatshops/completeordinance.doc

Swigart, L. (1994) 'Cultural Creolization and Language use in Post- Colonial Africa: The Case of Senegal', *Africa*, 64: 175–89.

Sylla, A. (1978) *La Philosophie Morale des Wolof*, Dakar: Sankore.

Tarkhanova, I. (2005) in discussion *'Russian dandies'* at Radio Liberty: http://www.svoboda.org/programs/ogi/2005/ogi.070805.asp

Tarlo, E. (1996) *Clothing matters: dress and identity in India*, Chicago: University of Chicago Press.

Taylor, L. (2002) *The Study of Dress History,* Manchester: Manchester University Press.

Taylor, P. (2004) *World City Network: a global urban analysis*, London: Routledge.

Thomas, N. (1991) *Entangled objects: exchange, material culture, and colonialism in the Pacific*, Cambridge, MA: Harvard University Press.

Thomas, N. (2006) 'Embodying Imperial Spectacle: Dressing Lady Curzon, Vicereine of India 1899–1905', *Cultural Geographies* forthcoming.

Thrift, N. (2004) 'Summoning life' in P. Cloke, P. Crang and M. Goodwin (eds) *Envisioning Human Geography,* London: Arnold.

Thuresson, M. (2002) 'French Fancies', *Japan, Inc.*, Tokyo, Japan: SRD Japan Inc., September.

Tran, K. (2005) 'Surfwear Makers Want Acceptance—But Not Too Much', *California Apparel News,* 20–26 May: 16–17.

Tschorn, A. (2005a) 'Denim's Star System: Movies Aren't the Only Craft at which Southern California Excels: It Also Sets the Pace in Premium Jeans Innovation', *Daily News Record*, 13 June: 58–9.

Tschorn, A. (2005b) 'Back to the Future: The Historic Denim Archive of Levi Strauss & Co. Charts the Past While Inspiring Jeans Yet to Come', *Daily News Record*, 13 June: 60–2.

Tulloch, C. (2004) *Black Style*, London: V&A Publications.

Veillon, D. (2000) *Fashion Under the Occupation,* (trans.) Miriam Kochan, Oxford: Berg.

Veshninsky, Yu. (1998) 'Sociokultyrnaya topografia Moskvi' in *Moskva i moskovskiy tekst rysskoy kyltyri,* Moscow: RGGU publishers.

Viazemskii, P. (1986) *Stikhotvorenia*, Leningrad: Sovetsky pisatel.

Vilmorin, L. de (2000) *Articles de Mode*, Paris: Le Promeneur.

Waldinger, R. (1986) *Through the Eye of the Needle: Immigrants and Enterprise in New York's Garment Trades*, New York: New York University Press.

Walker, A. (1974) *Hollywood, England*, London: Michael Joseph.

Wargnier, S. (2004) 'Eloge de l'Intermédiaire', in S. Richoux-Berard and F. Bonnet *Glossy*. Musée de la Mode de Marseille: Images en Manoeuvres Editions.

Weller, S. (2004) 'Fashion's influence on garment mass production: knowledge, commodities and the capture of value' Unpublished Melbourne University PhD.

White, N. (2000) *Reconstructing Italian Fashion: America and the Development of the Italian Fashion Industry*, Oxford: Berg.

Wigley, M. (1995) *White Walls, Designer Dresses: The Fashioning of Modern Architecture*. Cambridge, MA: MIT.

Wilson E. (1985) *Adorned in Dreams: Fashion and Modernity*, London: Virago.

Wilson, E. (1991) *The Sphinx in the City: Urban Life, the Control of Disorder and Women*, Berkeley: University of California Press.

Wilson, E. (1992a) 'The Invisible Flaneur', *New Left Review,* 191: 91–110.

Wilson, E. (1992b) 'Fashion and the Meaning of Life', *The Guardian,* 18 May.

Wilson, E. (2000) *Bohemians: The Glamorous Outcasts*, London: I. B. Tauris.

Wilson, E. (2001) *The Contradictions of Culture*. London: Sage.

Wilson, E. (2003) *Adorned in Dreams: Fashion and Modernity*. London: Virago.

Wolff, J. (1985) 'The Invisible Flaneuse: Women and the Literature of Modernity', *Theory, Culture and Society*, 2(3): 37–47.

Wolff, J. (1995) *Resident Alien: Feminist Cultural Criticism*, Cambridge: Polity Press.

Wollen, P. (1993) *Raiding the Ice Box: Reflections on Twentieth Century Art and Culture*, Bloomington Indiana: Indiana University Press.

Wright, G. (1991) *The Politics of Design in French Colonial Urbanism*, Chicago: University of Chicago Press.

WWD (1999) 'NPD: department stores taking a bigger slice of apparel pie', 30 April: 4.

Xu Xiaomin (2003) 'Paris of the East Again', *Shanghai Star*, 10 April.

Yohannan, K. and N. Nolf, (1998) *Claire McCardell: Redefining Modernism*, New York: Harry N. Abrams.

Yusuf, S. and W. Wu (2002) 'Pathways to a world city: Shanghai rising in an era of globalisation', *Urban Studies*, 39: 1213–40.

Zhang, Ruyun (2005) 'Greeting the world with our smiles. Interview with Chu Yunmao, Director of the City Image Institute of Donghua University' *2010 Shanghai Expo Magazine,* February, 87–8.

Žižek, S. (1997) 'Multiculturalism, or, the capital logic of multinational capitalism', *New Left Review*, 225: 28–51.

Zukin, S. (1982) *Loft Living: Culture and Capital in Urban Change*, Baltimore: John Hopkins University Press.

Zukin, S. (2003) *Point of Purchase: How Shopping Changed American Culture* New York: Routledge.

Index